Twixtujons

Twixtujons

✦

The Fabulous Realities of a Classroom

Richard Leonard

iUniverse, Inc.
New York Lincoln Shanghai

Twixtujons
The Fabulous Realities of a Classroom

iUniverse books may be ordered through booksellers or by contacting:

iUniverse
2021 Pine Lake Road, Suite 100
Lincoln, NE 68512
www.iuniverse.com
1-800-Authors (1-800-288-4677)

Because of the dynamic nature of the Internet, any Web addresses or links contained in this book may have changed since publication and may no longer be valid.

The views expressed in this work are solely those of the author and do not necessarily reflect the views of the publisher, and the publisher hereby disclaims any responsibility for them.

ISBN: 978-0-595-44387-1 (pbk)
ISBN: 978-0-595-88716-3 (ebk)

Printed in the United States of America

Twix-tu-jons (twiks'too jons), n. room 101 between the girls' and boys' restrooms. [1976]

To my loving mother

Geneviève Leonard

For making my world safe

Contents

Acknowledgments

Many thanks to Jerry Ahern, Kathy Barbagallo, Joy Barone, David Breindel, Georgine Capazzo, Dawn Cerasi, Kim Cinquina, Debbie Cirrincione, Patricia Doyle, Kethrin Gentile of inkonpixels.com, Natalie Giboney of freelancepermissions.com, Michele Gomez, Frank Joerss, Rachel Krupicka of iUniverse.com, Jennifer Mancuso, Robert Mancuso, Cissy Markun, Paul Prendergast, Georganne Serico, Joanna Shubin, and Roger Sorrentino for their interest, support, thoughtful reactions, and constructive criticism.

Special thanks to the following people for returning my phone calls after being subjected to multiple readings of *Twixtujons*:

Christina Burk—behavior analyst and poet—for patiently revealing the computer's mysteries to me (and launching me into the present), proofing and editing the text, collaborating on the website for the book, and creating the cover design.

John Thomas Clark—my new old friend, adviser, bibliophile, novelist, poet, and author of *St. Patrick's Captivity* and two collections of sonnets, *Othering* and *The Joy of Lex*—for inspiring a review of the book's ideas and imagery as a result of our many and varied conversations.

Geneviève Leonard—my first (and most influential) reader and adviser—for seeing the book's potential in a very rough draft and buying my first (and second) computer to make the book a finished work.

Robert A. Liftig—English teacher, essayist, author of *AP in English Language/Composition*, Professor at Fairfield University, and Writing fellow at Quinnipiac University—for always finding time to advise a longtime colleague.

Jane Nason—a teacher's teacher, an authority on the English language, a longtime colleague, and a mentor for many years—for interrupting her study of art history, painting, and American history in order to proof and tighten *Twixtujons*.

Andrea Rosenthal—poet, novelist, essayist, and author of *The Bookseller's Sonnets* and bi-monthly columns in *The Jewish Chronicle*—for rigorously analyzing the book's trajectory and voice, and offering enthusiastic encouragement throughout the process.

Louis Serico—history and social studies teacher, educational and occupational consultant, and longtime colleague—for always being generous with revisions, professional advice, artistic insights, and comical memory adjustments.

Jonathan Shubin—bibliophage, my second (and frequent) reader, closest friend and confidant for a half century plus five years—for being the book's unwavering advocate and supervisor from the very beginning.

Roberta Silman—author of *Blood Relations, Boundaries, The Dream Dredger, Beginning the World Again*, and other works—for sharing her professional experience, artistry, and wisdom with a stranger who taught her niece over twenty years ago.

Credits

Preface

I began writing *Twixtujons,* because my friend had cancer. At the hospital Marv sat in a large circle of people tethered to IVs, and like a merry-go-round, the nurses moved from patient to patient. I sat in front of Marv, and we spoke—once about my unexpected early retirement from teaching the year before. Since Marv and I were the only single men in our group of friends, we traveled together every summer and became very good friends; and on one trip—Marv reminded me—we had agreed to teach into our seventies.

At sixty-six, he retired. After being an "intrepid army typist" in the Korean War and a "jailbird union leader" after our strike, he said he was now a "tired geezer teacher." I retired at fifty-five, because I didn't want to correct papers and grade teenagers any longer. Marv didn't understand. If my students and I enjoyed one another—and we did—why retire?

After two months of chemotherapy, we settled into the circle's routine. Marv read his Truman biography, and I decided to write. Not poetry. I'd written a few inspired poems for several women—they were not much impressed. I thought about a novel. Many English teachers dream of writing one, but I never have and dismissed the idea immediately. Too complicated. But I felt like writing, quickly jotting down those flashes of memory that—like finger-snaps—call the mind to attention. There was too much going on around me in the circle.

My subject would be teaching. Write about what you know, I told my creative writing students. The classroom had been my home away from home for forty-nine years. For the first seventeen years, I listened and learned; for the last thirty-two, I taught—and learned. At my retirement party—a week before the doctor told Marv that he had lung cancer—Marv had warned me I'd be giving up a persona of educator, student advocate, academic colleague, and union leader. Sue and the other sweet cafeteria ladies—as well as sleepy-eyed students eating bagels before first period—would no longer greet me in the morning; and at the end of the day, pushing a huge broom, Tom the custodian wouldn't ask, "Going home, Mr. Leonard?"

Marv felt I should reconsider, or I'd become one of the ghosts he believed roamed the school building at night. "You'll look through the window of *your* classroom and see excited students sitting in front of *your* old desk, smiling and raising their hands, but you won't be able to turn the doorknob. Pressing your cheek against the glass and closing your left eye, you'll slide your face to the right side of the window to see yourself standing behind the desk or sitting on *your* file cabinet; but you'll just see a hand holding a piece of chalk and hear students laughing. No," Marv said, "you'll miss it; you'll miss the affection. There's no other profession like it. Now, like some teachers, you'll be that ghost someday—because you love the kids—but you're not ready yet." I think Marv could have written a novel.

I retired in June of 2000. Marv died in September of 2001. For that year and two months, I was able to spend a lot of time with him—and continued to record my thoughts about the years in the classroom. Marv's big complaint about dying was not knowing how things were going to turn out. Three years later, I completed *Twixtujons*. I began the book, because I needed something to do in the circle. I finished it, because I didn't want to be a ghost.

1

June 23: My Last Day of School

When I took early retirement in June, the senior class was very gracious to the retirees. Considering the quality of these students, I wasn't surprised. They were a smart and kind class, the best of both worlds for teachers. They invited us into the graduation tent to receive their public appreciation for our service to the community; this was a first in my memory of June graduations. With the exception of Hollywood movies, the public does not usually honor teachers at ceremonies.

We sat in front of the stage. The senior girls were to our left; the boys, to our right. Had I been wearing a cap and gown, and facing the next seventy years of my life, this could have been my high school graduation. Most of the speeches were thankful and inspirational. One was nostalgic. One was humorous. And one tried to be humorous and inspirational. But all the speeches told us to look forward; I looked back.

Forty years ago, I met Kathy on a blind date and, after one date, fell in love with this girl who looked like Zeffirelli's dark-haired Juliet. To my astonishment, Kathy agreed to wear my high school ring and became my first girlfriend, and for two years, the bridge between my college experiences and daily life. My intellectual journey didn't end at the school gates; our dates became take-home literature classes—and homework was never so romantic.

After I had studied *Othello* and struggled through Joyce's *Ulysses*, I discovered film versions were then playing at neighborhood-movie art houses. Kathy and I watched Laurence Olivier's Othello suffer the pangs of jealousy and Milo O'Shea's Leopold Bloom endure the ridicule of being a cuckold. Later at the Green Kitchen Diner on First Avenue over hamburgers, and much later sitting until dawn on the steps in Kathy's hall-

1

way—our private place between the fourth and fifth floor landings, hidden from neighbors below and her parents above—we spent many evenings discussing the nature of infidelity, Desdemona's murder, and Molly's monologue.

And when we saw Rod Steiger's powerful performance in *The Pawnbroker*, we decided to read the movie's source, Edward Lewis Wallant's novel, and compare the two works. The movie followed the book's plot and characterizations closely but at the end added the scene of Sol Nazerman's impaling his hand on the pawnshop spindle. Very late that night, Kathy and I agreed that the movie did not need to explain Sol's emotional death and rebirth with a crucifixion symbol. We agreed the movie was excellent but preferred the novel.

As for those evenings when we were not "playing school"—and Kathy was not typing my research papers—she was listening on the phone to the day's college adventure. Like a child testing his wobbly legs going up and down steps, I unveiled my latest epiphany; and like many intelligent girls of her generation who didn't go to college, she listened and encouraged her boyfriend.

Kathy and I never had a chance to see Franco Zeffirelli's *Romeo and Juliet* together. Sadly we had broken up the summer before I entered graduate school. A year later at the Paris Theater in Manhattan, Olivia Hussey's familiar face held me spellbound with flickering hallway images of dawn-breaking talks—and a dark final embrace. I wish I could thank Kathy again for those happy years when she made *my* education *our* passion.

I thought of my closest friend, Jonathan Shubin. It seems I'm always thanking him, because he's been a devoted friend for over fifty years. In the black-and-white photograph on my bookcase, we're the little boys waving wildly atop a Bronx Zoo camel. In the photograph on the wall, we're the two cowboys sitting high on Central Park ponies. Many years later I flew from New York to Kentucky to be his best man, and he flew from Oregon to New York to be mine. The night his mother died, he came to my apartment. The day I separated from my wife, he drove me to my new apartment in the city. We've always been there for each other, and today I thanked Jon for making my teaching career an important part of our friendship. There were those dry runs of my lesson plans to anticipate student questions; we rehearsed everything but the attendance taking—and jokes.

To help me become a better teacher, Jon would risk his job and break the law. And he did. The editors of the literary magazine, *Forum,* and I depended on the kindness of the student government—or strangers—for the money to publish each year. Once, Jon was that stranger, and he had to remain a stranger, because on a dreary Saturday in March, we entered his empty office without permission. After eight hours of running several copy machines—and nauseated by the toner fumes trapped in the unventilated copy room—we loaded seven hundred copies of the school's literary magazine into his station wagon and drove off. Jon is still in the business of helping me; he's already proofed and printed this book several times.

Next, I thought of my mother's loving influence—and my early interest in literature. When my parents separated in 1953, she traded apartments with Jonathan's family. They lived a floor above us in a studio and happily moved to our one bedroom apartment on the first floor. At first, we relished the much smaller apartment, simply because my father didn't live there; but during the following twenty years, it became a cozy home with hissing radiators and a history of warm memories. I smile when I remember my mother lying on her bed, made up to look like a sofa, reading *Gone With The Wind* with a French/English dictionary—and grumbling when she couldn't find the translation for the slaves' dialect.

One of my fondest memories from our new life was my habit of looking up from doing homework, because my mother had giggled—or groaned—while reading one of my school books. "Where are you, Mom? What part?" She'd tell me—and we'd laugh while taking turns unfolding the funny scene to each other. From Charles Dickens's *Great Expectations* in the ninth grade to D. H. Lawrence's *The Rainbow* in college, my mother thoroughly enjoyed my school-assigned reading. Most parents probably stop reading "with" their children when they stop reading "to" them. I was fortunate. I never cared much for school, but I always looked forward to the next book.

And she was the person directly responsible for my being honored today under this tent. Whenever the subject of college and dream careers came up in class, I confessed to the students that my dream was to drop out of college. Like most of my friends in the neighborhood, I wanted a full time job. Tommy loaded luggage at Kennedy Airport, Charlie stocked shelves at the A&P, and Wayne sorted mail at *The Daily News*. They had real jobs and made good money.

At my weekend job at the liquor store, I made the minimum wage of $1.10 an hour plus tips. And tips rarely exceeded ten cents a delivery in 1965. Raising my standard of living, the late Peter Jennings of ABC Local News—and two other generous customers—gave the astronomical tip of one dollar for a case of wine. But it wasn't enough. Without a full-time job, I didn't have my friends' wealth and freedom. Going to college cost me the good life. The students were eager to hear the particulars of my odd confession.

"What was the good life in the olden days, Len?"

"Instead of spending the best years of my life in discotheques dancing with attractive women, I spent them at the 42nd Street Library writing research papers. I worked very hard to be a teacher."

"You gave up fantasy women for us? Thanks, Len."

"I *postponed* dancing with attractive women. As of today, my dance card is full for the next two years. And I went to college for my mother."

"Your mother? What were you, a mama's boy?"

"Lucky for you, I was. And lucky for me. None of my friends went to college."

Over the years I've thanked my mother often for my very good life, but I'd love to thank her publicly for her relentless parenting, which was put to the test when I entered high school. I still could not go out on school nights and had a curfew on weekends. Why couldn't my mother understand that she was destroying a teenager's life? In 1959, nothing was more important to me than being with "the guys," or listening to Dion and the Belmonts on the radio and watching the girls dance with each other. Why couldn't she be like the other parents? I explained, I argued, I begged. I needed to go out. But I never convinced her.

During summer nights and winter weekends, I savored freedom—up to 10:30, my curfew. Since no one had a watch, I'd every so often look through the corner drug store window to get the time. I never intentionally broke the curfew. But sometimes, I'd forget to check the clock, because we were teasing the girls—or sharing the latest teenage wisdom. Since it was dark—and I never wore my glasses outside school—I was the last one to see the silhouette menacingly approaching us. Hearing someone say, "Here comes your ...," I knew who was coming and jumped off the stoop to intercept her. It was bad enough they saw her; I didn't want them to hear her.

"Do you know what time it is?"

"Is it later than ten thirty?"

"You know it is." *So much for faking surprise.*

"What time is it?"

"Ten forty."

"That's only ten minutes, Mom."

"Would you prefer a ten-twenty curfew?" *So much for bargaining.*

"What about Tommy and Charlie?"

"What about them?"

"They're in high school and don't have curfews."

"They're not my children." *So much for parity.*

"Their mothers let them stay out."

"I don't care what their mothers do." *And so much for peer pressure.*

But most of the time, we walked home without saying a word. My mother is a very strong woman. She had to be. By the time she was fifteen, she survived the deaths of both parents; and for four years during the German occupation of France, she endured malnutrition and constant fear. In the 1950s, when women conventionally tolerated bad marriages, she divorced my father to rescue me from an abusive home. My mother, therefore, was not going to take the easy way out and surrender to a nagging, rebellious teenager; she loved me too much. I never had a chance against a woman determined to give me an excellent education for a dream career.

2

Hitchhiking and Student Teaching

In the 1950s, we didn't hitchhike in Manhattan. We did "go hitching," though, which had more to do with the thrills of rodeo rides than transportation. Squeezing our fingers into the ridge below the window and standing on the bumper, my friends and I clung to the back of a moving city bus. If my fingers popped out of the ridge, I jammed them back in and felt my heart pound. I once went hitching with a very short boy who used his leg to prop up our taller friend, whose injured right arm dangled at his side. When the bus stopped at a light, the three of us hopped off and walked up to 2nd Avenue for the ride back home. The bus bucked on the cobblestone streets, but we were lucky city cowboys; I never heard of anyone's falling into a stampede of New York City cars.

I usually hitched up 1st Avenue, hopped off at 86th Street, walked up to 2nd Avenue, and then hitched down 2nd Avenue; but my favorite ride ran on Lexington Avenue, because traffic moved both ways back then. I'd hop off one bus, cross the street, and hop onto another. Uptown—downtown—uptown—downtown.

For a quick one-way hitch, coming home from a movie on a hot day, I'd hang on an open window of a bus, making sure my feet didn't touch the moving back wheel—and hope no one in the bus would slam my fingers with a fist. When the city made the back bumpers of new buses too narrow for our feet—and covered the cobblestones with tar—the rodeo left town.

In the 1960s, "hitching" meant something very different to me. To receive a college education, I became a highway hitchhiker. Since I didn't have a car, and the railroad was too expensive—and time consuming—I took the IRT #4 subway to Yankee Stadium in the Bronx, walked several blocks to the Major Deegan Expressway, and hitched the ten miles to Iona College in New Rochelle. Unlike Clark Gable in *It Happened One Night*, I didn't "thumb" a ride. I just stood on the entrance ramp and waited for cars to stop. And the daily commuters did; they knew that we hitchhikers—carrying books and wearing jackets and ties—were Iona boys. One week into the school year, the same cars stopped at the same time. "Crowd in, boys, and leave the snow outside." Sometimes, there were twenty of us, but we always followed the "first-come, first-go" rule. We Americans love a line. There were rumors that Ed Sullivan and Frank Gifford gave rides to Iona boys; my celebrity was Jack McCarthy of St. Patrick Day's parade fame. During those four years on the road, I was never late for a class. And more important, I always made it home at night.

After my last class of the day, I hurried to the "hitching corner" where fellow students with cars—and local residents—picked me up and dropped me off at the Deegan. From there, a good ride took me to the Bronx—Fordham Road or Yankee Stadium subway stations; a great ride took me down the FDR Drive in Manhattan to 73rd Street, four blocks from my house. An oddity of those times was that we called an apartment—even my studio apartment—a house. If I got to the Deegan early, I could be choosy. After the driver had leaned over and rolled the window down, I'd ask, "Where you going?"

"Manhattan."

"East Side?"

"FDR Drive."

"Great." I'd get in. "Thanks."

Limousines usually were the sure thing for the FDR. They were going to either the United Nations complex on the East River or the business district in midtown to pick up their important clients. "Get in back, kid, and make yourself comfortable." And I'd scramble into the huge back seat. Sitting behind *my* chauffeur, I stretched my legs into the horizon and enjoyed the wonders of car air conditioning.

But standing on the Deegan for an hour made me desperate. I didn't ask any questions; I just got in. I knew they were going south, and that was close enough. One afternoon, a young couple in a noisy little coupe stopped. Since it was getting late, I gladly squeezed into the tight back seat behind the smiling young woman leaning forward. Once I was tucked in—and she had slid back into her seat—she turned her head to ask me where I was going.

"The East Side."

"Is the East Side in Manhattan?"

"Yes, it is. So is the West Side. And Central Park is in the middle. Where are you going?"

After slowly shaking his head back and forth, the driver turned his head. "Manhattan. Third Avenue and 86th Street, and that's on the *East Side*. Unlike some people in this car, I know where we're going."

"Unlike some people in this car, I didn't study the map of New York for the past two years." She poked him in the ribs. "This is our first time to New York. This is a belated honeymoon vacation. Will we be close to where you're going?"

"Fifteen blocks. This is a great ride, thanks."

"Great ride? Snug as a bug in a chug-chug, you mean. If you hiccup, you'll pop out the window."

They had to be the happiest honeymoon couple in the State of New York. After twenty miles of front-seat teasing and poking, Anthony and Melissa pulled up to the corner of 86th and 2nd Avenue. This time, Melissa got out of the car and pulled her seat forward. I placed my right heel on the sidewalk, grabbed the window post, and yanked myself out of the seat. And I collapsed. As I was looking up at Melissa and the sky, she screamed and Anthony, who hadn't seen my fall, shouted, "What happened? What's the matter, Melissa?"

"I don't know. He just fell down, Anthony. He's lying on the sidewalk. Anthony, get out of the car. I think he's having a heart attack." By the time Anthony, Melissa, and a crowd of passersby were leaning over me, I began to feel the pins and needles. I had been sitting on my foot during our happy journey into New York City. "Don't move; we'll call an ambu-lance." Poor Melissa.

"No, I'm okay. My foot fell asleep. I'm sorry."

"Oh. Well, don't apologize, you poor guy. Not your fault. I'm half your size; I should've been the bug back there." After Anthony and Melissa had helped me gather my books, Melissa patted my shoulder. "Imagine if you *had* popped out the window; we'd never forget this honeymoon." Poking each other and waving goodbye, Melissa and Anthony slid back into their "chug-chug" and made a right hand turn onto 86th Street for 3rd Avenue.

During my four years of hitchhiking, I remember only three rides: Jack McCarthy, who was a great storyteller; happy Melissa—and lucky Anthony—who will always remember the pins-and-needle attack on their honeymoon in New York City; and Martin Lobenthal, who changed my life.

I met Martin in April of my senior year. I left school a period earlier, because the philosophy professor had cancelled class. I wasted many hours waiting for rides, and that afternoon I'd use my new-found time doing a term paper at the 42nd Street Library. But I was the only person on the Deegan, and that was a problem; nobody was stopping. Being too early on the road was just as bad as being too late. Drivers felt comfortable picking up teenage boys in jackets and ties—when there were many of them. I looked down at my watch and figured that in forty minutes I'd be sur-rounded by the regular afternoon shift of Iona hitchhikers. When I looked up, a yellow Buick convertible was pulling over to the curb. The driver's sun-burnt head and sunny smile turned to me. "Hop in, hop in, hitch-hiker!" he shouted in a voice as gleeful as the color of his car.

As soon as I pulled the door shut, he hit the gas and swerved back onto the Deegan. "Hang on. I'm a terrible driver." He was also an honest man; steering took a back seat to communication. He was the most animated man I had ever met, and I liked him immediately. "Where are you going? Where do I drop you off?"

"Manhattan. The East Side—or anywhere south from here."

"I'm going to the West Side. Greenwich Village. My new home. But I'm going down the FDR. Is that good for you?"

"Seventy-third on the Drive is great."

"Great … I teach in the Bronx, but I took the day off to move. I live with my sister and her family in Mount Vernon. Ten minutes from Iona.… You are Iona, right?"

"This is my last year. I'm going to Fordham next year for a Master's degree in teaching."

"School won't teach you to be a teacher. You go to school for the license to teach. Only teaching will teach you how to teach—up to a point, of course, because teachers are born, not made. But you'll be a good teacher." His optimism shone in his smiling eyes.

"How can you tell?"

"Hitchhikers make good teachers. Every one knows that. They're independent … trusting … patient … resolute … adventuresome … fearless … and, most important, they can stand for hours—all necessary requisites for the good teacher. But teachers are not necessarily good drivers."

At 73rd Street, he swerved off the FDR onto the service road to drop me off. He wished me luck in teaching, I wished him luck in his new city home, and after waving goodbye with both hands, he grabbed the wheel and aimed the car for the FDR. Walking the three blocks to my house, I realized it had taken me four years to hitch a ride in a convertible.

After Iona, I never hitchhiked again. I took the subway to Fordham and had the luxury of studying with the attaché case across my knees; even a crowded, noisy subway car was preferable to standing on the highway on the best of days. On a normal day, I took the subway in the morning down to 302 Broadway at the Southern tip of Manhattan for my education classes, and then in the afternoon, up to the Fordham Rose Hill campus in the Bronx for my English classes. In the evening, I took the subway back home to Manhattan. Traveling was simple—and predictable—but still time-consuming.

When I began to student-teach in February, the subway became my second home. In the morning, I took it up to Roosevelt High School in the Bronx across the street from Fordham. After teaching three classes, I took the subway all the way down to 302 Broadway for my education classes. After lunch, I took the subway back up to the Bronx for my afternoon English classes at Fordham. By the time I made it back to Manhattan in the evening, I had spent two hours writing papers—if I had a seat.

One early February morning, while I was hurrying up the stairs to my first classroom on the second floor, where I'd spend several months student teaching, I heard a voice that made me smile. I followed it past my floor to the third floor, but the crowd of students prevented my catching up to it. At the fourth floor corridor, he was standing in the midst of several smiling students, but directing his merry lecture to one desperate student in particular.

Student: "I had to work overtime last night."

Teacher: "Well, son, I'll tell you:

      Life for me ain't been no crystal stair.

      It's had tacks in it,"

Student: "But you give too much homework."

Teacher: "And splinters,

      And boards torn up,

      And places with no carpet on the floor—

      Bare."

Student: "I got other homework to do, too."

Teacher: "But all the time

      I'se been a-climbin' on,

      And reachin' landin's,

      And turnin' corners,

      And sometimes goin' in the dark

      Where there ain't been no light."

Student: "Damn, you're good, Mr. Lobenthal."

Teacher: "So boy, don't you turn back.

      Don't you set down on the steps

      'Cause you finds it kinder hard.

      Don't you fall now—"

Student: "All right, you win. Can I do it tonight?"

Teacher: "Langston Hughes would insist, Bobby. And read his poem

'Mother to Son' for inspiration."

I waited for Bobby and his friends to finish their jousting with Mr. Lobenthal and walk to their classes before I approached him. "Hello. Remember me?" He turned his smile toward me.

"No.... No, I don't ... Yes ... yes, I do ... I remember your face, but I can't remember your name. I'm very sorry. When did you graduate?"

"Last year."

"Last year?" His gleeful voice dropped. "How old are you?"

"Twenty-two."

"What?" He almost whispered. "Twenty-two?" His smile never left his face, but his eyes squinted to frame this mystery, to corner it before he had to apologize to someone whose name he had forgotten completely but whose face was vaguely familiar.

"I'm the hitchhiker you picked up on the Deegan the day you were moving to Greenwich Village. I told you I was going to be a teacher. Remember?" His eyes widened.

"Remember?" He placed both hands on the sides of his head and yelled. "I'd remember you on any highway in New York! On the fourth floor of Theodore Roosevelt High School in the Bronx one year later? No! What the hell were you trying to do? Retire me to the Mary Muldoon Home for Teachers?"

Martin Lobenthal was my first school mentor—and school friend. Since my cooperating teacher and I didn't always get along, she happily allowed me to spend time in Martin's class, where I observed a master teacher connect with at-risk and angry black students. Evoking Dr. King, he called them the "marvelous new militancy." But he let them know that violence was not the solution. "You know, I'm your favorite black teacher...." And they'd laugh with this white man who respected them and their black authors. "But don't just listen to me; listen to Dr. King." And once more, he'd quote King. "Again and again we must rise to the majestic heights of meeting physical force with soul force."

Martin also made it difficult for them to stereotype—and hate—the white man's world when he bragged that Dr. King and he shared the same dream, the American dream of freedom—and that it was no accident they shared a first name. "Our mothers were soul sisters." The students laughed as much as I did.

From the back of the room, I watched Martin and his "black brothers," and thought of Brother Hayes and Mr. Gurney, my two favorite high school teachers. Martin knew what they had known. If he wanted the students in front of him to learn, he had to make them feel special—and safe. Remembering teenage angst and using humor, the three of them were not afraid to show their affection for students. Brother Hayes encouraged us to do well on his algebra test to make our girlfriends proud. "Maybe Trixie'll let you hold her hand at the show." Mr. Gurney tolerated our practical jokes in class, because he understood it was the teenagers' way of showing their fondness for the teacher. And when Dr. King was murdered in April of 1968, I watched Martin and his "militants" curse white racists for an entire class period.

Unlike the bus-hitching days that took me in circles up 1st Avenue and down 2nd Avenue, hitchhiking to college became the metaphor of profound change in my life; meeting a man in a yellow convertible—and our serendipitous reunion the following year—the turning point. On my first day of student teaching, I observed this man with the smiling eyes—in the busy corridor of a school—use poetry, respect, and humor to change a student's attitude toward a homework assignment. His relationship with this student—and all the students—reminded me of the teacher's special gift. Martin was right that day in April; good teachers are born.

Martin's wisdom went far beyond that revelation. Since he was a vice president under Albert Shanker in the United Federation of Teachers, he suggested in June that I look for a job in Westchester County because of the impending September strike in the city; and he loaned me his car for the search. All I knew of Westchester was my hitchhiker's trail to college, so with a map of this unfamiliar county—and the steady radio reports of Bobby Kennedy's murder—I crisscrossed Westchester County, interview after interview, in a yellow convertible.

When I signed a contract with the Yonkers School District and eventually moved to Westchester County, my life in the city—and a plan to teach in a New York inner city public school—came to an end. If I hadn't met Martin that sunny day in April, my memories of the classroom would tell a different story with different characters. Perhaps I would not have written this book at all.

3

My First Day of School

It was the first day of school, and I was a new teacher. I was never an excellent student. A late bloomer, very late, I began to bud in college. Now I was the nervous leader of the class. I would not eat breakfast—and lunch—for a month. I became an English teacher, because I was an English major in college, and the schools needed teachers. Even though I had received my Masters degree from Fordham University and my permanent New York State Teacher's license, I knew I wasn't a real teacher.

As soon as I entered the massive brick building guarded by eight towering columns, I turned left for the main office to pick up my assignment for the year and a list of the students. I looked for my mailbox. There it was, *Mr. Leonard,* but it was empty. *Did the principal change his mind about hiring me?* Then I turned and saw rows of manila envelopes lying on the counter, which separated the visitors from the principal's secretary. I found mine, heavy with directions, student medical forms, the names of the students, and the key to my homeroom.

This was another "first day." I already had experienced four "first days" of school: grammar school, high school, college, and graduate school. My mother laughs about the large woman in the black-and-white habit chasing me in the schoolyard, but once Sister Jean Margaret caught me, I sat, listened, and daydreamed. In high school, I was no longer a big shot eighth grader and respectfully listened to the Irish Christian Brothers. In my first year of college, I wanted to have a job like all my neighborhood friends, who didn't go to college, and I pretended to listen. In graduate school, I eagerly listened to the professors, who knew so much about literature.

But this first day was a true break from the past. I didn't need to find a seat and wait for the teacher. I didn't need to follow the new rules. In high school we didn't have to use the fountain pens mandated by the nuns anymore. This made writing easier and chewing safer. One can chew a fountain pen for only so long before the ink tube ruptures. I didn't need to write the room number and the name of the teacher on my spiral notebook. Today, the students had to listen to me.

I had thirty minutes before the first class. Sitting alone in the classroom made me more nervous, so I left for the faculty room to look for the other new teachers. When I opened the door, I saw older men trading summer stories and smiling; on the opposite side of the room, serious young men speaking softly. I sat with the serious young men.

Since I sat at the end of the couch, I faced the door and saw the growling shadow first. Opening the door, he banged it twice against the wall. The room became silent. "Who sits in this room?" The shadow banged the door against the wall a third time and entered the room. He was a big man with very short hair. He turned to us, and the contorted face behind the thick glasses growled more loudly, "Why are you sitting? You! You! You, virgin teachers, do you have tenure? No? Do you have seniority? No? And you sit? You pathetic creatures, get up! Get up! Get up now!"

Like children, we quickly stood. I knew he wasn't the principal. Maybe the assistant principal? He sat on the couch, and the older teachers clapped and slapped their knees. This was the annual ritual for Roger Sorrentino, who played the madman with gusto for his audience on the other side of the room; in fact, they had been waiting for the show to begin. On the first day of school for the past ten years, he had frightened new teachers, waiting for the first day of their careers to begin.

Over the next few days, I would learn that Roger was a master teacher. Like Mr. Gurney, Brother Hayes, and Martin Lobenthal, he passionately taught—and played—in the classroom; and, of course, the students loved him. When they asked for loose leaf, he scolded them for thinking "paper grew on trees"; when they misbehaved, he called them "ungrateful and uglitudinous"; and when he taught literature, he enhanced the lessons with his vast knowledge of psychology and philosophy, which brought the work to life. Reading and studying the difficult autobiographical *Long Day's Journey Into Night*, his students appreciated the complexity of the play's naturalism and pitied Eugene O'Neill's doomed characters.

Since I desperately needed guidance to survive the month, I asked Roger to observe my lessons and share his magic. But while Roger was mentoring me, he discovered my other—"certainly more troubling"—problem. I considered chow mein and pizza exotic. I ate lentil soup without a "squirt of lemon," drank coffee (pre-Starbucks) without a "dash of cinnamon," and never tasted Gewurztraminer wine or a Manhattan Special Coffee Soda. I was "gastronomically bereft." But he was a gourmet, and by the end of the month, he introduced me to Indian, Thai, and Szechwan cuisine—each with many gulps of water—and during our meals taught me some magic for the classroom as well.

I found Roger's fearsome entrance therapeutic on that first day. When he smiled and extended his hand like royalty from the couch, I laughed with the others and shook it. We were still standing. For the time being, I forgot my nervousness. I realized some of the older teachers had been his victims in the past. I felt good about our initiation, because I now shared something with these veterans. The first day of my lifelong career began with a bang—literally.

I remember nothing else about my first day of classes. Sitting across from Roger, I thought of next year's virgins.

4

Role Models

I was not an angel in elementary school; I didn't know any boy angels. The girls sat with folded hands, wings at their sides. The boys corkscrewed themselves to tease the girls around them and to punch the other boys whenever Sister Mary Illuminata was preoccupied with her class of fifty or so students.

The nuns, with few exceptions, were always angry with us boys, and for good reason. Despite the smacks, the sideburn twists, the shin kicks, the whirling rulers, the snarls, or all of the above in a paroxysm of righteous discipline, we ignored their pursed lips: *Moments of pleasure ... hours of regret.* Unlike young girls, we lived for the moment.

High school was different. There were no angels, because there were no nuns—and no girls—only Irish Christian Brothers, who convinced the freshmen they were in boot camp. Not infrequently, I saw a Brother lifting a freshman off the tile floor, because he broke a rule. Some boys never broke the rules: Don't pack your books while the principal speaks over the PA, or don't speak on the stairs on the way to lunch. During the first few weeks, most of us learned the rules the hard way.

Our remaining three years of high school were tranquil. As veterans we all knew the drill, but we always enjoyed the shocked faces of the new freshmen, who made the mistake of thinking they had entered a nunless haven for boys. We also knew that we were neither angels nor saints, and every morning before class, we broke not just one, but two rules.

Perhaps like other Catholic schools in the city, Rice High School did not permit the students to patronize the stores in the neighborhood, but one block away, we gathered with friends for our last coffee and cigarette of the school day at the huge Rexall Drug Store, long gone now, on 125th

Street and Lenox Avenue. Here we were breaking another rule: no smoking on school grounds. The Brothers considered Lenox Avenue school grounds. I guess we thought there was safety in numbers, since we occupied every red-cushioned silver stool at the shiny counter before 9 a.m. We were wrong.

The revelation came to us in the apparition of our principal, Brother Patrick Synan, who impressed all the mothers during the freshmen parents/teachers night with his "dark, dark eyes" and "Cary Grant's good looks." (Today's mothers would see George Clooney.) But to this day, when I think of him, I see his form, arms akimbo, floating in our cigarette smoke at the sunlit door. No one ever saw Brother Synan enter the drugstore; we just knew he was there because of the familiar sounds of our exodus. My friends and I stood at the men's cologne counter in the rear of the drugstore. As a result, we produced the last ripples of sound to splash against the back wall. Under the slowly turning ceiling fans, the students no longer enjoyed the freedom of the store's white noise to share stories and homework.

First, we became aware of the gradual cessation of conversation that made our voices louder. Next, ice cubes clinked in Coke glasses, and coffee cups banged and rattled against saucers and nearby glass display counters of watches and perfume. Finally, stools squeaked while cigarettes dropped to the floor tiles until it was our turn to ditch them—without last deep drags—sweep our books off the counter, and prepare ourselves to walk past Brother.

Since we occupied the farthest corner of the drug store, we joined the procession at the end, making us conspicuous rebels. Brother Synan was going to choose us for punishment, I was sure; he couldn't punish half the school. We walked across his shadow, out the door, and down Lenox Avenue to school. We never turned to see if he was behind us; we assumed he was, because my friends and I were the last ones out. And we never said a word, fearing he was two steps behind us. Of course, we knew only God was omnipresent, but we weren't going to take any chances. We never heard of anyone punished for breaking two rules at the same time. The ritual was impressive enough to keep us out of the Rexall for days.

Several years ago, Andrew McCarthy, Donald Sutherland, and Mary Stuart Masterson starred in the excellent film, *Heaven Help Us,* which contains only one scene (in an otherwise realistic depiction of a Catholic high school and the Brothers who ruled fairly and unfairly) that blatantly misrepresented the extent of the students' rebellion. The boys in this school relaxed at the off-the-limits luncheonette across the street. Once in a while, the Brothers raided the boys' "hangout."

As I was watching this scene, I was in my own heaven of things remembered—until the raid. I almost called out in the theatre. No! No! The boys wouldn't run from the Brothers. And the Brothers wouldn't chase them. They wouldn't run from the Brothers, and not die. Not in my high school of the early sixties. Brother Synan knew that, and he also knew that he didn't have to say a word to get our attention. All he had to do was stand by the door with the sun at his back and wait.

5

Call Me Schoolmaster

When I began to teach, I was twenty-two; however, students had to ask me for permission to use the bathroom. I became an important person the very first day. How many people in the world have that kind of power? For seventeen years, I had asked permission to go to the bathroom or ignored the urge to go, because a teacher stood in front of the room. Now I had the power, but times were different. The teachers of the fifties and sixties were all-powerful; we weren't.

In the fifth grade, Sister Mary Anthony denied Margaret's request to go to the bathroom. "No, you may not." That was the end of it. A few minutes later, I looked over to Margaret, because a dripping sound came from her direction. I saw a puddle under her seat and whispered, "Margaret. Margaret. A pipe broke under your desk. Move your shoe; it's getting wet." Margaret's face bunched up into a teary mess, and she ran out of the room. I had a crush on Margaret, but her dark maroon skirt clinging to the back of her legs changed that forever. She was no longer an angel, but we were still friends, and I didn't laugh with the class. No one, not even Margaret, was shocked by Sister's decree.

Every Monday morning, a parish priest Father Reilly visited all eight classrooms of St. Catherine of Siena to remind us boys and girls of the mortal sin of missing Sunday Mass and the punishment of burning forever in hell. "Sister informs me that Leonard, Costigan, and Russell missed holy Mass yesterday. Why?"

"I was sick, Father." He glared at Tommy.

"I had a fever, Father." He glared at me.

"Me, too, Father." He looked down and wrote in his pad. Before he left the room, the entire class knelt in the aisles for his blessing.

And at the end of the year, he solemnly distributed the report cards to the "Promoted" students and the "Left-back," inconsolable students. In the eighth grade, Father Reilly spoke to the forty-nine students in the class, one by one, about our futures. Mine was bleak; I was not a conscientious student, too busy dreaming of Annette Funicello, a Mouseketeer who chose Spin over Marty on the Disney TV show. When I wasn't feeling sorry for Marty, I dreamt of being a soldier in the typical war movies of the fifties when the invasion of Normandy was heroic—and black-and-white bloodless.

Always, after seeing a World War II or Korean War movie, my friends and I would come home, get our toy M1 rifles, and shoot at one another from behind parked Chevys and Fords until it was dark. We even created the game of "Who dies the best?" Each boy chose a weapon for his death—rifle, machine gun, grenade—and ran toward the enemy. My specialty was dying slowly from a bayonet wound while sliding down a parking street sign. *Apocalypse Now* and the other Vietnam movies of the seventies put blood, fear, and horror in colorful war movies, ending forever the joy of children playing war after a Saturday afternoon matinee.

When my turn came Father Reilly advised me that college was out of the question. Three years earlier, I had been "Promoted On Trial" to the sixth grade. I should study auto mechanics in high school. I believed him, but my mother didn't. She never saw any mechanical talent in me; she saw laziness and daydreams. I wonder how many mothers sent their children off to a trade school because of Father Reilly. I went to college and graduate school, and became a teacher that decided who graduated—and who went to the bathroom. I became a teacher of the late sixties, but like the actors in the new, realistic war movies of the seventies, teachers faced new roles.

For two years, my wife dropped me off at school every day on her way to work in Connecticut. One day, the car broke down just as we entered the teachers' parking lot. We got out of the car and went to work. She opened the hood; I held her coat and an umbrella, since it started to snow lightly. Father Reilly would have been proud of my wife. She knew her engines.

When she fixed the problem, she closed the hood and asked for her coat. I gave it to her. Then it began. Whoops, whistles, and howls competed with the wind. Windows in the three buildings around the parking lot framed gleeful faces of students who enjoyed my chivalry.

"You were a big help out there, Mr. Leonard."

"Yes. Thank you."

"What kind of man are you?"

"A secure man."

"You hold a steady umbrella."

"The wind means nothing to me."

"What does she see in you?"

"You're too young to understand."

For the entire day, that's how it went, and not just that day, but every time something happened that allowed them to see the human being in the teacher. I still gave them permission to go the bathroom, but they knew I went, too.

My authority extended to the cafeteria. Lunch duty was mandatory for young teachers. My teachers never had a problem with us students, but our students had a problem with us teachers (if they didn't have us as classroom teachers). I assumed they would listen to me. Why not? I was a teacher; I was an authority figure, but I was not their teacher. My authority was law only in the classroom where grades and familiarity defined my power.

In 1968, teachers were responsible for a clean cafeteria after the lunch period. No trays could be left on the table or under it. We picked up greasy plates, leftover soda, and wet napkins. As a result, we were on top of the students to take their leftovers with them at the end of the period. If we weren't, administrators—or the cafeteria manager—made us clean up. Today, thanks to unions, teachers no longer have this duty.

In the cafeteria, we joked with the students to show them another side. We wanted to be respected, but we wanted to be liked. For some, I was a young man to tease or flirt with; but for many others, I was a father figure, a very young father. It took a few years to realize that the more appropriate image was the grandfather who enjoys the children for part of the day, sending them home for the difficult parental work.

I became softer, and soft words firmly delivered worked well in the classroom and anywhere else in the building where grades had no effect. Mr. Fiore became Fiore; Mr. Prendergast, Prender; and Mr. Leonard, Leonard, Len, Lenny, and occasionally Le Nerd. The nicknames allowed the students to get close without diminishing our authority in the classroom, cafeteria, hallway, or auditorium.

As the authority figure in the cafeteria, teachers also kept the peace. We anticipated fights and stopped arguments. Fistfights were rare in my student days; they were not in my early teaching days. Our presence in the cafeteria rarely deterred angry students from fighting. There were so many fights that teachers didn't wear ties for angry students to grab.

When a fight did break out, I jumped in, furiously mindful of the danger. Always, students who saw me leap half-crazed into a fight marveled at my exuberance. After all, I was not a Physical Education teacher. I was a slim teacher-in-training whose Catholic school need for order masked his fear, but the post-fight brain chemistry that left me battered told the real story; I had some difficulty concentrating on my work for the rest of the day.

During a fight, I had the good sense to survey the scene to determine which student I would grab from behind, avoiding a motorcycle boot or a fist. Only once did I make a mistake. I was teaching a class on Emily Dickinson when those unique sounds of a fight interrupted my loving praise. I opened the door and saw at least ten tumbling, punching, kicking, cursing boys, surrounded by horrified and happy students preferring the spectacle to lunch.

I thought I had picked the right boy when one flailing fist found my face. Shortly afterward, the fight magically ended. I released the boy, found my unbroken glasses (also magical), returned to my classroom, and asked the class where we had left off. I was the teacher. I was not going to let them know that post-fight adrenaline, not Emily Dickinson, ruled my brain, but they wanted to explore this other side of me. After all, how many adults break up fistfights during a normal workday?

"Mr. Leonard, you were awesome."

"Yes, Carmela, I was. Let's get back to work."

"You're the man, Len."

"It's my job."

"Are you all right? You got punched."

"I can take a punch, Gloria."

"You looked like that girl in *The Exorcist* when her head spun...."

A knock at the door interrupted our fun and my chemical restoration. I opened the door, making a joke about the second fist looking for me. One of my favorite students stood in the hall with his hands in his pockets. He was one of the boys in the fight. He wanted to know if I was all right. I told him I was. He then confessed that he was the one who had hit me. He apologized several times before I convinced him that I'd learn to live with this humiliation. For the rest of the year, I enjoyed the role of the frightened teacher. "Jeff, do you have enough time for this essay? I can move the date back. And what grade would please you?"

One beautiful spring day, I was speaking to some students in the cafeteria when I heard an explosion of screams and curses. I looked to the other side of the room. Students had knocked over chairs to get out of the way of some terrific fight. I ran toward the huge circle. What was I going to find? *What did lifeguards think about while swimming to a shark-attack victim?* I pushed through. Rocking on his back in a fetal position, Frank, a senior in one of my classes, was having a seizure. Repeatedly, he banged his head on the floor.

Holding his shoulder to restrain him, I put my other hand under his head. I looked up to the circle of students and shouted for someone to get the nurse. No one moved. In my most authoritative voice—and channeling my fear—I ordered them to get the nurse. "Now!" They had no idea that I was as shocked as they were. I had never seen anything like this.

Finally, Ann came. She and I held Frank while other teachers moved the students out of the cafeteria. I have always admired school nurses. They're calm, friendly, and competent. Ann was no exception. When she arrived, I knew what the students felt when I broke through their circle. Somebody who knew what she was doing was in control.

Finally Frank became still. Ann asked for a stretcher, and several teachers carried him away. Rubbing my bruised knuckles, which had cushioned his head, I sat against the wall on the floor. It was my turn to become very still. This was my third year of teaching, and I thought I had seen it all. It was my first day of school again.

When the bell rang, I got up and went to class. *If a teacher heard a bell in his sleep, he would stand up.* I opened the door, sat at my desk, and looked out the window. I was drained; I had just experienced the equivalent of five fights in a row. June was the first student to come into the room. When she saw me, she asked if I was okay.

"Tired."

"You were the only person to do anything."

"I was the only teacher there."

"But we couldn't move."

What seemed natural to me was a revelation to June. She and her senior classmates, who were the ruling class among the students, were not in charge of their world. Of course, they couldn't move; they were frightened teenagers. They needed their teachers; they needed me. Suddenly, my exhaustion became exhilaration. I was the teacher of my schooldays, a leader of students—and even a hero to some of them.

At the end of the day, I went to Ann's office to check on Frank. His mother had picked him up, and Ann was tending to new emergencies. I thanked her for coming so quickly and being the best nurse in the world. "I think I love you, Ann. You saved Frank—and me. How's he doing?"

"Not good. This was an unexpected relapse for Frank. He wants to go away to school next year, but that's out of the question now. His mother won't allow it."

For many suburban upper-middle-class students, going away to college is a rite of passage. My city friends and I never considered leaving home for an education. Why would we? There were many colleges in New York City.

When Frank came back to class two days later, I asked him how he felt. He said he felt fine, but he was different. Since he sat in front of my desk, we often spoke about baseball and movies. I asked him if the Mets were playing that day, but he pretended not to hear me. He didn't say anything else, and he didn't look at me. I told myself he was embarrassed. Things would return to normal after a few days of conversations, but they didn't. He spoke only to answer a question about our work. He never looked at me, and he never smiled. I thought I'd hear from his mother, but I never did.

I was sympathetic, because I knew that public embarrassment is the teenage nightmare. Acne, braces, and glasses cause pain to most teenagers who believe happiness belongs to the beautiful. Since I wore braces *and* glasses, *and* had acne, I hated the injustice of teenage life. Of course, I never dreamt of a girl with braces, acne, or glasses.

I felt somewhat comfortable with myself when I kept my glasses in my pocket and my lips wrapped across my teeth. Never smiling also helped. For my acne, I used antibiotics, a steam machine, a sun lamp, Retin A, and radiation treatments, which I'm told can cause thyroid cancer later in life. If I couldn't be one of the beautiful, I was going to be inconspicuous, the universal defense against teenage embarrassment. To Frank's horror, his personal nightmare became a public exhibition in the school cafeteria.

During a normal lunch period, he was enjoying his free time with friends and eating lunch when he was jerked out of his chair and thrown to the floor. He never extended his arms to protect his face. He twitched and rocked himself into students until there were only chairs for him to knock over. Terrified, friends and strangers surrounded Frank and stared.

I did what any teacher had to do. I held him while convulsions rocked his body. I tried to control his movements, so he wouldn't hurt himself. I spoke to him. "It's okay, Frank. You're all right, Frank. You're okay, Frank." At some point, teachers moved the students out of the cafeteria, and the nurse came. When his body became still and his cheek rested on the floor, a thick discharge oozed from his nose. I smelled urine and asked for a nearby newspaper to cover him. To June and others, I was in control. To Frank, I was a witness. I saw everything.

And he hated me.

In 1968, my first year, I had much to learn about my role as a teacher. Since I knew nothing about the profession, my goal was to avoid being a fool in the classroom. I copied what I knew best, the method of those teachers who had taught me throughout those years in Catholic school, which both helped and hurt my early years. I learned the value of discipline from them, but not the patience, which they didn't need to exercise, because no one ever defied them. Public school was different; today was different.

During my first four years of teaching, I became an authority figure—and much more. I realized that my students' world was not the simpler world of my youth when the teacher's word was absolute, and we listened, because we always had. Broken families, drugs, civil rights, the Vietnam War, and the military draft changed everyone's perception of authority. Students became more than faces behind desks; they became confused and angry voices, and teachers could no longer ignore what they didn't see. They had to listen.

Today, teachers can not predict what will work with students. The good lesson plan, steady discipline, and good intentions should get the job done, but teaching is not a science. The teachers of my day were sure of their roles in schools; Frank and my other students taught me that I never would be.

6

Land of Leonard Trainees

To understand my passion for teaching, I need to consider the person I was before teaching. I was rarely at the top of my class, I was rarely a game-winning athlete, and I was never the most popular kid in the neighborhood. I was an above average student in high school. After eight years of ruler-waving nuns in elementary school, I appreciated the Irish Christian Brothers. I enjoyed studying Latin and literature—and having male role models.

Since my mother wanted me to attend college, I did. But I wanted to start making money. None of my neighborhood friends went to college; they worked. Living at home, they had money to spend and often treated me, their poor friend, to movies and drinks. In January of my first year, two non-neighborhood friends from high school failed out of college; I barely survived. My mother and Brother Synan, then Dean of Iona College in New Rochelle, convinced me that college was worthwhile. After a disastrous first year, I was an above average student for the remaining three years.

In 1965, I became an English major, because I enjoyed the English survey courses of the first two years. I read books all the time. What was the big deal? Of course, I never considered the many hours I'd be spending in the library doing research papers. I did have an advantage over my literature classmates. My girlfriend.

Kathy had gone to secretarial school. After work and on weekends, she accompanied me to the 42nd Street Library. For several hours each day, she took down my pencil underlining in shorthand and then erased the underlining. At my home, she first typed the notes, which I organized, and then the final paper. (I didn't know how to type.) Kathy and I deserved those good grades.

Fordham University accepted me into the graduate program at a time when young men all over the country were applying to graduate schools for deferments. The alternative was Vietnam. Fortunately, my improvement over the last three years of college impressed the acceptance committee. I chose the education program, because I had made one entertaining speech my senior year in Speech 101 to a receptive audience. Perhaps, this indicated a talent for teaching and a solution to my draft status—and career choice. I did very well at Fordham.

The first four years of my teaching career in Yonkers, the fourth largest city in New York State, were the most significant years of my life. Like all new teachers, I taught the difficult classes the veterans didn't want—the non-academic/preparatory students who didn't go to college. After some early problems with their rebelliousness and my inexperience, we began to like one another. I became the "preparatory teacher" to all the other students and teachers in the building. For the principal, however, I was a teacher who could control large classes of students who did not want to be there.

I understood my survival depended on discipline, so when a student was disruptive, I took no prisoners. Their behavior slowly improved, and eventually the battlefield became a classroom with students sitting quietly, taking notes. I earned the students' respect and respect for myself.

My classes grew and grew. Whenever an academic teacher failed a student or "threw" one out of class, the guidance counselor came to me. I was still young enough—and insecure—to be flattered. "You can deal with these kids," and "You're the only one he'll work for." I loved the attention. The large classes of "troubled kids" were confirmation of my new and surprising talent. Veteran teachers do not fall for these compliments.

The second year was another milestone in my career. My schedule included one academic class. I was a confident "preparatory teacher" but didn't know if I'd be a successful "academic teacher" working with "smart kids," many of whom were better students than I had been in high school.

They were highly motivated, sophisticated young people who left home for prestigious colleges. I had to prepare them for the New York State Regents Exam, my first—as a teacher.

At Fordham, I had taken a seminar in Ralph Waldo Emerson, because all the other courses were full. At the time, I had no idea that my "bad luck" would give me material for future lesson plans every September; the American renaissance in literature began with Emerson, Thoreau, Whitman, Hawthorne, and Melville. For the first homework assignment, the students defended their favorite epigrams from Emerson's essay, "Self Reliance." Naturally, they found the essay difficult. Well, yes, I agreed, it was difficult. I explained that Emerson was college material and that I wanted a sense of their potential. I added that after Emerson, they would find the other authors simple reading.

Feeling safe with my honest appraisal of Emerson and eager to share their potential, they became positive about the assignment. Students enjoy knowing they do demanding work. Taking a cue from Emerson to revolt against society, Mark, one of the brightest students in class, claimed to be self-reliant in a terse sentence below his name and refused to do the assignment. I wrote A in one corner of the paper and F in the other corner.

"What do A and F mean?"

"I gave you the F."

"Who gave me the A?"

"Emerson."

"Which one counts?"

"That's up to you."

"Which one goes in your book?"

"Who gave you the assignment?" The class laughed. "Sorry."

"That's not fair. Emerson tells us to be individuals."

"Exactly. Then, why do you want the A? I represent society. For your rebellion to be meaningful, you must choose the F. Next week, you'll find out that Thoreau spent a night in jail to validate his civil disobedience."

"Can I do the assignment over?"

"You realize I'll own you." This time, Mark laughed with the class.

I remember going to the teacher's room afterward and announcing that I had just taught a wonderful essay. Of course, I camouflaged my gloating. "I really enjoyed that class.... Those kids are very smart, very smart." I sat in the huge, ancient armchair fit for a king, ate my lunch, and relished this new feeling—until I remembered beginner's luck. But after each successful lesson, I became less and less the beginner. I became more secure, because teaching gave me the respect for myself I needed.

Lesson plans are key. Students like amusing teachers but don't respect incompetent ones. When I wasn't correcting homework in the evenings and on weekends, I was working on lesson plans. Often, a plan requiring several hours to write up lasts for only one class; the same plan in another class may last two or more periods. Jonathan read all the literature for that first "academic" year and anticipated student questions for me the evening before the lesson. After his rigorous questions and challenges, I was ready for anything.

I dreaded developing new plans. Perhaps, the fear of failure had something to do with it. Unlike the college research paper, which loses its importance the day of its submission to the professor, the lesson plan can make or break a teacher's day or week. Curious young minds demand a rational, interesting, and most important, insightful roadmap that guides their journey through a literary selection. Students test the teacher's lesson plans every day of the year.

But before every formal lesson, I asked the students for their opinions. "What did you think? Good? Bad? Do I know how to pick great authors?" Always, the students raised their hands to claim some ownership of the discussion. My next question was even more unthreatening. "If you didn't like it, do you know why?" I wanted them to know their contrary opinions were important. I always looked for a hook, something in their criticism to coincide with my interpretation. "I know what you mean. I felt the same way about the ending of *Huck Finn*. The return of Tom Sawyer ruins it."

My favorite lesson plans built on student comments. Once students felt safe to voice their impressions, they became interested in the divergent views and criticism that a good lesson plan encourages—and sometimes adopts. (Over the years, I frequently revised lesson plans.) At the end of a discussion, I would ask students if opinions had changed about the work. I was always happy to hear, "I still don't like the book, but I'm glad I read it." (I admitted I found it difficult to watch opera singers and football players, but I appreciated their talents.)

The students liked the works of Twain, Cather, Fitzgerald, Salinger, Wilder, Miller, Williams, and Albee; they struggled with those of Emerson, Thoreau, Dickinson, Hemingway, Wharton, and Steinbeck. I defended the work without attacking the student critics. While teaching Emerson and Fitzgerald, I was romantic; Twain, realistic; Williams, naturalistic; and Albee, existential. I believe this made a difference in my teaching. I was passionate about the work of each author, and passion is contagious.

I made sure the students respected themselves. Often, I reminded them that their maturity and intelligence permitted our doing sophisticated work. They became LTs (Leonard Trainees) and, like doctors, could proudly exhibit the designation after their names. On the last day of class, I presented them with professional-looking diplomas with an official seal, thanks to Jonathan and his printing connections. The diplomas came in three colors: blue/LT, brown/LT2, and purple/LT3 for first, second, and third timers. The criteria for the diplomas were simple—pass the exam and laugh at my jokes.

To add solemnity to the ceremony, I played "Pomp and Circumstance" while I called out the names. Smiling, they walked to the front of the room, shook my hand, and received their diplomas. Intermittently, chords of the rock song, "Wild Thing," interrupted "Pomp and Circumstance," which delighted the class, because they knew that my girlfriend called me "Wild Thing," the man who made her "heart sing," the man who made "everything groovy." As soon as they recognized the beginning chords, "Pomp and Circumstance" resumed, and I called for restraint by reminding them of the serious nature of the ceremony. They'd play along with me until another burst of "Wild Thing" spiked through "Pomp." I wanted them to remember my class.

The following September, I would miss last year's seniors until I began to know my new classes, and year after year, I met wonderful young people, most of whom I never saw again after graduation. Teacher-student relationships are existential. (Mark will always be that Emersonian teenager rebelling against homework.) Fortunately, those of us who thrived on the love shared with students may believe we were successful teachers. And in the land of LTs, I finally found something that made me better than average.

7

LTs at the Movies

Schools are family. Like parents, we teach and protect students. Like children, students rebel and show affection for anyone guiding them. I once informed my college-hitchhiking buddy and old friend Jerry Ahern, who found his daughters' rebellion at home exasperating, that his children like many others often begin sentences at school with "My dad went …," "My mom said …, and "My dad and mom are…." At many *Forum* and yearbook meetings, I listened to my editors play "dueling parents."

"Really? You know what I hear at home?" In a struggling high voice, Jerry mimicked his daughters. "My teacher said this. My teacher is so funny. My teacher is the best."

Students move back and forth between home and school with the expectation that life will hold no surprises. Parents act this way, and teachers act that way. When students see teachers outside school, they're either shy about the encounter or ecstatic about two separate worlds coinciding. Life is magical.

In 1981, after I had moved to my school's town, twenty miles north of New York City, "Lenspotting"—seeing me around town—became public revelation at the beginning of class Monday morning. "Hey, Len, you drink wine with dinner?" And "Why does a skinny man like you drink skim milk?" Seeing me—and my wife, Mary Jo Bellafortuna, whom they had never met—became the holy grail for Lenspotters. As far as LTs were concerned, there was a new member in our school family.

"What does Mrs. Leonard look like?"

"She's a beautiful brunette with dark eyes, and has excellent taste in clothes—and husbands—Thomas. And she's not Mrs. Leonard. Her name is Bellafortuna; she kept her maiden name."

"Do we call her Mrs. Bellafortuna?"

"Call her Bellafortuna.... Like Cher."

"Does Bellafortuna sing?"

"No, she cheers. In high school, Bellafortuna was captain of the cheerleading squad. Now she's my cheerleader."

"Does she ever play nurse, Len?"

"This is the reason you'll never meet Bellafortuna, Thomas. You can't control your feral impulses."

"Come on, Lenny. I'm kidding. Bring her to the play this weekend. I'm in it." "Yeah. Me, too. Bring Bellafortuna ... What does she wear when she cheers, Len?"

"Last weekend, scarves and mittens. We went to one of those upstate Christmas tree farms. I sawed; she cheered:

Leonard! Leonard!

He's my man!

If he can't do it,

—nobody can!'

"I bet you cut down a big tree, Len."

"I bet his tree is bigger than the one at Rockefeller Center. He's Bellafortuna's quarterback."

"Careful, Matt."

"Hey, Len, it must've been freezing up there." Looking at Tara, Matt shivered and hugged himself.

"No, Matt. Bellafortuna knows how to keep *her man* warm." Seated, Tara did a fitful hula-hula.

"That's very attractive, Tara. Actually her pantyhose kept me warm." For several moments, the classroom became a lawn of statues. One. Two. Three.

"Her pantyhose? You wore her pantyhose?"

"Best thing for a cold day. Ask a professional football player. Broadway Joe Namath swears by them."

"You must like big women, Lenny."

"They stretch, Tara.... And he has no idea he's going to meet you."

"Who?"

"Your future husband. He has no idea that his life will change forever. For all he knows, life is one long party after another. He's probably going to a party tonight. He's smiling. Maybe he has a girlfriend. A nice girl. Probably pretty. He's in a good mood; life is good. All that will change, Tara."

"He's a lucky man if he's going to meet me."

"He has no idea … Okay, folks, pass up the Wharton homework. And thanks for coming." Conversations like these at the beginning and end of classes elevated Bellafortuna to mythical heights.

When my wife and I saw *Body Heat* at the movie theater on our new street, my meeting Dana and Suzanne at the refreshment counter became a potentially historic event for the two eleventh grade Lenspotters.

"Mr. Leonard, what are you doing here? You're seeing *this* movie?"

"I wanted popcorn."

"But isn't this a bit sexy for you?" Dana tilted her head to soften the revelation. Suzanne nodded in maternal agreement.

"My wife gave me permission."

"Your wife! Bellafortuna's here? Where's Bellafortuna?" They had hit the jackpot and dropped the cat-and-mouse chit chat. "Really? Bellafortuna's here? Where?"

"She's watching our seats."

"Can we say hello?" A Saturday night movie was never this good. A Lenspot—and a spouse.

"No. You'll scare her."

"What's Bellafortuna wearing? We'll find her!" They had the power and loved it, but since we sat in the balcony—and they sat downstairs—they never found us.

I've always loved balconies. In the golden days of movie palaces, we cigarette smokers climbed the steep steps to our seats beneath the twinkling lights of the 72nd Street "Low ese," where we legally puffed our smoke into the galaxy. When I gave up my Luckies in the sixties, I no longer sat in the balcony; but I still looked up to admire the stars through the clouds of smoke.

This night, my wife and I were sitting high above several hundred sold-out seats. Leaning into each other, we sat in the middle of a row of strangers, and the huge ceiling fans moved the heat against our faces; there were no stars above us here, no galactic space to cool us—just two teenage girls looking up to the balcony for me and Bellafortuna.

During the first adulterous scene in the movie, William Hurt looks through a window to see Kathleen Turner, who's standing inside her home. With her left hand on her hip, she slowly moves the flared fingers of her right hand down her thigh, directing his eyes across her red skirt. Hurt breaks a glass door with a chair to reach her. Turner gasps. With my wife pressing against me, I saw Turner's wedding ring, scene after scene, but I didn't wonder about her husband. I wondered about the audience. Did they approve?

Turner unbuttons and opens his shirt just wide enough to kiss his chest and neck. She turns her back to him, and he slides his right hand down her skirt and his left across her breast. She slowly turns back to him. Beneath a warm starless ceiling, I watched him tug her red skirt up and up and up until her panties appeared, and he was able to slip his hand beneath the elastic and squeeze. And I gasped. My students and I were watching this together.

Turner lies back on the rug. While the fan in the background of the frame cuts through the humid air behind them, Hurt removes her white panties; his dropping them casually behind them on the red rug fills the frame. I remembered that the juniors and I had discussed the theme of corruption and the red-and-white symbolism in *Gatsby*. Did they remember?

William Hurt says to Kathleen Turner, "It's not right." I agreed, but she's more convincing, "Please do it." She convinced me—and reminded me—that Dana, Suzanne, and I were listening to the language of seduction and passion.

After several torrid scenes on silk sheets, Hurt whines, "Give me a break here," but Turner doesn't and he surrenders. Dana and Suzanne gave me a break, though; after the movie they weren't waiting for me in the lobby—or the street. There were, however, no breaks Monday morning in class.

"Mr. Leonard, what did you think of William Hurt breaking the glass door?"

"Didn't see it."

"How could you not see it?"

"My wife covered my eyes."

"She probably thinks you're too delicate." Suzanne pursed her lips.

"No, she was worried about later. She was afraid her quarterback would break through the bedroom door." Dana fell across Suzanne's desk, and Suzanne fell over Dana, two squealing tag-team wrestlers.

We were family, and certain teachers were fair game. On the other hand, families come together during difficult times. There were no references to Bellafortuna—or my divorce—the following year.

8

No LTs at the Barber

Since the first grade, I have loved snow. During my forty-nine years in a classroom, as student and teacher, snow in the forecast was more exciting than the advent of a holiday. If we were lucky, we had a week to look forward to it. Every night, the weatherman drew waves across a map that indicated a sure thing—when this and that came together. Every morning, students and teachers confirmed one another's fantasy.

"They're always wrong."

"Not this time. It's coming."

"I love snow days."

"If I don't see you tomorrow, read the next chapter in your text."

The day before the storm was electric. The sky might be dark, but hearts were light. It was going to snow. Students smiled, and teachers frowned, winced, and made vague complaints. Snow was worrisome. The students understood. Teachers were the adults; they were the "kids." They loved snow days; teachers loved school. At lunch among themselves, the faculty smiled "kid" smiles. They were going to have a day off.

That night I watched the weather channel to enjoy the certainty and the dire warnings of the approaching storm. That night, I listened for the snow against the window. I listened for the plows. I listened for the silence of roads closed to cars. In the morning, I waited for the phone-chain call to make it official. Then I called three teachers who eagerly waited for my call.

More often than not, the call never came. I ran to the window. Nothing but cars and people, without umbrellas and boots, going to work. The satellites and the computers were wrong. With a sigh of relief, the weatherman announced that the storm spared our community. Yesterday's sure thing "skirted" the metropolitan area, closing schools and delighting unsuspecting students, teachers, and administrators somewhere north or south of us. That day, teachers and students consoled one another. "They're always wrong!" But I reminded my students of Keats's "Heard melodies are sweet, but those unheard/Are sweeter." The great joy was their imagining a day off. Yesterday's dream was better than the day off. For the weatherman, Keats, and me, the students had one word, "Baloney!"

On those days the dream materialized, I watched the commuters, using their umbrellas as shields against the blizzard to reach the train station, walking in the roadway, because the sidewalks were under a foot of snow. I sipped my coffee and listened to the radiator hiss until my stomach growled. After a leisurely breakfast, I read a novel or corrected papers. If the snowstorm took place in January, I called my dentist and grabbed a snow cancellation for my bi-yearly check up. I'd brave the three-block walk.

On the way back, I'd walk into the barber shop and take advantage of the empty chairs. I had an excellent barber, but he was no LT. He knew how to trim and thin my hair. There was never the danger of my leaving his shop looking like a raw recruit in boot camp; however, there was a price to pay. Under the black sheet, which shockingly highlighted gray hair, and over the clicking of the scissors, I patiently listened to the ritualistic questions and comments.

"Another day off? (click, click).... It must be nice? (click, click).... How would I know? (click, click).... Someone has to open up. (click, click).... I should be a teacher. (click).... You have to go to school a long time to be a teacher? (click).... How many days you work a year? (click).... You're off the summer, and Christmas, and Easter, and the Jewish holidays. (click, click).... You work half a year? (click).... If your wife is a teacher, you have the whole year off, right? Ha! Ha!.... Blow dry?"

But he was an excellent barber. I endured him—and my neighbor, a friendly woman, who also worried about my time off. I never defended myself. I never informed him—or my neighbor—that snow days (usually two or three) were "built" into the calendar, and that if days lost to snow exceeded the allotted amount of snow days, the teachers had to make them up over spring break. I just tolerated the clicking monologue.

On icy days, the superintendent also canceled school. Two hours later, the streets looked fine. On one such day, I decided to get a haircut. Through the window, I saw only one customer in the shop. When I opened the door, I also saw the pain in the barber's eyes. Here I was again, a man who worked now and then, depending on the weather. But I was a customer; he gave me a weak hello. Feeling his pain, I looked down.

I hung my raincoat on the rack, sat near the radiator, and picked up a newspaper. Between gazing out the window and reading my horoscope, I heard the barber say to the captive head above the black sheet that schools must be closed, because "the professor is here again." Wink, wink in the mirror. Without ever looking at me, he continued with his winks and assessment of my good life. My status had fallen from 2nd person to 3rd person somewhere between the door and the radiator. I stood up and walked to my raincoat. "Professor, where are you going?"

"The professor doesn't want you to cut his hair."

Too bad; he was an excellent barber.

9

Rookie and Veteran

A new teacher has an audience of many witnesses. It is impossible to hide the many mistakes, because some students watch him, sit near him, and wait for mistakes. And some witnesses become players in a farce. I have seen sympathetic students, kind human beings—embarrassed by the mistakes and laughter—laugh at the teacher.

The new teacher doesn't need an entire class to make him entertaining; one student can turn a good lesson into a long running comedy. I was that new teacher in 1968. I met several students who challenged my authority. And I broke all the rules. I raised my voice too often and made threats I couldn't keep. Worst of all, I took it personally; I took the classroom home. What was I to do? Sure, I was a successful straight man in a comedy, but I wanted to be a teacher.

Since I couldn't inspire them, and I couldn't threaten them, I went for the kill. I did the unimaginable. I ignored ethical education. I decided to fail anyone who disrupted my class. This solution is unthinkable for those who don't teach, for those who have support from administrators, or for those who are blessed with charisma; but I didn't qualify.

My plan was simple. I would break my students' average into two parts: 60% for academic achievement and 40% for participation. If the students were disruptive, then they were not participating. Jerry was my target, a junior performing and enjoying a good show at my expense. He played the martyr when scolded and vehemently swore that the letter A was an O on a spelling test. Jerry loved the show more than the others, because he was the writer, director, and audience. I spent more time threatening Jerry than teaching the other students. The show could not go on.

Unfortunately, Jerry did well on his tests and homework, leaving me powerless to control him until I discovered a new source of power, an unorthodox approach to discipline. Jerry, therefore, received 46/60 for his work and 10/40 for his successful comedic direction; Jerry failed the marking period with a 56. I wrote the average in red on top of his last paper. The next day, I handed out the papers, returned to my desk, and waited. While other students spoke quietly about their grades, Jerry held his paper in front of his face; I could see only his hair and one red ear. Then, his paper shook and moaned.

"What's the matter, Jerry?"

"You failed me!"

"You failed yourself."

"You gave me a 56%."

He was angry. For the first time in eight weeks, Jerry was on the defensive; he was not in control. He was feeling the heat of anger and confusion. Out of the spotlight for the first time, I enjoyed the show; I was directing Jerry.

"I explained to the class how it would work, Jerry. You knew the breakdown."

The students were smiling, but for a change, they were looking at him. I knew the "here we go again" smiles well and enjoyed their new focus. I no longer resented these happy faces. I wasn't going to be a pushover.

"How could you give me 10/40 for participation? I participate a lot."

"You did, yes, but not enough to cancel out your disruptions. Do the math."

"This is an English class!"

"Lower your voice, Jerry. Every time you interrupt a lesson, you lose a participation grade. I did you a big favor here."

"You gave me a 10. What favor?"

"Your disruptions far outweigh your participation. Think of a scale. Think of feathers and marbles on a scale. Your disruptions are the marbles; your feathers didn't stand a chance. See?"

"I'm seeing the dean!"

This was wonderful. Unlike some deans who don't support their teachers, but do support students, our dean was consistent. He supported no one.

Go ahead, Jerry, I thought, but please come back quickly and complain. The class was watching and realizing there was a new show in town.

Jerry came back, sat down, and put his head on the desk. When the bell rang, he left the room without speaking to anyone. It took some time, but eventually Jerry accepted the inevitable and forgave me, and from then on, he was all feathers.

My behavior with Jerry was extreme, but pragmatic. Nothing else had worked. I spoke to him. I joked with him. I even pretended I liked him. But he was smart enough "to drive the teacher crazy" and pass the course. This all took place during my first two months of teaching. Some new teachers never finish the year. I was not going to be one of them.

Jerry became one of my favorite students. When his clowning entertained the entire class, there was no victim. Once, however, he became his own victim. Despite Jerry's newfound respect for me, he frequently fell asleep. Like many students, he worked too many hours after school at his job and insisted he needed the money. Jerry swore he wouldn't fall asleep again, and for a good stretch of time, he succeeded until the treacherous lesson of *who* and *whom* as relative and interrogative pronouns. In all fairness to Jerry, he did try to revive himself by going to the bathroom, but I couldn't let him go twice in ten minutes.

Several minutes into the minefield of grammar, I looked over at Jerry to see if he could maneuver through this dangerous terrain without my guidance. Once again, he succumbed to the most pleasurable seduction allowed to students in a classroom.

Nothing was ever so humorous to me as watching a student resist the forbidden fruit of sleep. For most students, the struggle is valiant. The chins balanced on wrists like golf balls on tees, the head jerks, the bobbing heads, the flickering eyelids, and the lips working like the last gasps of gills were signs of a lost struggle, a sweet surrender to sleep.

I was always eager to share my glee with the other students. I'd simply smile and point to a sleeping student, and the rest of the class understood the significance of the moment; we were going to play. If there was a camera available, we took a picture. Then we surrounded the sleeping beauty and waited for his "personal space alarm" to wake him.

Once a student slept so soundly that I left him to wake among the strangers of another teacher's class. Unfortunately, my students and I didn't enjoy firsthand his bewilderment. Later at lunch, the lucky teacher informed me that he awoke near the end of the class and sat quietly for the remaining minutes, looking around the room for a familiar face to confirm that he was awake. The room was right, but who were these people?

Jerry never displayed signs of a struggle. He accepted the futility of resistance; his lids slid over his eyes, his cheek settled on the cool desktop, and his arms dangled near his knees. His only chance of staying awake was to revive himself with generous scoops of water against his face, but that was no longer an option. Once confined to his seat during a challenging lecture, Jerry never had a chance. I wished he had fallen asleep during my first eight weeks, but that was a compelling time for him.

I suppose his nose was congested, because his mouth was working mightily, perhaps causing the suction of pages of the adjacent *Warriner's Grammar* to flip into his mouth. The class and I gathered around Jerry and agreed that, "He'd rather eat it than read it."

Unlike most students, Jerry slept through our conversation above him. (Everyone has the ability to focus on something.) After several minutes, I decided to return to teaching and clapped several times for the students to sit and for Jerry to wake. After the third clap, Jerry's head popped off the desk. I smiled and turned toward the board when I heard a mournful whine. I turned to see Jerry slowly shaking his head back and forth. Like an elephant's trunk, the grammar book swung beneath his face.

Jerry in his sleep could disrupt a class, but even I enjoyed this spectacle. Apparently, one of the pages, which had fallen into Jerry's mouth, sucked his tongue dry and became part of his face. What was he thinking at the time? Had I grabbed his tongue to teach him a lesson? Had his tongue gained several pounds during his nap? Finally, saliva returned to his tongue, freeing the book and cementing an image I've shared with my students through the years.

During the same year, my fourth period comprised a class of non-academic students who found themselves lumped together, because they were academically lazy, emotionally disturbed, or vocationally bewildered. While I was introducing myself to them, a husky, balding boy ran between the class and me to a desk on the other side of the room, chased by the weary-looking dean of discipline. "Coach" appeared to be seventy years old; therefore, his attempt to kick Evan, just before Evan found a seat, surprised me and delighted the class.

Evan remained in the first seat in the first row for the entire year. He participated but couldn't control the urge to call out, and his reflections had the effect of deflating the serious mood of the moment. During a discussion of a scene in Harper Lee's *To Kill a Mockingbird*, I asked the class how the children opened the gate to Boo's house without making a sound.

"I'd pee on it!" I ignored him; the class laughed. Evan sat sideways on his chair to face the class. I directed my next question to the other side of the room.

"How did the children do it?"

"They did it the wrong way."

One arm on his desk and the other on the back of the seat, Evan prepared himself for battle. I pretended Evan didn't exist; he knew better. Maria raised her hand. I would take the class back.

"Yes, Maria?"

"They spit on the hinge."

"Very good, Mar...."

"They did it the wrong way. You can't compare spit to pee. You cover more ground."

"All right, Evan."

"They'd have to spit all night!"

"Get out, Evan!"

"Why?"

"You know why."

He didn't. He was destroying my lesson plan, a beautiful lesson plan that had required several hours of work. On some level, he knew the laughter was his undoing, but he loved the attention; he played to it.

"I'll go to the bathroom and check it out."

"Get out now, Evan!"

As he left the room, he wiggled the doorknob.

"Sounds squeaky!"

The class roared. I turned toward him with one thought. I could kick him all the way to the bathroom.

I learned that Evan was not a bad kid. He never said anything to hurt anyone's feelings. He just needed attention. The students'. Mine. Anyone's. The entire school knew Evan; he was outrageous. He simply said whatever was on his mind. Fortunately—and unfortunately—he was fond of me. He never challenged my authority, but he loved to "play" with me. I learned to play back and maintain the students' respect.

His notebook, familiar to the students, was infamous. On the front and back covers, Evan had written "I hate Leonard" over and over in different colors, in different sizes. He wanted me to react. The class already had seen it, but I was the prize. He wanted me to ask him about the notebook. I didn't. I wouldn't play his game.

Frustrated, Evan announced to the class, "I hate this man. He makes me work!" The class laughed. I ignored him, so he added more of his comments onto the covers and voiced his discontent with me again. "He makes me come to class!" I ignored him. After a short period of time, I heard, "And he can't teach!" He—and the class—watched me. I ignored him again. He was becoming desperate. They groaned when I wrote the homework directions on the blackboard.

When it became obvious to Evan that the verbal attacks did not work, he became physical. Evan weighed 220 lbs; I weighed 160. When he grabbed me in a bear hug from behind, I was powerless to move. I threatened him with failure, detention, expulsion. He didn't believe me, but he was sure of one thing; he had my attention. Not just in the classroom, either. I was his toy in the cafeteria, in the hall, anywhere students and teachers came together.

I was not only uncomfortable with my feet skimming the floor but also painfully aware of probably being the only teacher in the building's history in this unprofessional position. The more I squealed, the happier he was. I was a schoolmaster puppet. Only one tactic worked; I played dead. He shook me, lost interest, and released me. Again and again.

Once, while I was sitting behind my desk during an exam, I felt Evan grab my neck. This was a new line of attack; he preferred crushing my chest. I couldn't see him, but I knew it was Evan. The assailant was stealthy, swift, and strong. I couldn't play dead; I was watching my students take a test. My only hope was that they wouldn't notice.

One by one, they looked up. Maybe it was my hoarse whispering to Evan or my breathing, which was becoming labored. Evan was showing no mercy. Every time I moved my head up and away from him, he tightened the grip. The class was watching Evan playfully strangling me; no one was laughing.

Why was he persisting? His audience didn't seem to appreciate his efforts. In fact, they looked perplexed. Some adjusted their glasses. Some stared. They all looked troubled. I found it disconcerting that they couldn't make eye contact with me. Evan had lost his mind, completely. Since they were all looking at my chest, I looked down with great difficulty. Eyes bulging, I pushed my head forward (yoga, they must have thought). When I was able to look down, Evan released me.

He was not behind me. He was not in the room. He never was. I had shut my desk drawer on my tie, which became as taut as the strings of a banjo under my chin. I opened the drawer, freeing my creased tie, and loosened the noose with great difficulty. The class, relieved that I was not suffering a stroke, fell into their test papers, which could not muffle their laughter. I smiled. Evan had not tried to kill me. And then I laughed, because I must have looked ridiculous and because their laughter was affectionate. After we dried our faces, they continued with their tests. Of course, at lunch, Evan laughed more than anyone.

During my thirty-two years of teaching, I developed a teaching style that did not depend on major reprimands and threats; my first year taught me the importance of self-control. If a problem could not be solved with an aside or a scowl, the student and I went into the hall for a conference. This occurred, perhaps, with one or two students a year, who found school in general to be overwhelming. In most classes, discipline was never a problem.

Since I rarely lost my temper, Tim was unaware of it. He was a pest. When he challenged my patience, he had no idea of my anger's heat; and I had no idea of its proximity. Tim enjoyed side conferences with his friends more than the theme of group action in *The Grapes of Wrath*. But a long stare usually worked wonders with him. In our two years together, I think I perfected the stare. Tim didn't anticipate what lay at the end of the stare; he assumed it was interminable.

Unfortunately, he also couldn't gauge my enthusiasm for literature. Ma Joad is one of my favorite characters. The scene, in which she protects Ruthie from Pa, because Ruthie revealed to the other children in the camp that her brother Tom had killed a man, moves me as no other scene in fiction. Discussing it, I found a rhythm with the class that makes teaching an art form.

Apparently, the girl next to him offered Tim more than art. I approached him and lowered my face uncomfortably close to his. My voice did justice to my anger; I sneered to Tim to be quiet. I expected to see fear. Instead, Tim made a face at me. I just had given Tim a-once-in-a-lifetime-fearsome face I rarely used, and he mimicked me. Now, he insulted both Ma Joad and me. Rarely do teachers throw honor students out of class. I told Tim to leave the room.

He came to see me after school. By then I was more troubled by my temper tantrum than by him. He apologized for disrupting the class, for making me angry. I gave Tim some very good advice: Never, never mimic a crazy person. He shook his head and swore he never had mimicked me.

"What was that face you made?"

"I didn't make a face. First, I thought you were kidding. When you told me to get out, I couldn't believe it."

But he did make a face, a face he had never seen. That evening, my friend David suggested to me that Tim wasn't making fun of me. On the contrary, Tim was trying to understand my face, because he had never seen the unfamiliar person glaring at him; he was confused.

Neither Tim nor his classmates had ever seen me lose my temper, and it changed something else about the world that they thought was constant—a "nice" teacher is always nice.

Tim had never seen the "mean" me. He mirrored my face. If I were possessed, he was going to find me. I apologized to Tim for throwing him out, but warned him the monster might return, if he interfered with a great lesson again. For the rest of the year, Tim and I never saw that face again.

Students have a great capacity for forgiveness. If they feel the teacher likes them and respects them, they will excuse occasional outbursts or moodiness. Tim never held a grudge against me; however, he appreciated the danger of testing the "good guy."

10

Administration

My first professional encounter with an administrator took place the week before school opened in 1968. He had been a history teacher who coached football, had recently lost his wife, and had beaten colon cancer. The changes in his life, the politics of student rebellion concerning the Vietnam War and the Civil Rights Movement, and the rise of teacher unionism tested him every day.

When I entered his beautiful office in the beautiful building that was Gorton in the sixties, he looked up from his large mahogany desk and saw a very young man pretending he knew what to do in a classroom. My interview with him was a courtesy to him, since I already had signed the contract at the Board of Education an hour earlier; he asked me only one question.

"Who do you like?"

"Who do I like?"

"Football."

"I don't follow football."

He bowed his head, slowly moving it from side to side. I think he was doing the universal head movement for "And now this."

The late sixties was the end of one generation of teachers and the beginning of my generation. We old-timers would begin retiring in 2000 with the advent of PowerPoint presentations in the classrooms. In 1968, the old timers longed for the days of the benevolent dictator who knew how to run a school. Students did not talk back to teachers, and teachers did not talk back to an administrator. The halls were quiet; the classrooms were quiet. But those days were gone. Students were no longer afraid of teachers, and students—and many teachers—were no longer afraid of administrators.

When the students saw me on the first day of school, they saw the establishment, a reason for rebellion. The previous spring, Dr. King and Bobby Kennedy were murdered, and the Students for a Democratic Society occupied the administration building at Columbia University. My students were going to challenge me, as many students challenge teachers; but in this climate, they were going to do so with a new-found political passion.

As a first-year teacher, who had to pay his dues, I was assigned the preparatory students. Because of learning disabilities, emotional disabilities, disciplinary problems, drug problems, or chronic indolence, they were grouped in the same classes. They were called "prep" students, and we were called "prep" teachers. The academic student body and administration had little respect for both of us.

Since my students knew I couldn't count on an administrator for support with discipline, after-school detention for disruptive students was a useless exercise; I was the only one to show up. Survival of the fittest was at work here, and they believed my fitness would not survive their success with new teachers; three months into the year, another first-year teacher, a young man my age, resigned from his math position—without giving notice.

I don't remember much of my first three months. I know I struggled with classroom management and often lost my temper, but one incident is memorable. I was returning graded tests with a passionate lecture about the power of an education, and my students were listening. It was one of those rare times when all was right with the world. I was a teacher; the students respected me. Why else would they listen to me?

But I learned unfortunately that my lectures did not have staying power. I had to be interesting and entertaining. "Maybe we're boring! Why can't education be fun?" whined the college education professors around the country. Obviously, I wasn't entertaining. I had to tell the "bored" students to be quiet so that I could be heard by the few who weren't bored. I never said "Shut up!" It always sounded awful to me. And where would I go from there?

"Keith, keep quiet."

"I wasn't talking to anyone."

"Your lips were moving."

"I was talking to myself."

"Say goodbye."

The class laughed. Keith laughed. I smiled. At times like these, I loved my students. Humor works for the new teacher if the class believes it's not a plea for mercy. But humor can easily turn an attentive class into an opportunistic one. After all, freedom is worth it, even at the expense of a "funny teacher."

The kids laughed for as long as they could and then stopped when it was obvious, even to me, that my joke was not that funny. All thirty stopped smiling and braced themselves for the return of my lecture. I was holding their papers in both hands, acutely aware of the progress I was making when whispers curled up into my happiness. I looked down to see two girls, Grace and Beverly, chatting below me; they could have been sitting in Grand Central Station.

I was going to lean over and say, "Polite people don't...." Instead, I roared, "Shut the hell up!"

But that wasn't enough; I wanted to punish them for every whisperer who knew I was struggling. Growling, I raised both arms over my head, like a biblical figure, and threw the test papers at them. Unfortunately, most of the papers slapped the top of Grace's head, fluttered around her body, and like autumn leaves, surrounded her desk. She glared up; I glared down.

And the class was perfectly still. Now this was entertaining. I wonder if reality TV would be interested in the following concept: Five people who have never taught must survive a week in the same class; the students must decide their fate at the end of each day with an up or down thumb.

Grace kicked her desk into Beverly's desk, jumped up, and banged out of the room. It took several minutes to pick up the test papers in the quietest room in the building. I didn't expect anyone to help me, and no one did. I walked up and down the aisle to hide my discomposure, picking up where I had left off; I pretended I was in control. Grace did not run to the bathroom to hide her tears. She would return, steely-eyed, to confront this crazy new teacher with her indignation. I would discover that the class was well acquainted with her temper and feared it.

There was a knock at the door. When I opened it, an administrator motioned me out of the room with his finger, the same finger that threatened students and teachers in the good old days. Would I lose my teacher deferment and go to Vietnam, because my tolerance for teenage rudeness was chalk thin? I didn't care. Not then, but I would that night when the television screen framed boys in body bags coming home from Vietnam. His moving knuckle ordered me to come closer. Moving his bowed head from side to side, he moaned, "Leonard, are you nuts? You can't use language like that." He didn't mention the paper assault nor give me time to justify my behavior. He walked away. The less he knew, the happier he was.

If this had been 1969, just one year later, and I had thrown papers at Grace's head, students would have boycotted my class. In 1969, in the lobby of the school, the girls staged a sit-in for the right to wear pants in school; they won that right in one hour. In 1999, I could expect a visit from the principal, the guidance counselor, the chairperson, and the school psychologist, because a parent made an angry phone call to the president of the Board of Education, who called the superintendent, who called the principal.

But this was 1968, and the protests at Columbia were still abstractions—pictures on television—for simmering high school dissidents. Our students were still in transition; they knew they were angry, but they didn't know what to do about their anger. If I didn't know what to do with my "reluctant learners," as they were euphemistically called, they didn't know what to do with their "loony teacher."

Grace came back to class the next day and quietly ignored me for a week. She made me the happiest person in the world, because this was the beginning of a truce that would lead to a normal classroom, where teacher and students worked together. The episode with Grace was my last display of despair.

I showed anger again, but not desperation. In fact, I became angry less often and learned to use the silent teacher stare, which is a thing of beauty framed in the right face. Something changed in my classes; we began to like each other. Like two boxers who hug after a bloody fight, Grace and I especially liked each other.

Whenever someone spoke out of turn, she wheeled her desk around to make eye contact with the offending student. If that didn't work—and her patience lacked endurance—she'd make her discontent clear with an exasperated "Shut up! Shut up, I said!" Satisfied that the class was being respectful, Grace faced the front of the room, and I continued to teach.

First-year teachers, and many experienced teachers, are uncomfortable with the obligatory observation/visit from an administrator. They speak to themselves while teaching: "Be funny; don't make too many jokes.… Be informative; don't be boring.… Keep order; don't be too strict.… Encourage student participation; don't digress."

During the early years, I was my harshest critic; therefore, I was fortunate to meet some nurturing administrators who rejected my severe criticism and advised me properly. Some administrators today choose the pushy parent's self-serving complaint as the educational reason to harass, and even fire, a new teacher. Why mentor a young teacher with potential if it means they have to take political heat? In my friend's school on New York's Long Island, the teachers posted a sign in the faculty room that says it all for them: "You are as good as your last parental phone call."

One day, long after I had made peace with my students, I arrived late to class. When I opened the door, the students were celebrating my tardiness with loud, happy conversation. You can be the most loved teacher in the school, but your absence is their talk time.

"Cream rules!"

"Okay, folks, let's start class."

"The Allman Brothers are gods!"

"All right, enough now!" Someone sang a few lines from "Sweet Melissa."

"If I have to tell you one more...." Someone began to air strum chords from a Cream song.

"That's it. Three hours of homework tonight."

Schools of Education around the country make it very clear that homework should not be used as punishment, but I didn't have a water cannon handy, and this threat had worked in the past. I used it again.

The class became quiet, aware that the battle of the bands was leading to another battle. They would sing another day. For several weeks, they seemed happy with the class, but I feared my pioneer-teaching days of the recent past returning when whispers and yawns naturally had led to head-turning conversations. The room was quiet, except for the clanking of a radiator. When I began to take the attendance, a student approached my desk.

"What is it, Steve?"

He leaned toward me and whispered, "There's a lady in the corner."

I looked up and saw Marjorie Elvove, the district-wide supervisor for all English teachers in Yonkers. She was writing in her notebook, which could only mean that she was documenting my lack of classroom control, my unorthodox threat, and my lack of self-control. When I thanked Steve, I didn't whisper. The class was watching, and I didn't want to reveal my concern for her presence.

I taught the class, sure that the incompetent-teacher police had found the faker in the building. Two thoughts dominated my lesson. Mrs. Elvove saw the real me at the beginning of the class and knew I was impersonating a teacher. And my students might see the real me who wanted to appease the administrator.

Since I could not fool Mrs. Elvove, I decided to preserve my integrity and fool my students for the rest of the period. I pretended to be upset with them; I was not going to be "nice" for the administrator. I didn't want them to see my sudden return to normalcy as hypocrisy to impress the outsider. It never occurred to me that this new behavior would be strange to them, since I never stayed angry with students. I didn't fool them; I confused them. But they said nothing. If students like a teacher, they'll be on their best behavior to make the teacher look good during an observation.

Usually, after every observation, the good administrator will meet the teacher as soon as possible. Mrs. Elvove and I discussed the lesson over cafeteria pizza.

"You were late to class. What happened?"

"I teach a class on the other side of the building. Sometimes, the halls are so crowded, you can't get through…."

"Say no more."

"Usually, I get to class on time."

"When you get your own classroom, you'll wonder how you ever taught all over the building." This woman was terrific.

"My kids were rowdy. They're usually good."

"Kids will take advantage of a situation…. You *were* angry."

"I was angry." I trusted her. "Too angry."

"Your reaction was honest. They accepted it. I saw the boy warn you that I was in the room."

"He's a good kid."

"You have good kids. Near the end of the period when they were waiting for the bell, the girl next to me told me that you were a *good guy* and that you were having a bad day."

I often think of Mrs. Elvove and the effect of her words on my confidence. I had made class management mistakes, and my lesson was mediocre, but she evaluated the students in my class, considered my inexperience, and most important, my students' protection of me, and concluded I had potential. The students realized that Mrs. Elvove's presence caused my erratic behavior and accepted it; she was the boss, and I was a first-year rookie.

When we met the next day for class, we resumed our normal relationship, but I have never forgotten the power of the outsider to affect me. As a result, for many of the following thirty-one years of observations, I made it a rule to ask my students about my behavior in the presence of the administrator at the end of the period. Years later, one wise guy thanked me for not beating him and the others when they gave the wrong answers. At that point in my career, I was able to laugh. Then I hit him on the head with a folder.

A friend of mine told me that he had developed the habit of lightly slapping his students' arms, as he walked up and down the aisles; it became their joke, their game. Once, when he was observed by his principal, he omitted this little familiarity, but my friend hadn't anticipated the students' leaning away from his approaching figure. To the principal, he seemed to be parting the Red Sea. Since he didn't get the joke, the principal was uncomfortable with the appearance of corporal punishment. He probably had left the classroom for administration as soon as his resume looked good; he no longer appreciated the unique relationship between students and teacher.

And recently, I was told a story by teachers who had to endure a lecture on differentiated learning by a consultant hired by a school district. The administration's latest embrace of a fad was the elimination of tracking students according to ability. Since the veteran teachers had strong reservations about the one-room schoolhouse-on-the-prairie classroom, they asked for a demonstration lesson. The consultant declined. He said he knew when he was "being set up."

He felt that these teachers were hostile and were going to sabotage his lesson. I've never heard of a teacher "setting up" an administrator, but I've known many students who wouldn't tolerate a teacher unable to prove his ideas. Imagine doctors refusing to demonstrate their theories to their colleagues in the medical profession. Fortunately for our profession, some administrators are also teachers.

I never felt I had to impress Dick Krell, the head of the English Department at Eastchester High School. He came into my room so often, the class and I considered him one of us. Like Mrs. Elvove in Yonkers, he was intelligent, supportive, and experienced in the classroom; he was a teacher's administrator.

I first met Dick outside his office. I was desperate; I had to get out of Yonkers. I became disillusioned with the school system after our eight-day strike in the winter of 1972 and the racial strife at Gorton that was destroying my love of teaching. I had two friends, teachers at Eastchester, who had spoken on my behalf, but I hadn't heard anything from the administration.

Dick was a gentle and unpretentious man, so our meeting proved to be his adventure for the year. I didn't swing into his life on a vine, but I did startle him with my eager salutation and proximity. He had locked his office door and turned into me; I was that close. His head snapped back, and his eyes darted to my shoes, to my forehead, to my shoes, and back to my forehead. When he was sure I wasn't a specter, he blinked and looked at me.

Once I mentioned my two friends, who taught at his school, he relaxed. But why was I standing before him? There was a procedure to follow for an interview. I told him I hadn't received a response to my request for one, hence the ambush. I smiled; he didn't. He wrote my name in a notebook and promised to look into the matter. Apparently, he sensed the urgency of my predicament because within two weeks, I met with him and Dr. Frank Driscoll, the Superintendent of Eastchester Schools, for the interview of a lifetime.

Dr. Driscoll was a short man, packed with intelligence and passion. He was also anti-union. Administrators are anti-union—unless they are talking about *their* union. It was my misfortune that Dr. Driscoll began the interview with a reference to my role in the strike. He knew the answer, of course.

"Were you on strike over there in Yonkers?"

"Yes, I was."

"Eight days?"

"Yes, eight days."

"After losing sixteen days pay, I'm sure you regret the strike?"

"No, I don't."

"You don't? You don't regret all that money you lost?"

"I'd do it again." Dr. Driscoll's face became red. His neck and head zoomed out of his collar toward me. His voice rose.

"What about the students?"

"They supported us; they brought us coffee on the picket line."

"You deserted them!"

"The Board of *Education* deserted them!"

My face became very red, and my voice rose.

"You broke the law; you broke the Taylor Law!"

"It's a bad law!"

I turned to Dick; he looked very uncomfortable. He was sitting against the wall to our side, and I forgot he was there, something, I'm sure, he never forgot; he said nothing. I stood up.

"Well, thank you, Dr. Driscoll, Mr. Krell. Thank you for the interview."

"Where are you going?" Dr. Driscoll looked surprised.

"I'm arguing with the interviewer." I shook my head in disbelief.

"That has nothing to with your teaching. Sit down."

That was Dr. Driscoll. He didn't smile. He probably didn't like me much, but he had heard good things about me, and that was more important than our personal differences. When he told me to sit down again, I did. I don't believe there are many people like him in positions of power—certainly not in education today. A principal once told me that he would have done the same thing.

"No, you wouldn't."

"Yes, I would."

"You would say that I was not a 'good fit.'"

"I would even hire you."

"No, you would say that it 'wouldn't be a good marriage' or that we 'weren't on the same page.'"

"I wouldn't say that."

"Stop it. You'd kill me with administrator-talk."

The more he insisted, the more I laughed.

At the time, I didn't know what to make of Dr. Driscoll. Did I really have a chance of being hired by a man who wanted to drag me across his desk? He still had to observe me, and I was sure he wouldn't like what he saw. Would he see a chalk-waving teamster in corduroy bell-bottom pants? Or a free spirit, a loose cannon, who didn't have the good sense not to argue during an interview? Would I even hire myself?

To prepare for my observation, I called my friend Lou Serico at East-chester for advice about my lesson. He told me that Dr. Driscoll was a conservative man and that I should dress appropriately. That was a prob-lem, since I didn't wear ties any longer. Most teachers at Gorton didn't wear ties because of their potential danger in breaking up fights. For Dr. Driscoll, I would risk my life.

My problem, once again, was to preserve the appearance of integrity for my students, but more important, to avoid their embarrassing questions about my change of dress during the observation itself. Any physical change in the teacher—haircut, watchband, pimple—arouses the students' interest and intolerance for anything that contradicts their sense of order. A student once noticed that the silver color of my watch didn't match the gold color of the clip on my watch band. I decided to wear a tie every day for two weeks before the observation, hoping to acclimate them to my new look, but every day they had something to say.

"Is that a clip-on?"

"No, it's genuine neckwear."

"Neckwear! Who says 'neckwear'?"

"He says 'trousers.' Why wouldn't he say 'neckwear'? So, why are you wearing neckwear?"

"I want to look swanky."

"That's a funny-looking tie…. Swanky! Who says 'swanky'?"

"I didn't know you were interested in fashion."

"I know funny looking."

"You think this is funny looking? Come up here and look at this care-fully."

Several students rushed my desk. I chose the biggest critic and held my tie up to his face.

"Yep, that's funny looking."

"What is?"

"Your tie!"

"That's not a tie."

"What is it?"

"It's a mirror."

There was nothing more gratifying to me, during classroom teasing, than to turn a group of students, ready to have their way with me, against one of their own—especially if that student was popular and clever.

Shocked, they turned to the boy holding the end of my tie; they made monster faces, pointed, and screamed at him. He had me cornered, but like a martial artist, I leapt over him. Dazed, he didn't know where to look. Realizing that he had been ensnared, he laughed with us. He could be gracious, since he had directed many pointed fingers at me in the past.

For two weeks, they asked about my swanky new look; and I thought maybe I had run out of time when finally they stopped several days before the most important observation of my life. Dr. Driscoll and Dick Krell observed a senior class, discussing Cleaver's *Soul on Ice,* and a junior class, analyzing Robinson's "Mr. Flood's Party" and "Miniver Cheevy."

After the second observation, my students left the room. I walked to the back of the room where Dr. Driscoll and Dick sat. Without getting up, Dr. Driscoll complimented my senior class, reached into his jacket pocket, and gave me an envelope containing the contract. He told me to sign it and send it back as soon as possible.

Meeting my students the next day, I wasn't wearing a tie. They demanded that I wear a tie; they liked the swanky look. I said my charm depended on my changing wardrobe. They asked me about the two strangers in the room, and I asked them for their routine assessment of my behavior. Was I natural? Was I myself? A little nervous, they thought, but pretty much the same as usual.

I never told them what I had done. How could I? For the entire year, I was candid with them, and they with me, about my behavior during the observations. How could I confess to staging a performance that was totally for someone else's benefit? What happened to my integrity? After two weeks, they stopped asking me about the ties, and I never wore one again until I began teaching in the fall at Eastchester High School.

It took me two weeks to send the signed contract back, and only after Dick had telephoned me. I knew I had to leave, but during my four years at Gorton, I had become very much attached to colleagues and students. I would still see my friends on the weekends, but I would never see my students again. Marjorie Elvove knew what to say when I expressed my sadness at leaving them. "You'll love the kids at Eastchester just as much."

I was fortunate, early in my career, to know Mrs. Elvove, Dr. Driscoll, and Dick Krell, who understood our profession. Certainly, good administrators still work in our schools, but today's corporate culture in education, with superintendents' hopping from one district to another for higher salaries, has often robbed communities of administrative experience.

Superintendents do not have to worry about the long-range consequences of their decisions. In five years, they will be in another school district, once again implementing "innovative" programs, which were innovative twenty and forty years ago, appointing administrative underlings to support them, and hiring expensive outside consultants to train the faculty and impress the Boards of Education. These decisions, of course, will make the superintendents' resumes look good for the next hop in five years. Fortunately, the most important educator in a school district prefers to remain in the classroom.

11

A Mob is Ugly

My never having children played an important part in my relationship with students, but I never saw myself as a parental figure in their lives. According to the admissions from smiling grandparents in TV ads, I resembled a grandparental figure: I enjoyed the students for the period, and then they were somebody else's responsibility. Like most grandparents, I didn't experience the parental anxiety of broken curfews, wild friends, drugs, car accidents, sex, diseases, etc. My anxiety was usually selfish. Do they understand the material? Is the class interesting? Am I a good teacher? Why are they so quiet? Do the students like me?

I knew my subject well; I spent many hours working up lesson plans. And my seventeen years of Catholic education stressed the benefits of discipline. Teacher knowledge and classroom management are necessary for student edification, but achieving a personal rapport with students transcends formulas. I knew teachers who ran effective classes but failed to connect with the students. The students learned the curriculum but didn't enjoy the classes—if they felt their teachers didn't enjoy them.

When the Eastchester School District hired its teachers, it conducted an orientation program for them, which included a speech by Dr. Driscoll. After my four years in Yonkers, I knew that most administrators had little to say to those of us who chose to remain in the classroom, but Dr. Driscoll was different. He had hired me despite our argument the preceding spring. When he spoke, I wanted to listen.

Every student, he said, should leave the school building with at least one good thought about the day. Dr. Driscoll wasn't referring to grades. He was referring to students' feeling good about themselves. When they're walking home or sitting at their kitchen tables, they should remember

65

something about their day in school that makes them feel special. "In the main office today—in front of everyone—Mrs. Cirrincione and Mrs. Martucci said I was excellent in the play." "Ms. Dalton waved at me in the library." Or "On the lunch line this afternoon, Mr. Prendergast, the nicest teacher in school, said I wrote a sensitive essay." A student should look forward to a new school day, because the faculty and staff are there. Dr. Driscoll believed the school building is the students' home away from home.

I had never received better advice. Recently, I counseled a new teacher to make sure the students knew that he liked them. A successful teacher likes his students and demonstrates his affection for them in some way. My young friend understood this, because he remembered his "kind" teachers; he knew they liked him.

I remember Brother Kearney, my Latin teacher in 1959, addressing me in the cafeteria, "Good job on the quiz, Leonard." I didn't care about my quiz grade; I cared that he had spoken to me using my name. At Rice High School, teachers rarely addressed students outside class, and more rarely used their names. I assumed they had more important things on their minds.

Letting the students know too soon that you like them may be dangerous. If my young friend is too quick to reveal himself, he'll lose control of the class. Students will choose freedom over kindness. They may easily confuse kindness for weakness, so the teacher must wear a mask. Young teachers want respect and popularity, but usually they can't earn both at the same time. For every new class I met, I wore the September schoolmaster mask. Sometimes, the mask would smile, but only when my face surrendered to an unexpectedly funny moment. After I had established myself as the leader in the class, the mask faded, but my students remembered it.

In an English class, girls are usually better behaved than boys, because they enjoy literary analyses more than boys; girls talk, boys listen. And small classes pose fewer problems than large classes. Of course, a small class of girls appreciates freedom as much as a large class of boys, and one student is enough to cause a mutiny.

Twenty years ago, I had a class of six girls that fooled me with the size of the group; my schoolmaster mask faded prematurely in the presence of six sweet girls who initially responded to gentle reprimands. But they couldn't resist their instincts to be free. They spoke out of turn, and they spoke while I spoke. They had their way with me. I became desperate; I had lost control of my class while we were smiling. My schoolmaster mask returned, but it was too late; they had seen the "real me." I growled and I warned, but they frowned at this masquerade; I was too nice to be "mean."

There were too many distractions, and I spent too much time on discipline for the class to be meaningful. The class was a failure, which meant that I was a failure. When June arrived, I was happy to see them go. I didn't blame them. They were nice girls, but they were immature and needed a class leader, a disciplinarian. I was too friendly, and they treated me like a friend. Most students would do the same.

I remember an easygoing substitute teacher leaving a note in my mailbox about the rudeness of one of my classes. They were honor students and an "easy class." When I spoke to them about the complaint, they swore he was a "mean sub," because he had decided that they should stop the whispers.

I promised myself that I would never underestimate a class again. Some years later in the bank, I met one of the girls from that infamous class. Ironically, she hugged me and gushed that our class was the "best class ever." I realized that she saw our class as a family, large and noisy.

Several weeks into each school year, I became the teacher that students teased, but respected. There was never a plan for the breakthrough day when I would reveal the "nice teacher" lurking behind the September mask. In the margin of my lesson plan, I didn't prompt myself with the annotation to "be nice." Somehow, within weeks, Mr. Leonard became "Len," and I trusted the relationship we had established enough to smile freely and relax. Like a family, then, the students and I shared experiences from our lives and wove them into our literature discussions.

In 1975, I told my tenth graders that I needed to confess something. Students love drama. I confessed that I had once screamed at several women in a saloon, and I felt terrible. "I was a brute."

"Why did you scream at them?" Noreen was shocked.

"They wouldn't dance with him!" James wasn't; he was going to play.

"Nothing like that, wise guy ... I better not tell you. You'll never forgive me."

"Of course, we will! What happened?"

"Well, all right. That night, I was having an onion and cheese sandwich...."

"That's disgusting!"

"Wait a minute! How can I confess something to people who think a sandwich is disgusting? I know you'll never forgive me." I pressed my lips together, shut my eyes, and slowly moved my head back and forth.

The boys laughed, and the girls told them to shut up. "We promise to forgive you!" At this point, the girls would kill to hear my confession.

"All right, here we go. Before seeing a play at La Mama, ETC on 4th Street, my friends and I were having dinner...."

"An onion and cheese sandwich is dinner!"

"Excuse me. Do you want to hear this story?"

"Sorry." James was afraid of the girls who *really* wanted to hear the story.

"... at McSorley's Ale House on 7th Street. McSorley's is the oldest bar in New York, and they didn't allow women in."

"Who cares? Women don't eat onion and cheese sandwiches."

"That's the point of my story. Why would a woman want to eat in this place? It's a man's place. Sawdust covers the floor, and knife carvings scar the thick pine tables. It's a great place for guys to drink beer without the pressure of being attractive to women."

"No fear of that!" James smiled when the class laughed.

"Listen to you. You're mocking me."

"The next mocking person will die." Noreen glared at James and turned back to me. "Go on, Len."

"Well, we were eating our sandwiches when several women gathered outside the bar, but one of the bartenders locked the door."

Some of the boys clapped, but most of the students looked at me and waited to hear more. I didn't smile.

"There were six or seven women chanting something about their rights, and a television crew was filming their protest. We didn't care; we knew we were right. There were hundreds of discos in the city. Why did they have to come here? This was a saloon."

"Why did they bother?" The boys were on my side.

"They wanted to integrate the bar on principle; they were feminists. Gulping our beer and chewing onions, we wanted to preserve our manhood and drive back this female invasion."

"What did you do, Len? Throw an onion at them? Curse them out? 'Shoo, shoo, go away, you darn girls!'"

"I wish I had said *darn*." Today, of course, women would quickly echo our invective, but in 1970, women cursed discreetly. Discretion didn't stop us that night. Never before had so many men cursed female strangers in a public place.

"Len, I can't believe you're a male chauvinist pig!"

"I never thought I was. I didn't see how this would advance the rights of women. I wanted to preserve the tradition of McSorley's."

"How would you like it if someone stopped you from going somewhere, because you were a man?" The girls looked concerned; the boys sat back and became the audience. I was on my own.

"I wouldn't like it. But there was something far worse than our discrimination against them. Looking at these women, I saw surprise in their faces. They knew they were not wanted, but they didn't know they were hated. I looked around the bar, and I saw what the women saw. The men were ugly, because they had become a mob, and I was one of them."

"What happened? Did the men kill the women?"

"No, we didn't *kill* them, but they didn't get in." (Not that night. Soon though, thanks to the U.S. Supreme Court.) "But I had to leave; I felt awful."

"I knew you weren't a pig." The girls smiled; the boys didn't.

"No, I didn't leave to support the women; I left, because I didn't want to be one of the men. A mob *is* ugly. Remember yesterday we read Colonel Sherburn's speech to the cowardly and hateful mob in *Huck Finn*? That night, we were that mob."

"I knew he'd find a way back to work."

And we did return to our discussion of *Huck Finn*, but I had made my confession to these tenth graders, because I wanted to share my revelation about humanity—and myself. Our reading of *Huck Finn* had nothing to do with it. Like a family, we discussed ideas that came from our daily lives; we didn't need to relate these ideas to the literature, but we frequently did, sometimes years apart from one another. In the process, the literature came to life.

The next day, Natalie, who was disappointed that I was a chauvinist pig, proudly presented me with a poster of the words, **A Mob Is Ugly**, superimposed on the smiling faces of men and women. "Why the women? And why the happy faces, Natalie? We weren't happy."

"You were before the women tried to get in. Who knew you were ug … that ugly anyway?"

Natalie made the sign truthful and universal. All men and women have the potential for despicable behavior. Weeks later, when we studied Hawthorne's "Young Goodman Brown," I reminded them of my rage that night. Hawthorne had written that the fiend, the devil, "in his own shape is less hideous than when he rages in the breast of men." I remember watching an interview with a cordial, handsome, smiling Ted Bundy who savagely killed many women. And where would con artists be without their smiles? Would anyone buy the Brooklyn Bridge from Uriah Heep? Natalie's poster made the human condition clear.

We placed the poster above the blackboard behind my desk, where it remained for twenty-five years. At times, graduates drove around the parking lot to view the poster through my windows. In 1992, the Health Department evacuated our school because of a pesticide misapplication dangerous to the students and the staff. The clean-up crew threw everything that was not washable out of our rooms. After several weeks, the teachers returned to the classrooms to discover the walls, which teachers love to decorate to mark their territory, bare. The **A Mob Is Ugly** poster was gone.

In the past, whenever students became noisy, I looked up at the sign and pointed to them. They laughed and got back to work. This became "our thing." They knew about the sign before they were my students because in small schools, teenagers fondly share stories and traditions. The juniors, during their first month in my class, wanted the sign back. They wanted to be the ugly mob; it was our joke, our tradition.

They complained about its absence until Eric made a new one with his computer, but he left out the pictures of the smiling faces; in fact, there were no faces at all, so I asked for their photographs, which quickly covered the white spaces around the lettering; they were marking their territory. This was their room—and when they were noisy or playing a joke on me—I pointed to their pictures. I called them degenerates, yahoos, the dead zone, and the ugly mob; and they were proud. Now, their notoriety was public and personal.

During the 1980 graduation exercise, the valedictorian proudly referred to being a degenerate in Mr. Leonard's class. Watching the parents turn to one another made me uncomfortable with Mario's admission—and our private joke.

Today, students love nothing better than playing jokes on their teachers. In the late fifties and early sixties, we didn't play jokes on our teachers. Mr. Gurney, a history teacher, was the exception. He was the master of the deadpan. When he revealed that he was in the secret service before becoming a teacher, we believed him. After many such revelations, we caught on and always looked forward to the next story. We loved every minute of his world history class, and I believe he did, too.

He had no patience for corporal punishment. He relished making fun of those teachers who relied on their leather straps for discipline. But the Brothers were proud of their straps, which were different in size and shape from the others, and often gave them names. If a Brother forgot his Enforcer, Persuader, or Snapper, he'd borrow one from a Brother next door: "Go to room 443 and tell Brother Murray that I find your behavior worthy of his Reformer."

There were black straps with white tape at the end to enhance grip and brown straps folded over for "sudden and certain revelation." There were short straps and wide straps. The Brothers drew them from belts like six shooters and from satchels like swords. Gurney disapproved of the straps and said there was enough leather in the building to open a shoe repair store.

We knew there was serious friction between Gurney and the strap-packing Brothers, so we were not prepared for his announcement; he had undergone a conversion because of our bad behavior. "I have failed you, but I now see the light." He reached into a brown paper bag and uncoiled a soft, tan leather belt. It was four feet long, and he bragged he would be the most fearsome teacher in the school. He named it "Sparky," because sparks would fly when "leather met sinner." But when he raised Sparky over his head, he hit himself in the back. We cupped our faces, watched his demonstration through parted fingers, and enjoyed the show. He was playing with us again.

Gurney allowed us to play jokes on him, something we did to—and for—very few teachers. Sometimes, we'd decide our strategy just before class. For instance, instead of saying the prayer "Hail Mary," as we did in English before every class, we said it in Spanish. Unexpectedly, he continued with the prayer "Our Father," which forced us to surrender, since we didn't know the "Our Father" in Spanish.

One Friday—before he entered—we turned our desks to face the back of the room. No one turned at the sound of the door opening. We heard his school bag slide into his desk and his slow, heavy steps across the room. It was his practice to enter the room only after the collision of school bag and desk. He said nothing. We began giggling, but we understood that no one was to turn his head. We heard the chalk tapping the blackboard. He wrote for twenty minutes but said nothing.

He judged we were weakening by the fidgeting and said, "Tomorrow, you will be tested on the material on the…." We never heard the rest. Like bumper cars, our desks made sharp left and right turns and banged into one another. He could take a joke, but he took his teaching seriously. As we scribbled in our notebooks, Gurney sat at his desk with his hands behind his head.

Another plan was simple; no one was to speak a word in class. And, of course, no one was to smile. This was our most daring practical joke. It would be individual—not group—defiance. We waited for his customary entrance. When the bell rang, his school bag slid into the desk. He came into the room, lifted the school bag onto the desk, and reached in for his notes and text.

"Last night, you read Chapter Ten?"

We nodded.

"Yes, you read Chapter Ten."

We nodded.

"Greene, what did the chapter cover?"

Greene looked at Gurney and squinted to find the answer.

"Detention after school, Mr. Greene." The formality of the address indicated that he was not in a good mood. This joke would take many casualties. How long could we keep it up?

"Mr. Myers, you look half alive. What was the subject of Chapter Ten?"

Myers looked toward the windows to our left.

"The pigeons don't know, Mr. Myers. The chapter is in your text."

Meyers flipped through several pages.

"Mr. Myers, keep Mr. Greene company after school."

Whispering the wrong answer to someone who didn't know the answer to a question was our favorite game—being on the "griddle"—because the "poor unfortunate," not the whisperer, received the detention. He could be your best friend; it didn't matter. For this joke, however, we would all be on the griddle, one by one.

"Mr. Maloney!"

Maloney shrugged.

"Mr. Crowley! ... Mr. Waterman! ... Mr. Leonard! ... Detention!" Gurney's hand covered his mouth, but his eyes gave it away.

"Mr. Clark, who was our first president? He knew. "Mr. Clark?" Tom squeezed his chin. "Mr. Clark?" Before the griddle got hotter, several boys broke down. Over the giggling, we heard Gurney groan, "I'll see you all after school to make up the lost time. I hope it was worth it." Certainly, it was. We loved his class, and we did well on the New York State Regents Examination in June.

My teaching style took something from my experiences with Mr. Gurney. We played jokes on him, because we liked him, and we wanted him to like us. Sometimes, we went too far, and his pale face turned Irish red, but he never held a grudge. The day after a joke—and detention—he'd slide his bag into the desk, and we believed our class was special. He liked us; therefore, he let us play. His great talent was walking the line between play/work and chaos.

Looking back on my teaching career, I now understand that Gurney and I needed the same response from our classes. In his day, he had to be a tightrope walker. I remember a kind science teacher who suffered, because we took advantage of his kindness; he wanted to play, to "be liked," but he didn't know how, and we ruined many of his lessons. Today, more teachers play with their classes. Thanks to Gurney, I played with impunity.

Over the years I used the **A Mob is Ugly** poster to tease my students, but in 1983 several spirited juniors wholeheartedly accepted that characterization. When they played a joke on me, they left a note signed, The Ugly Mob. They took my possessions, leaving ransom notes that threatened their destruction if I didn't postpone a test or cancel a homework assignment. Eventually, I discovered the identities of the three intelligent, imaginative boys, and we played throughout their junior and senior years.

Their boldness reached a climax the Christmas of 1983. When the doorbell rang, my mother and I were exchanging presents—and since I was still in my NY Mets pajamas, a recent student present—I didn't answer the door. It rang twice. Later in the day, we were leaving the apartment to enjoy our Christmas dinner at a French restaurant in the neighborhood. I opened the door and saw a large, beautifully wrapped package at my feet. I brought it into my kitchen where I placed it on the table. My mother recalled the bell, and I wondered aloud if I had disappointed a thoughtful student; I felt terrible. My mother made it worse by commenting on my popularity.

I opened the package; our restaurant reservation could wait. When I pulled out my classroom garbage can, my mother's enthusiasm about her son's popularity changed to shock and confusion. "Why would someone give you a garbage can?" But the significance was clear to me. For some inexplicable reason, as I walked back and forth in the front of the classroom, passionately expounding, I'd bump into the can. They always laughed as I kicked the can out of my way; I pointed to the Mob poster, they smiled, and class continued.

After explaining my Charlie Chaplin routine, my mother criticized my being as immature as the students, and we hurried out of the apartment to avoid losing our reservation. It was in the elevator that I had the chilling realization that the garbage can gift was a means—not an end—to their public playfulness. Above the panel of buttons, a Polaroid picture had captured the colorful presence of the gift several feet in front of my door.

They had taken the photograph from the side—from the stairs leading up to the roof. They must have been disappointed, since the image in the Polaroid lacked crucial elements for their mission to be successful: There was no man in the photograph wearing Mets pajamas, bending over a box. There was no disheveled man looking to his right at the camera. And there was no shocked man protesting their presence. The Ugly Mob, therefore, had nothing; they had signed the photograph. The first day back in school, I would be greeted by students who saw a photograph of a garbage can and a door. But there was no proof it was my door.

Craig, Terry, and Carlos graduated in 1985 and attended good colleges. And I missed them. For several years, we kept in touch; however, college, job, family, and geography interfere with relationships. In no other profession does a person know and lose contact with so many people, year after year. This is the great revelation for young teachers who believe in the permanence of their relationships. Recently, a young teacher complained to me that, after one year of college, even the e-mails ended.

I regret never going back to thank Brother Synan, Mr. Gurney, and Brother Hayes.

The Ugly Mob was not the only gang to invade my privacy, to play a joke on me, which must have amused the neighbors on my floor. Jamie and Linda were one year behind the Ugly Mob and decided to be uglier than their predecessors. They certainly challenged the boys' cleverness and daring with practical jokes that made us laugh seventeen years later when we met recently for coffee.

First, we recalled the "dog" incident. After a yearbook staff meeting, I drove Jamie and Linda to their homes. When we arrived at Jamie's, her mother and sister were walking their dog, Shadow. Since I had once worked with Jamie's mother, I rolled down my window, and we had a conversation about school, and the yearbook, and the fleeting nature of time. I then gave her my usual assessment of Linda and her daughter's degenerate behavior in school, and we laughed at the absurdity of my comments—and my attempt at humor. "You have to watch these crazy kids!"

When I waved goodbye, I made a face at the girls. Apparently, my grimace underscored their enjoyment of being the subject of a conversation that lasted for more than ten minutes. Smiling, they waved and hugged each other. I rolled my window up and drove off. I was in a good mood. Was there another profession as respectful and satisfying as teaching?

As I was turning at the corner, a dog barked at the back of my head. I hit the brakes and turned; there was a dog on my backseat. "What … the … hell?" When the dog barked again, I understood why Linda and Jamie found it difficult to wave goodbye.

Yes, seventeen years later, the girls—young women now—and I laughed and rocked, disturbing the tranquility of the patrons who were drinking their lattes and reading the bookstore's magazines and travel books. "You girls were good." I admitted. "I had become a stranger in a strange land."

"Good? We were great!" Gleefully, they reminded me of the "umbrella" incident. Ah, yes. Jamie and Linda had made it snow in June. "Remember, your mother thought it wasn't funny."

That was true. I was visiting my mother. We had decided to go to a movie on a rainy afternoon, and as we were leaving her building, she asked me to open my umbrella, something I rarely do when I'm alone. In her courtyard, a sudden, short burst of snow fell on our heads and shoulders. After the initial surprise of a June snow shower, we recognized the snowflakes were small pieces of paper, but we didn't connect them with my umbrella, not until my empirical mother looked at the evidence.

My mother didn't think it was funny; I had littered. It took me several minutes to pinch each piece of paper off the ground. I assumed Jamie and Linda were the culprits. On Monday, I suggested that they could learn something from the old Mafia who spared the lives of family members and "citizens." In April, they insisted, they had placed the pieces of paper in my umbrella, and from the window in the guidance office, they watched me run to my car—without ever opening my umbrella. They swore they had no idea my mother would suffer "the hit" two months later.

Often, whenever students were successful with a joke that didn't disrupt my teaching, I shared the joke, the names of the "degenerates," and my reaction to the joke with the class. I knew some students might be inspired, and perhaps I wanted them to be, but I wanted to celebrate their cleverness and, of course, their affection for me. If students don't like a teacher, they don't spend their time planning and executing elaborate jokes. And if they don't respect the teacher, there's no humor in their simple jokes.

Sometimes, I shared a joke-on-me story with students, even if it didn't involve them. I confessed to being surprised once before during an umbrella opening; my wallet fell on my head. After the customary "What-the-!" I remembered the police report I had filled out, several months earlier, after I believed I had been a pickpocket victim at Penn Station. Worried about thieves, I thought I had shoved my wallet into the front pocket of my raincoat, which was behind the umbrella hanging on my bent arm. "You stuck it in your umbrella!" a student screamed.

"It could happen to anyone."

"No, it couldn't." They became a chorus. Even the girls felt I needed a reality check.

"It does. I just admitted it."

"Why? Why did you admit it?"

"I never want you to think I'm perfect." They moaned.

Before we left the bookstore café, Jamie and Linda wanted to remind me that they had come to my home. They must have known about the Ugly Mob's Christmas morning joke. Fortunately, I had not been sick much throughout my years teaching. Despite the initial joy of students, they don't appreciate a substitute's extended stay. Quickly, they become bored with the free time and miss their regular teacher. In 1977, my juniors prepared for my hernia repair with a countdown in the corner of the side blackboard: **5, 4, 3, 2, 1 Days Left Before Shave & Surgery**.

Nine years later, during Jamie and Linda's senior year, I got the flu, which made the students happy for a day or two. After a week, they sent a class card with all their scribbled names and complaints about the substitute teacher's meanness. And they missed me … "really." Of course, I appreciated the sentiment and looked forward to my return. The day came. With an attaché case in my hand and a newspaper under my arm, I pulled the door open and almost walked into a lattice of duct tape at my doorway.

Through the tape, I saw my neighbor at the elevator. "Don't kiss anyone."

"Thanks for the tip, Don." I didn't try to make a connection between the tape and his comment. I was going to be late for work my first day back, and I was now in a bad mood. "Take the elevator, Don. This'll take me a few minutes." The smart way to remove masking tape is to remove it slowly at the ends. I tore at the center. When I realized I was becoming a mummy, I stepped back to free myself. After methodically removing the tape, I found the reason for Don's bizarre remark; a sign on the tape warned, "Quarrantine—Rare Disease—Do Not Enter Under Any Circumstance."

Jamie stopped the story because of our laughter. It had taken them almost an hour to run the tape back and forth across the doorway, because they were afraid I would hear their laughter and open the door. They were able to run only one line of tape at a time before they had to run down the stairs to laugh safely. Only when they were in control of themselves, did they return to my door. But sometimes, just approaching the door sent them down the stairs.

Of course, I knew they had done this. But what was my reaction the next day? I didn't remember; they did. Did I retaliate? They told me, yes, I had. Without looking at them, I passed their desks and said, "You misspelled Quarantine! Ugly, very ugly." That was it; I said nothing else, which worried them the rest of the day. I never mentioned *this* incident to my class. There is such a thing as too much inspiration. Mr. Gurney taught me well.

Sometimes, the jokes are clever, and sometimes, they go too far—depending on the circumstances during the "attack." One year, I couldn't find the Regents examination papers to grade for New York State credit and my students' final grades. When I went to the bathroom near my room, I realized I had left the exams on the desk. Five minutes was long enough for their disappearance.

Anyone observing the administration of the test to students in the cheat-proof rows of silent gymnasiums, the cathedrals of many small towns in America, would confirm the solemnity of the ritual. After all, state examinations are sacred documents. Teachers circle the bowed heads of students rendering the proper responses to their state.

I had not shown respect for their catechism. I ran from desk to desk. No. Had I put them in my desk drawer? Filing cabinet? Coat closet? No! No! And no! Did I ever bring them to the room? Were they lying unguarded in the gymnasium? I had never lost exam papers. And this was my last year. No, they lay on my desk when I left the room. I felt like Ray Milland in *Lost Weekend.*

Finally, I went to my friend's classroom next door. Kathy, a superior English teacher, was grading her own papers. Seeing me, she smiled and said, "Look up."

"What?"

"Look up." I looked up.

"Is there a pigeon up there? A monkey?" Kathy was a friend to all creatures, great and small. When the seniors released frightened animals in the

cafeteria on Prank Day, she ran between the screaming students—and flee-
ing teachers—to rescue every single mouse. She had a much easier time
grabbing the chicken.

"No."

"A mountain lion?"

"No." She shook her head.

"What am I looking for? Not a snake, I hope."

(Several years ago, while Kathy and I were crossing the parking lot outside my room, a student called us over to see his pet. From the trunk of his
car, he lifted a huge boa constrictor for his "show and scare" of the day. He
was half-successful. With choreographed dignity, I left Kathy gushing over
the snake and escaped into the building to "care for my waiting students."
Once inside, I found them all at the windows.

"Okay, folks, let's start class."

"You have to see this, Len."

"I know. There's a serpent out there." When I got to the window, I saw
Kathy wearing the snake like a shawl around her neck and down her
arms—and smiling for a camera. Jane Goodall never looked so happy. "If
that snake eats you, Barbagallo, can I have your desk calendar?" My students and I laughed.

"We're coming in, Leonard." No one laughed.

"If you come near my classroom, I'll call the police. There are children
here." I walked to the door and locked it.)

"So why am I looking up, Kathy?"

"Not here."

"Listen, I've got a problem. Someone's playing a joke on me; they took
my Regents."

"Go back to your room and read your blackboard."

"You know, don't you?" Of course, she did. Students trusted her. They
shared all their problems—and amusing stories—with her. Kathy Barbagallo was a very popular teacher—and the "social worker" on the staff.
No one in the building had a bigger heart. And as my good friend—and
comrade-in-arms during fierce English department battles over the latest

educational fad—she easily read my moods and enjoyed the joke. "You're an evil woman. You shouldn't be around children."

"Children don't steal my exam papers."

"They're afraid of you, Kathy. The blond hair and quick smile don't fool them. That's why they make these sacrificial offerings." Action figures from *Star Wars*, *Harry Potter*, and *Lord of the Rings* covered the front of her desk.

"I'm a sweet person, Richard."

I made a sick face, turned, and ran to my room.

LOOK UP! HAVE A GREAT SUMMER

—THE MOBETTES.

I looked up. There they were, balanced on the fluorescent lights above my desk. I stood on a student's desk to retrieve them and save my reputation. The Mobettes were Emily, Sarah, and Danielle, three wonderful senior girls. Emily never forgot my lobbing a "wake-up" eraser at her the first week of class. With chalk in her hair, she rushed out the door and sucked her classmates' gasps out of the room. Returning five minutes later, she promised retribution—and two years later—she kept her promise.

The "Mobettes" were lucky not to be in the building. Relief then anger replaced confusion and fear. In their defense, they never thought I'd miss their message. Each letter was a foot high. At the time, Kathy enjoyed the joke. It was funny. In retrospect.

During my last year, I didn't think a junior's programming the computers in the room to make burping noises during my American literature class very funny. I looked around the room to confront the offending student among his hysterical peers with my stock reprimand, "Well, that's very attractive." Realizing I was reprimanding a computer, I joined the hysteria.

I avoided playing jokes on individual students. Their teenage sensibilities make it difficult to laugh at themselves. I preferred to go after the entire class. I certainly avoided funny-noise jokes. But once, a self-defense tactic accidentally targeted an innocent student. During the creative writing class, my stomach growled. Every one looked up. Since the students and I sat in a circle, the students couldn't be sure of the growl's epicenter. One boy opposite me couldn't resist the opportunity of accusing me.

"Mr. Leonard, was that you? Was that your stomach?" I looked up at him and pretended to appreciate his joke.

"Ha, ha, very funny, Louis. No, it was Lorraine."

"It was not!" Lorraine, who sat two seats away from me with Jill between us, grabbed her desk with both hands to steady herself. I chose Lorraine, because she was the lady of the class, well-dressed and well-mannered. In fact, she was my star student and editor-in-chief of the literary magazine, *Forum*. I turned to Jill.

"It was Lorraine, right?" Jill turned to Lorraine.

"Yes, it was." Jill's voice was certain; she wasn't playing along with me. I was shocked.

"What? It was not! It was not me!" Lorraine bounced several times on her seat to restore order in the world.

"Yes, it was!" Jill defended *her* perception of world order.

While the class laughed, I lowered my guilty face to the desk. Never did I think that Jill would agree with me; I was being absurd. But the growl was so loud that I guess it spread outward and reverberated, confusing Jill's sense of direction. She trusted me. Of course, I confessed. I wanted to share Jill's hilarious comedy of errors—and I was afraid Lorraine was going to strangle me.

12

Being Observed

Spotting the principal with his "observation" clipboard under his arm near our classrooms, we nonchalantly warned the other teachers. "Guess who's baaack?" The reactions varied. A few teachers shrugged and returned to their classrooms; most protested indifference: "Who cares?" Some enjoyed sharing their anxiety. "Again? Not again!" But not me. No one feigned indifference more than I did. "Let him come."

Since many things can go wrong with a lesson, most teachers don't welcome the principal's "visit." Too many variables test the lesson plan: time of day, day of the week, students' attitude toward the material, students' attitude toward the teacher, and teacher's attitude toward the material—and the students. My lesson plan for E. B. White's 1939 pilgrimage to Walden Pond may inspire students in a morning class to plead for a sleepover-school trip to transcend society at Thoreau's pond; but in an afternoon class, it may inspire them to transcend my class. No wonder teachers are apprehensive about the principal's face at the door window.

Some principals politely asked, "Is this a good time?"

What could I answer? "Not today. The students are transcending."

Some principals suddenly appeared at the door, and glancing down at each desk in the first row, followed the wall to the back corner of the room. After several seconds, their large, incongruous faces rose above the bowed heads of the students and, like a submarine periscope, turned to survey the room. One year, the principal's face turned ninety degrees when he spotted the English chairperson's face in the other corner of the room. Both faces swung back and dropped. The principal slid his clipboard off the desk and followed the wall out of the room. "Where are you going?" I wanted to say. "The students love the lesson—and my jokes are funny today."

There are administrators who believe classrooms must reflect military order: "Your shades are crooked, and your blackboard needs erasing. And why isn't your *aim* for the day posted?" I was fortunate never to have known a four-star high school general. But several of my principals did study the bulletin board next to them. I never took a graduate course for an administrative license, but maybe this is a technique to relax the teacher: Don't stare at the teacher. Don't be conspicuous. Make believe you're waiting for a bus.

One year, on the bulletin board, I tacked a line from Frank McCourt's *Angela's Ashes* that occupied the principal's attention for some time: **If you have anything to say....** I omitted the anti-climactic last two words, but revealed them to my students.

On young Frank's first Communion day, his grandmother spat on his hair to comb it. When he asked her to "please stop spitting" on his head, she responded, "If you have anything to say, *shut up*. A little spit won't kill you. Come on, we'll be late for the Mass."

Granted, McCourt's grandmother—and my nana, for that matter—might have ignored issues of self-esteem, but I found it useful to counter certain student recommendations: "Let's read a shorter book." "Let's have class outside." And their favorite, "Can we just talk today?" Simply raising my hand signaled the class to chant, "... *shut up!*" When the principal tried to joke about the propriety of the quote, I laughed and then explained that my students found my tough-love approach refreshing during this "you-students-are-really-really-the-greatest-ever" era in education. I'm afraid today's young—untenured—teachers would face a court-martial.

Some principals never looked up. If I didn't see their pens move, I wondered if they were napping between observations, something I appreciated from my days of observing master teachers during my student-teaching training in 1968. At Alfred E. Smith Vocational High School in the Bronx, I had the responsibility of observing different teachers working with the same students for one week. There were talented teachers who made the students forget the clock above the door that ended—and interrupted—excellent classes. And sadly, there was one teacher who made the clock an object of intense interest for all of us trapped in the room. When the bell rang, I ran to the door with the best of them.

Some principals gave a heads-up on the lunch line: "I'll be in this afternoon, Richard."

"This afternoon? Really? That time again? Great." For the next forty minutes, I cheerlessly chewed my sandwich and recalled the morning lessons to remember unexpected, challenging student comments. Usually, most observations went well, and when they didn't, the principal usually found something pleasant to say. "Interesting bulletin board."

(The two nuns who observed my class in 1973 had nothing pleasant to say to me; in fact, they said nothing. They entered my room without an introduction, and to save themselves, they hurried out of a hellish classroom where they saw the teacher smile at an exasperated student who struggled with his antagonistic classmates.)

I learned early in my career that teachers must have auxiliary lessons to fill the free time before the bell or to replace a lesson plan when half the class is off somewhere in the building attending meetings for class officers or performing winter concerts for elementary schools or senior citizen centers. And in the 1970s, my public school students observed all Catholic and Jewish holidays. To validate their devotion to Saint Patrick, they insisted he was an apostle. They also took off for sunny Fridays in May. Why repeat the same lesson the next day for the politicians, entertainers, born-again devotees, and pagan sun worshipers?

My favorite bail-out lesson was an exercise that illustrates the necessity of being specific for effective communication. On the State English Regents, many students lost points for lack of specific references. For this lesson plan, on slips of paper, I drew an exotic figure combining geometric shapes. From the smiling volunteers, I chose a student to sit in front of the room with his back to the class. He was not to use his hands to describe the figures on the paper. He was not to turn to look at the class. While he described the figures using shapes, size, and space relationships, the other students drew the figure. When needing clarification, the students called out questions to focus the description. The students enjoyed both roles in the exercise.

The day of the nuns, Justin sat in front of the room with his back to us; I always sat with the other students to appreciate their perspective. The nuns had no idea Justin was a favorite of mine, a kind and intelligent boy. And they didn't know that Justin had trouble being specific. Just the day before, I wrestled Justin for concrete evidence that Harvey Merrick—the sculptor—in Willa Cather's "The Sculptor's Funeral" was an important man. Justin thought Harvey was important, because he was an artist. When I pushed Justin for an example, he became frustrated. "He was hated by the crooked people in his town, because he was important—and different."

"That's not a specific reference, Justin. What people?" Then I'd smile, *because* Justin was reluctantly departing from his world of abstractions.

"When the family goes to bed, the townspeople sit in the parlor and rip him apart."

"What do they say? What does anybody say?"

"The Grand Army man says Harvey killed one of his cows."

"How did Harvey kill the cow?"

"He was watching the sun set when a cow … 'foundered in the corn-field.'"

"Sounds pretty bad to me. Anything else?"

"Someone sold him an eighteen-year-old mule. He thought it was eight years old. And they're laughing at him at his own funeral. Those crooks have no respect. They have no respect for his art. All they know is their little world of business deals."

"How do you know they're crooks, Justin?"

"Jim Laird, the crooked lawyer who works for all of them, says so. Jim says Harvey loved his art and that all the bad things they're saying about him is the only tribute a great man could get from this crooked town." Justin then sat back, troubled that he had to prove the obvious to me. After all, we all had read the short story, right?

When the two nuns opened the door to the classroom, they saw Justin behind my desk with his back to the class. Before I could stand to speak with them, they glided to seats across from me near the windows. I anticipated their confusion; they would observe an unconventional exercise, in which students mercilessly questioned the "teacher"—with his back to the class—in an English class about geometric shapes that resembled nothing in the real world. Realizing Justin was not a teacher, the nuns looked for one; and when they found me across from them, their faces relaxed. There *was* order in this public school classroom. They turned back to Justin.

Justin: "Draw a circle."
Classmate: "What? You're mumbling, Justin."
Justin: "Get a hearing aid, Terry."
Classmate: "Come on, Justin. What are we supposed to draw?"
Justin: "Draw a circle, Amy."
Classmate: "How big?"
Justin: "Small."
Classmate: "A Quarter?"
Justin: "Smaller."
Classmate: "A nickel?"
Justin: "I said small."
Classmate: "A dime small, Justin?"
Justin: "A dime's good!"
Classmate: "Well, say so, will you, Justin! Next time, say dime!"
Justin: "I just did, Phil. Now draw a box."
Classmate: "Where?"
Justin: "Inside the circle."
Classmate: "Where inside the circle?"
Justin: "All the way."
Classmate: "What do you mean all the way, Justin?"
Justin: "The points don't stick out."
Classmate: "Where are they?"
Justin: "Inside … touching the circle."
Classmate: "How many are touching?"
Justin: "All of them."

Classmate: "Why the hell didn't you say so the first time, Justin? What the hell is wrong with you?"

Justin: "What the hell is wrong with you, Melanie? Do I have to spell everything out? What the hell is wrong with you, you moron?"

The nuns were alarmed. The one in front turned to the other for professional—and spiritual—support. Never in their classrooms would students shout at one another. And what kind of lesson was this? When they turned to me, their eyes revealed the real disgrace in the room. Habits swishing and rosary beads jingling, they rose righteously from their seats and, in tandem, followed the shortest route diagonally across the room to the door.

When Justin, the class, and I discussed the necessity of specific references—and courtesy—in effective communication, the nuns were safely out of the room. They would never hear Justin's laughing classmates calling him the anti-Christ, who drove two shocked nuns back to the sanctity of their classrooms.

Often administrators—and once nuns—observed me through the years, but I rarely felt comfortable with "visitors" in the room. I was not an actor; my students were not the audience. And we didn't work with a predictable script. In one class, a lesson ran for a period; the same lesson in another class, for two. We followed my lesson plan—and the students' spontaneous responses. Sometimes, I jotted their revelations in the margins of my plan book for the afternoon class. Over time, some lessons became reliable—but never rigid—guides for our class discussions. Truth and time wrote our scripts.

Teaching is not performance art; but for casual visitors, for many of today's administrators who spent few years actually teaching a class of teenagers, the art of teaching may resemble a performance: The teacher stands behind the biggest desk in the room; the students sit on the other side and watch the teacher. For my students and me, the rapport did not begin and end with school bells. It began in September and ended in June. If the visitor imagined a stage, the students and I shared it.

13

Observing

On the last day of school before Christmas vacation in 1978, I brought the creative writing class to a rehearsal of *Saturday Night Live*. One of my students in the class was doing an apprenticeship at NBC and received permission for our "creative" field trip. The students and I looked forward to the school trip of the century. How cool were we? *Saturday Night Live*! We were going to see stars. We weren't going to a museum or a play. Everyone did those trips. We were going to see the exciting behind-the-scenes of one of the hottest show on television. And we were going to see the show before anybody else—Friday afternoon. Live.

Kevin, my "influential" student, led the fifteen of us to the balcony. We looked down to the left, and there was Gilda Radner, who stood on a stage, doing her drunk-rocker tribute to a rock star idol. Just one minute of her comedic brilliance made the trip worth it. Within five minutes, she and the director polished the funny scene with several interpretations. After ten minutes, we were tired of laughing. Gilda did it again and again, did it this way, that way, over and over. At the end of the song, she fell to the stage. She got up, sang, and fell, got up and sang.

After one hour, Gilda was still rehearsing her song, her movements, and her falls, and we were numb with boredom. We were no longer watching a funny woman; we were watching an artist create. Then, John Belushi did us a favor; he threw us out. I saw him appear below us to the right. He waved a guard over and pointed up to us. In less than a minute, the guard asked us to follow him.

On the train home, no one spoke. We had seen only an hour of the rehearsal, and we were exhausted. We had watched a wonderful actor at work. There was her vision—her plan. There was her dedication. There was her physical labor. And there was her experimentation to find the perfect performance. Belushi wanted to keep Gilda's journey private. No observers allowed. Just the voice of the director. And Belushi who wanted to keep it in the family.

Tomorrow night, people would laugh and applaud. And after Christmas vacation in the creative writing class, we would speak about the artist and her process. This trip was most successful, because we saw the sweat behind the glamour. I expected laughs, not revelation. I watched Gilda's performance that Saturday night. For her minute or two on stage, she was brilliant.

14

Trixie

For many years, when I was a young teacher, I brought a cardboard box, decorated with hearts and cupids, to school several days before Valentine's Day. There was a slot for cards at the top. I placed the red-and-white box on my desk, and on a side blackboard, I wrote the following assignment:

Due February 14:
Drop cards and drawings in the box.
DO NOT MAIL!
—The number of cards last year broke the mailbox lock.
—The postal worker has a bad back.
—Trixie may not understand.

NO FLOWERS PLEASE!

Every day, the girls—and boys—stuffed the box, and on Valentine's Day, we celebrated cloyingly sentimental cards, caricatures of Trixie and me, and many like the following, which I received after my surgery:
"To A Teacher
Whose Heart Is
As Big As His Head
As Big As His Ego
As Big As His Hernia!
Love Always, Terry (Period 7) HA, HA"

Trixie Laverne became my girlfriend in 1968, the year I began to teach, and she dazzled my students with her persona of athlete and teacher's girlfriend for twenty-seven years. I stopped seeing her during my marriage, which interrupted our unique relationship for five years. At one time in her young life, she had been a roller derby queen, who raced under the name of Boom-Boom, and had the scars, which were numerous, to prove it.

She loved me deeply, because I looked beyond the scars; I discerned her womanhood, her soul. And she considered me intensely attractive. I could have had my pick of beauties. She considered herself the luckiest woman in the world. When my students asked to see her picture, I repeated her little joke: "Let's spare the camera."

"Oh, man, that's cold!" The boys laughed, and the girls' shock turned to indignation within seconds.

"How could you say something like that about your girlfriend?"

"Wait a minute. That's not my joke. It's her joke. I would never joke about her looks. I'm not kidding when I say she's unattractive; it's a fact. And even if she were attractive, she wouldn't pose for a picture; she's very humble."

"She's not real! Who calls their girlfriend unattractive?"

"If she's not real and not my girlfriend, then why do I buy her Valentine gifts?"

"What did you get her last year?"

"A shower curtain …"

"Real romantic, Len!" Their eyes rolled to the ceiling.

"… with a huge picture of my smiling face … eyes shut, of course. She's self-conscious about her muscles. Roller Derby's not for sissies."

This was getting them nowhere. They wanted answers. They wanted to know something "real" about her. "Why do you love her?"

"I already told you. I love her spirit. 'She makes my heart sing. She makes everything groovy.'"

"That's 'Wild Thing.' That's a song by the Troggs."

"Really? Funny, that's her name for me. When she's in a romantic mood, she calls me her 'Wild Thing.'" Smiling and squinting, they looked at my serious face and considered the reality of my preposterous relationship; there was something "wild" about a teacher who bragged about his ugly girlfriend. For the rest of the year, we sang what became our song whenever discussing Trixie.

"She makes my heart …," I began.

"Sing!" they screamed.

"She makes everything …" I continued.

"Groovy!" they sang.

When I began to teach, I needed a girlfriend for protection. Almost any young male teacher is attractive to high school girls. Most of them love the attention. When the teacher speaks, students listen; some even copy his words in notebooks. What he says is very important, and the class will demand he repeat it. Some even become angry when the young teacher speaks too quickly and shout, "Slow down!"

To my great surprise, I was popular. I had never been popular. Now, it was not uncommon for boys to shout my name across the street when they saw me in town on Saturday, and for girls gliding past me in the cafeteria to sing, "Hel-lo, Mis-ter Leon-ard!" This was a very different world. I vividly remembered the one of my parish dance days when I depended on friends to identify slow songs (fast songs revealed my unusual rhythm) for my heart-pounding walks across the gym floor to girls who preferred to dance with their girlfriends. One of the few times I caught a girl off guard and danced with her, I inhaled her hairspray for the duration of "In the Still of the Night" by The Five Satins and believed I had fallen in love.

Students are very interested in the personal lives of young teachers. And in 1968, we shared the popular culture of the times. We both admired The Beatles and Dylan. We shared the same views on the Vietnam War, the Civil Rights Movement, and anyone over thirty. But as a young teacher, I needed to remember I was their teacher, not their friend.

One month into my career, I had to remind Ginger, one of my seniors, of that.

"Will you take me out?"

"No."

"Why not?"

"I'm your teacher."

"We're the same age."

"No, we're not."

"How old are you?"

"Twenty-five."

"You're not. You're twenty-two … twenty-three. You told us you graduated from college last year."

"Twenty-three."

"Just. I'm nineteen. Come on; we're almost the same age!"

I realized the distance I needed from my students and the need to appear older. Looking back to those days, I never expected time to be so obliging.

"I can't. I have a girlfriend who's stronger than I am. She'd kill me."

"What's her name?"

In high school, Mr. Gurney was my favorite teacher, no doubt, but he had serious competition from Brother Hayes, who never raised his hand to a student, and who convinced me that algebra was not Sanskrit. His talent for teaching and his kindness guided me through the strange language of mathematics, and his sense of humor introduced me—and hundreds of boys—to Trixie.

Sometimes students tried to take advantage of him. When that happened, Brother Hayes stopped teaching and sat at his desk until we settled down. And we did, because we were so fond of him. He was the only teacher I remember having that power. He spoke Swahili and had contracted malaria in Africa. I remember his suffering a relapse one year. He was our man from the pages of *National Geographic*, but he never spoke about that other life. Once, and only once, did a student speak disrespectfully to him. Before the day was over, Dave apologized; we made sure of that.

At least once a day, Brother Hayes referred to Trixie. If we did poorly on a test, he blamed her. "Did Trixie keep you out late last night, Healy?" or "Morgan, will Trixie respect you if you fail the Regents in June?" And if we all had done the homework correctly, he gave her the credit. "Trixie's an angel for doing your work."

Once a year, Rice High School and three Catholic schools for girls in Manhattan sponsored a boat trip with music and dancing from Battery Park all the way up the Hudson River to Rye Playland, twenty miles north of New York City. For those of us unacquainted with maps of New York State, Canada was the next stop.

Since Brother Hayes often expressed his admiration for Trixie ("she must be a saint to go out with you"), five of us decided he would meet her on this boat. We found five girls willing to play a joke on him. He was speaking to a couple of nuns on the upper deck as far from the music as one could be on the boat. When the nuns walked away, we surrounded him. We were all smiles.

"Brother, I'd like you to meet Trixie, my girlfriend."

"Trixie, this is Brother Hayes."

"Brother, this is Trixie."

"Brother, Trixie."

"Say hello to Brother, Trixie."

Looking over the top of his glasses, he studied the smiling girls and slowly pushed his glasses up his nose. He looked to his right and to his left, then whispered, "Boys, I have bad news. These girls are imposters. I happen to know that Trixie is good looking." Before he could save their feelings with a wink, the girls raised their knees and marched toward the music.

We had played a joke on him, and he played a joke on us. Unfortunately, the girls didn't anticipate the jokes going both ways. Perhaps the nuns didn't develop their sense of fair play. Of course, he tried to apologize, but it didn't matter to us; we thought he was terrific, and fifteen-year-old boys hate to dance, anyway.

During the St. Patrick's Day parade of 1963, we desperately wanted to win back the marching trophy from Power Memorial High School, our only competition, and the high school alma mater of Lew Alcindor/ Kareem Abdul-Jabbar, by walking in step and giving one-eyes-right and two-eyes-left in time to the judges on Fifth Avenue. At 86th Street, we turned right where our school buses were waiting near 2nd Avenue, and relaxed. As we approached Park Avenue, however, someone spotted

Brother Synan, our ex-principal, and Brother Hayes standing on the Park Avenue island, clapping for us. We hadn't seen them since the year before, because they were assigned to different schools. We fell back in line and gave them a snappy eyes-left. We weren't trying to impress any judges. We admired these men.

In 1991, several girls decided to join the fun and explore my world with Trixie more fully. "What did you do last night, Leonard?"

"I went to the movies."

"Did you go with Trixie?"

"No, she's saving for my birthday present."

"You don't pay for her!"

"Sometimes. Last night, I had only enough for my ticket, popcorn, and soda."

During Halloween, the girls wore outrageous outfits with signs identifying themselves as Trixie. Before class, they wanted to know if Trixie was my cat and, if so, did she audition for the musical. And after class, they wanted to know if she had ever scratched me in an argument. They sent me love letters from Trixie and left presents of cat food on my desk for my "purrfect love." I always shared my good fortune and the latest joke with my students to celebrate the joy of our love—and my magnanimous sense of humor.

But one morning, several girls startled me with their vision of Trixie. The day began normally. I was in the habit of going to school well before most teachers to prepare myself for the day. It was my ritual. I opened the door, flipped up the light switch, and as I walked to my desk, watched the fluorescent lights flicker to determine which one was buzzing on this cold morning. After swinging my attaché case onto my desk, I removed my coat and hung it at the end of the blackboard—not in the closet for fear of roaches. I pulled my chair away from my desk, dropped onto it, and enjoyed the view of the empty parking lot and gray-blue light of dawn.

Like Nick Adams in Hemingway's "Big Two-Hearted River," I was happy. I was in my predictable world. I need order to be happy. There were many variables in teaching, so like Nick, I appreciated the beauty of preparation. For now, the rows were straight, and the board was clean. I took my attendance book from my upper right hand drawer and opened it to my homeroom, which would begin in thirty minutes.

I used the Delaney Book (invented, I believe, by NYC teacher, Mr. Delaney), which neatly represents a classroom with rows of slots for desks and small cards, which slide into the slots. When a student is absent, the teacher flips the card over and draws a line through the corresponding date. If the student is tardy, he bisects the line. At a glance, I saw the previous day's attendance for all my classes. Like the baseball player who adjusts the peak of his cap and spits tobacco juice, I was ready to face the day's fastballs and curves.

In five minutes, I would join Faye, Paul, Sue, and Kathy for our daily breakfast coffee in the small back room of the cafeteria reserved for faculty. I relaxed in my green-cushioned chair, inherited from a retired colleague. Retiring teachers bequeath to friends their desks, chairs *with* wheels, and filing cabinets *with* locks, all of which they had inherited from their older colleagues years earlier. Depending on the kindness of senior teachers, young teachers may have access to a bottom drawer while conducting classes in rooms not their own. This explains the empire building by veterans. Like Depression-era survivors, they remembered the lean years.

Looking through the windows, I noticed that the gray-blue light was now pink and teachers were parking their cars; some were walking together to the school's entrance. I looked up at the clock and let my eyes happily travel across my inspirational posters, **Show—Don't Tell**, **Writing is Re-Writing**, etc., which had become landmarks of my world, to a gorilla sitting atop a book closet to the left behind my desk. Wearing a blond wig and a red teddy, a life-size rubber gorilla had been watching my morning ritual without my knowledge, and her name was Trixie. The sign around her neck said so. I knew immediately who was responsible for this wonderful display. Getting up from the chair, I walked to the door, flipped the light switch, and listened to the school sounds fill the building on my way to the cafeteria for my morning coffee.

I passed the culprits—Dawn, my editor in chief, and editors Jenn, Tara, and Nora, all excellent students—huddled in the back of the cafeteria. I stopped at their table. "Hello, girls." I took a sip of my coffee. They gave me a "Gotcha" smile. They were going to be the ugliest mob. As I was opening the door to our room, I announced to my morning coffee friends that I finally had an attractive new student wearing a red teddy in my class. After I had closed the door, I heard their self-restraint collapse. And I said very little about our rubber visitor during my first class. My students pointed to the gorilla and wanted answers. I stared up and scratched the back of my head. "Sexy, but not Trixie."

In time, the students forgot the gorilla was there, but when administrators observed a lesson, they looked anxious; they couldn't ignore the blond gorilla staring at them. Most parents politely listened to me on Parent/Teacher night; however, for some, the black, red, and yellow vision was too great an attraction, and they stared back.

(Parent/Teacher nights had always been difficult for me. Although the parents were not there to judge, but to meet the teacher who had at one time or another become the dinner table subject, I worried. My performance had to be flawless—and interesting.

And for that reason one year, I "exploded" at two parents. Two minutes into my ten minute speech to the parents about curriculum, homework assignments, and grade requirements, I focused on the man and woman sitting directly in front of me. Something was wrong. And then, I figured it out. Pointing at them, I said "Why are you here?" They shrugged, and the other parents shifted in their seats and turned to one another with a this-is-a-strange-turn-of-events look.

"Get out."

I must have looked fierce, because every unblinking parent in the room looked at the door; but these two stared back at me. They were not going to move. I decided to appeal to the other parents. "They're bad people. As usual."

For many years, I had taught their children. Four of them. Terrific students. But none this year. When I had taught them, their parents—a principal and a teacher in the city—were sitting where they always sat. Since I taught all four of their children over many consecutive years, they politely listened to my Parent/Teacher speech year after year, despite my warning that I'd be saying "nothing new again. You've heard this too many times. Why don't you go to the cafeteria for a nice cup of coffee?" But no, they came and sat in the same front seats, hearing the same memorized speech, making me feel self-conscious about my lack of creativity—and spontaneity.

"Get out." Smiling at my mock anger, they stood, shook my hand, and left.)

And Parent/Teacher night always seemed odd to me, because the parents didn't wear jeans, and they sat quietly against a backdrop of night-filled windows. This changed the comfortable familiarity of my classroom. I remember one night confessing that it was odd for me to stand before a class that remembered Ed Sullivan. The parents laughed and I felt comfortable again. And in daytime classrooms where students never age from year to year, Parent/Teacher night was a revelation—a time check—for me. When I was a young teacher, they could have been my parents. In my forties, they became my contemporaries. And when I approached my sixties, many of them could have been my children.

Perhaps the gorilla helped me get through the night that year; I wasn't the only point of interest. Traditionally, the next morning students report parents' reactions to teachers. "My mother thinks you're very nice," and "My father thinks you're skinny." Recently I had announced my turning fifty; actually I was forty. "My parents said you're a liar! No way, you're fifty!" I was curious about the impression the gorilla had made on the parents. When I asked the students, they were nonchalant. "They knew about Trixie before they came."

In May, one student threw the gorilla out the classroom window into the hands of another student standing near an idling car (I was told). I was without a prop until I convinced a video store years later to give me a cut-out of Michelle Pfeiffer in a leather coat with arms folded, promoting her latest movie, *Dangerous Minds*. When my classes complained that I was in a bad mood, I confessed that Trixie and I had had a spat. Then I pledged my love to Michelle and posed with the cutout for yearbook pictures. Despite several abductions, the cutout returned without nicks and tears.

In June, I met the mother of the gorilla abductor one day in front of the school. I told her about the funny incident, and she admitted the gorilla was in his bedroom. Then, she felt it was necessary to comment on my "strange fixation." I responded by asking her, "Do you find it strange he has a rubber gorilla wearing a blond wig and a red teddy in his bedroom?" She never answered.

Over the years, my students became skeptical about a girlfriend who occupied all my free time. For years, they confirmed her existence to students not in my classes. They even swore they had seen her at school functions. Then, one student became an accomplice. Steve, a junior during my last year of teaching, surprised me with the declaration that Trixie and he were dating behind my back. I was completely unprepared for his playful defiance.

"Really?"

"Oh, yeah, we're an item." Teenagers don't say "item." He was using my language against me.

"How is that possible when I see her every night?" Touché.

"When you bring her home after your dates, we meet." He knocked the sword out of my hand. "You need more sleep than she does." He kicked the sword across the room. "She's a vivacious woman." This good kid was beating me at my own game. "She keeps you around, because she feels sorry for you."

"Don't you know what she's doing? No, you wouldn't. Very sad. She's playing with you; you know, boy toys."

From that day to my retirement, Steve and I dueled over Trixie. Who bought her the better presents? Who took her to the nicer restaurants? Who took her dancing? ("Len, if you don't retire this year, Trixie and I are going to the prom.") When I was a young man, my students believed in Trixie. Maybe that wasn't her real name, but they believed I did have a girlfriend who inspired some of my farfetched stories. ("No, I don't mind her being stronger than I am; I feel safe in bad neighborhoods. No, she never makes me do anything I don't want to do.") In my forties, they understood that the stories were fanciful, but there was likely a person in my life. In my fifties, Steve changed the rules and played my game against me. Trixie was played out.

15

Obie

Obie was never played out. Many years ago, my mother gave me a rubber toy whose eyes, ears, and nose popped out when his limbless body was squeezed. Five inches tall, he became a fixture on the front of my desk during tests. Since my vision was poor, I told my students, he became my eyes; he was my test monitor. I warned them that darting, cheating eyes disturbed him and would trigger an alarm. "He sees everything! You have forty minutes. Good luck."

"Will Rubber Boy take a bribe, Len?"

"My people don't take bribes."

"What about rubber candy?"

"No, he's not a cannibal."

Leaning against my filing cabinet that usually supported my lesson plan—and Obie—I taught and taunted confident students who enjoyed the game more than I did. While they were answering my review questions, for instance, I'd reach for Obie. If their answers were going in the wrong direction, I'd slowly raise him. If wrong, I'd squeeze. Therefore, once my hand began to move, hands rose and answers changed until I lowered Obie. Of course, students who just wanted to play became frustrated with the correct answers and shouted, "Squeeze 'im! Squeeze 'im!"

If there were remaining minutes at the end of class, we played "The Obie Challenge." I called for a volunteer and chose the most passionate hand. They understood the rules of the game: If they laughed, smiled, looked away, or closed their eyes, they lost the challenge. With their backs to the blackboard, they faced the class and waited for me to raise Obie. Shouts of support forced me to close the door.

"Are you ready?" After they blinked and smiled all the happiness from their faces, they solemnly nodded.

As Obie came closer and closer, I whispered, "Obie wishes you had a rubber nose," or "Obie wants to kiss you, but he can't rubber pucker up." Then, at eye level with the challenger, I squeezed. Very few students were able to resist laughing and running back to their desks. Just seeing the eyes, ears, and nose pop out within two inches of their faces was enough for a smiling surrender. Some students successfully resisted the urge to laugh or smile, but I denied their victory. They insisted on a rematch.

"No, Obie has to rest. He's had a long day." They begged to hold him, but I'd refuse.

"Squeeze 'im!" Before putting him in his "sacred chamber," I held him up one more time, and they cheered. Then, I locked him safely in the top drawer of my filing cabinet.

Sometimes, I forgot to lock the cabinet. Perhaps, as I was sliding the drawer in, someone asked me a question, which distracted me. (One year, a student found a way to make a duplicate key.) Or perhaps, I wanted the drawer to be unlocked for the game to continue. And for twenty years, it did. Then one sad day I told my classes "degenerates" had kidnapped Obie and left me a ransom note written with colorful letters crookedly cut from a magazine: "Give us all an A+ or you'll never see Rubber Boy again!"

"The person who stole Obie never learned how to use scissors; therefore, who in the room never received the *Cut and Paste Award* in kindergarten?" They laughed. "Do you think this is funny?" They did. "All right, let's get back to work and see if Holden Caulfield would think this is funny." My students never had a problem separating work and play, and we continued our discussion of the quixotic gesture in *The Catcher in the Rye*. Eventually, I'd find Obie in my school mailbox or on my desk after school.

Each year, the newcomers in my class knew the oral history of Trixie and Obie, and wanted posterity to know about their own daring and imaginative exploits. After years of ransom notes and threats, new abductors—once again, all the clever *Forum* editors—decided that a picture was worth a thousand laughs. And so, after the next abduction of Obie, I began to receive photographs of their captive in imminent danger. To heighten the humor—and poke fun at my criticism of sentimental subjects—they personalized the notes by scratching yellow messages on the photographs.

One photograph showed Obie at the edge of a toilet bowl with the following note on the tiles behind the flushometer: "Dad, save me. I can't swim!"

Another photograph included the two red doors leading to the cafeteria with Obie's head protruding from between the shut doors. Across the top red background, the girls had written, "I'm sorry, Dad. I had to cry even though I know it is sentimental and even though I am a boy." Of course, I passed the photographs around the room at the end of class. It wasn't a joke, a game, unless we laughed together. Of course, I maintained my mock horror, which made me the biggest player in the class.

In 1998 Scott, Dominic, and Johan played the game without my participation and without even Obie. While my class and I were wearily reviewing for the state exam on a very hot day in June, these senior boys decided to make my class memorable on the scale of a July 4th firework celebration.

Halfway through the class, I noticed the students looking over my head and smiling. As usual, I was sitting with my back to the window. Geese, I thought. Before I could turn to appreciate their flight, two boys opened my door and began taking pictures of me. This was June, their last chance to capture memories. I was flattered.

Smiling, I sat up in my seat and said, "Fire away!" And they did.

But my juniors were screaming, "Obie!"

"Not yet, we have five minutes left to review. Then Obie will come out. Okay, guys, no more pictures. Get out. We've got work."

My juniors were now standing and pointing. I turned and saw at least ten Obies bouncing against all three windows. The seniors had gone to the library, which was above my room, for the predictable permission of Mary Dalton. Mary was my good friend, who threw surprise birthday parties with cake and funny presents for me every year in her office. As the school's vibrant librarian, inspirer of reluctant readers, and conspirator extraordinaire, she allowed them to dangle the Obies from her windows to be photographed behind me as evidence of their mighty feat and our special relationship.

After twenty years of students' stealing Obies as souvenirs, the original one no longer exists; it was lost long ago. I never bought Obies, but I never ran out of them. My students made sure of that. I left the filing cabinet drawer open, and they stole Obie. We made up the rules of the game, and we played our game.

16

Motivation

My friend Jane Nason and I saw *Ferris Bueller's Day Off*. Obviously, we were the only teachers in the theater. I remember only one scene from the movie; Ben Stein is standing in front of a class waiting for an answer to his question about the Great Depression and ignoring the dead stares of his students. The audience found the scene very funny, and they laughed, and they stopped laughing when the scene ended. Jane and I didn't stop. Well into the next scene, we continued to laugh, because we had been the Ben Stein character in real classrooms, and we were laughing at ourselves.

Ben Stein has asked his question. Normally, a good teacher waits several seconds before calling on a raised hand; this allows all the students in the class to consider all the possible answers. There's no danger, however, of one or two students dominating this class; no hands are up. One boy is asleep, drooling on his desk, and is startled awake by the chalk scratching the board; he fingers his mouth, curious about its wetness.

Ben Stein appeals to his students with no success. Only he—and we—responded to his questions. "Anyone?" … We turned to each other. "Anyone? Anyone?" … We giggled. "Anyone, class?" … We laughed. "Anyone know what this says?" … We howled. "Does anyone know what Vice President Bush called this in 1980? Anyone? Something d-o-o eco-nomics. Voodoo economics." Unable anymore to express ourselves in sound, Jane and I pointed. He has asked his class several questions and accepts their silent stares. One could say these are not motivated students.

At the time, of course, in my three-dimensional classroom, I found this lack of response frustrating and exhausting—not funny. I had a class years ago that convinced me that I could no longer teach English. Even though Marv, a great teacher, had taught the same class the previous year and warned me about their apathy, I took responsibility for my own recurrent Ben Stein scenes.

Hearing Meryl Streep, on the Actors Studio, admit to James Lipton that she suffered terrible doubts about her talent encouraged me. Sometimes she feared that she could no longer act. Imagine that. The wonderful Meryl Streep feared Ben Stein moments. I believe that teachers, like actors, are artists who don't understand the nature of their talent; and, therefore, some teachers fear its loss.

As a teacher I believed in the potential of all students. They were "fertile minds," "sponges," "hungry baby birds," etc. I knew this particular group was a difficult one, but I had had difficult classes in the past, and somehow I had motivated them. Why couldn't I reach these students? Later, I would realize that I confused potential with personality. Apathy is a personality trait, and personality will serve or pervert potential. Furthermore, one or two students have the power to establish a class personality that will dominate individual personality—and potential—every time.

Some administrators have always believed that the majority would save the minority of reluctant learners; some have eliminated tracking to expose the weak or "bad" students to the strong or "good" students. They believed that the less receptive students would be motivated by the majority of hungry birds. Absolutely not. It had been my experience through the years to witness the opposite to be true. The bored and the ill-behaved, the minority of the reluctant learners, will convince the hungry minds that knowledge is not food for thought.

The art of teaching deals directly with student personality—as well as student potential. Motivation is the essence of teaching. Some students love books, teachers, school, since they are internally motivated. For whatever reason, they find the classroom enjoyable, or at least tolerable, under the worst conditions. Now for others, who don't clap and cheer at the sight of a book, teachers depend on external motivation, on themselves, to avoid looking like the Ben Stein teacher.

An excellent way to motivate students is to let them know they have something to say. Often, they don't realize they do. They need time to think about the question. By the time they have an answer, someone has answered it. The teacher should assume they need more time—not because they necessarily lack potential—but because their minds work differently. Some are divergent thinkers who consider their answers "weird" rather than offbeat and original. Some students are shy. Some students' potential lies in other areas. And finally, of course, there are students who would rather be somewhere else.

On the first day of school each year, I gave the same lecture to my students on the subject of appreciation. I warned them that it would be dangerous to say, "This is boring" about any assigned reading. They were taking the chance of confessing they were "boring" people. Perhaps they had missed the point or hadn't developed a general appreciation for the author's style. But they could learn to appreciate the work.

I told them about Enrico Caruso, who refused to terminate his performance during L'elisir D'amore at the Brooklyn Academy of Music, even though he was coughing up blood because of lung cancer—or about Maria Jeritza, who fell during a performance of La Tosca and sang the aria "Vissi D'arte" lying on the stage rather than interrupt her performance. There was obviously nothing boring about opera, but I found it boring. I just didn't appreciate this art form, and I, therefore, was a boring person.

On the blackboard, I made a list of activities people enjoy: books, baseball, opera, football, ballet, swimming, bird watching, traveling, movies, concerts, chess, paleontology. I admitted to being bored by opera, football, and bird watching. Compared to the person who appreciated all of the activities, I had fewer things in life to enjoy. But one could learn to appreciate the work and enjoy the author's virtuosity. Before every work to be discussed, I asked the class what they thought of the reading. I remember one student being frustrated. "I didn't like it last night, but I know I'll think it's good after we talk about it."

In some classes, I asked the students to write their answers in their notebooks. This non-threatening, simple strategy is effective, because it gives everyone a chance to think. For apathetic students—or for complex subjects—motivation must be creative. Teaching Thoreau is always a challenge, but students must understand him (and Emerson) to appreciate the development of American literature. Teacher enthusiasm is the starting point. Teaching the works of different authors, I became those authors. I accepted and defended their ideas as if they were mine. I believe passion about an author, more than anything else, motivates students to remain open-minded.

I decided that the students would appreciate Thoreau if they became Thoreau themselves. I gave them a week to read, "Where I Lived, and What I Lived For," the second chapter in *Walden*. In class the following Monday, I asked those who agreed with him to gather on one side of the room and those who didn't to gather on the other side. I gave them a day to confer. Using passages from the text, they had to prepare questions and anticipate questions from the other side; they had to attack and defend Thoreau's position on such subjects as imagination, property, nature, art, the post office, news, and reality. The romantics and the realists argued for a week during the great Thoreau Debate. I sat between them. My job was to moderate. They became angry with one another and sometimes became personal. The enthusiasm was contagious.

Thoreau believed that, "A man is rich in proportion to the number of things that he can afford to let alone." The class became a battlefield for the period. The romantics argued that simplicity gave freedom to those who didn't need to work for gas for cars they didn't own. The realists wanted to know how they planned to travel from here to there. The romantics quoted Thoreau: "In our own time, and on the journey, we'll appreciate the scenery—and the moment." Like Thoreau, the romantic students wanted "to live deliberately."

Back and forth, the students related Thoreau's epigrams to the world of their everyday lives. The romantics argued that Thoreau's ideas were actually realistic. "Look at the destructive power of pollution and mindless materialism," they argued. For confirmation, they quoted Thoreau: "We do not ride on the railroad; it rides upon us."

In unison, the realists accused them—and Thoreau—of being metaphorically dense, impractical, and unrealistic. For these students, progress and science were the stuff of reality. But a boy from the back of the room shouted "No!" and read from his edition of Thoreau's essay: "Shams and delusions are esteemed for soundest truths, while reality is fabulous." And he added, "Do you really believe money is the source of happiness."

"It couldn't hoit!" shouted a realistic classmate from the other side of the room.

After two or three days, the Thoreau debate ended. I never revealed the winner, and they never asked. At that point, they realized the process is more important than the outcome. From then on, my students took ownership of the authors by comparing them. For instance, "Thoreau said that before Steinbeck" or "Whitman is a sexy Emerson." The success of the debate was the result of students' stimulating opinions.

Back in the early seventies, I was assigned to chaperone the gymnastic show in the auditorium one Saturday evening. On some nights chaperoning assignments may be very difficult. The teacher stands in the back, making sure no one enters without paying, or he hangs over noisy students in the audience who scream out the names of friends on the stage. He makes threats that usually can not be kept, because the students are unfamiliar to him. And all this takes place in the dark.

The gymnastic assembly was considered a good duty. I didn't mind giving up my Saturday night, because if anyone dared to disrupt this display of grace and strength, he would suffer the anger of our respected Athletic Director, who coached the gymnastic team. Tonight, my job was to keep the aisle clear near the stage when the athletes ran up the steps to the stage. Then it happened. One of the gymnasts saw me. When the curtain closed to change the equipment, she jumped off the stage, ran up the aisle to me, and gushed, "You won't believe what happened last night at Vicki's party. We had this huge argument about who was better: Emerson or Thoreau. What do you think of that? Isn't that cool? See ya Monday." Maeve turned away from me and disappeared up the steps. Driving home, I wondered if the audience saw us and the effect of her spontaneity and her exuberance on me; we were close enough to the spotlights to reveal a very proud English teacher.

If the students had a stake in the literature—in "their" class—they appreciated the year's work. Before the discussion of every work, I asked for their opinions. "Did you like it? Why? Why not?" This was my favorite part of the lesson. Often, I could anticipate the responses to questions. But this was different; they were responding to their raw encounter of a new author. Since they were comfortable in class, they didn't hesitate to speak up. At this point in a new lesson, I listened; I didn't try to persuade them. I did respond when I heard something original, something that was a revelation to me. Then, I would admit that I had never considered such an interpretation. This admission always surprised them, and I think the honesty also motivated them to be serious readers.

At the end of every lesson, I asked again for opinions now that we had finished the discussions after we had pulled the novel, or the short story, or the poem, apart. Most of the time, they appreciated the work, even if they had not enjoyed it. Even this simple request for their opinion was powerful motivation. I remember one of my frustrated students in the pre-discussion of a work yell out, "Yeah, I didn't like it. It's not my kind of book, but it has something to say." He was going to remain open-minded about the year's work. Knowing his criticism was valid made the work worthy. After all, criticism of unworthy material is unimportant.

In the 1970s, I taught Shirley Jackson's "The Lottery." This excellent story deals with tradition and discrimination in an extraordinary way. For the harvest to be good in June, the people conduct a yearly lottery to determine the "winner," who is then stoned to death by the town—and the winner's family. The students have no idea that a good corn crop will demand a human sacrifice at the end of the story.

To emphasize the realism of the story, I concocted an outlandish story for my juniors that I needed to ruin their weekend. I apologized. I had no choice but to give them many hours of homework over the weekend; it had to be done. "Why?" they wanted to know.

"For you," I swore. "Well, the State Education Department." I sighed in frustration. "The curriculum of the state government in Albany mandates that this work be completed before nine a.m., November 12, which is Monday; they just sent special bulletins to all the principals in the state."

"It's their fault! It's not fair! Why do we have to suffer?"

"You're right, certainly."

"So we don't have to do it!"

"No, you do. Governor Rockefeller is behind this one."

To a student, a homework-free weekend is as good as a snow day. A weekend of homework is five nights of heavy homework in a row.

"Wait a minute. Let me see…. I think I have a plan, if you're willing to participate. All of you. Every person must agree. If you get the X and don't do the work, everyone in the class will fail."

"We are! We are! What X?"

"Well, we could have a lottery, and the person who draws the paper with the X does the assignment for the entire class. Ten hours will become twenty hours of work. Now before you agree, think carefully, but not too long, because time is running out."

"Do it! Do it!"

Of course, the solution made no sense, but a homework-free weekend is the good life, and the odds were favorable that they wouldn't get the paper with the X. They never considered the impossibility of one person's doing twenty hours of work; they wanted no homework.

I put the slips of paper, one with an X, in an empty trash can. I flipped a coin to decide where to begin: right side or left side of the room. I dropped the coin, and the class groaned as I crawled under the desk; they thought I had dropped it on purpose. "Stop fooling around!" I flipped it again and caught it; they applauded. "Sign him up for the Yankees!" We would begin on the right side; the right side of the room cheered. From that point on, they were no longer a group. As I approached them, I heard, "I'm going to get it, I know it."

"Don't cheat, Len."

"I never win anything."

"I hate you, LeNerd."

Of course, as I moved down each row, no one picked the X, and the odds of a lost weekend became a reality for the remaining students. The tension and the playful/angry comments escalated. "You're an ugly man, Len. Trixie must be blind." One by one, they drew their slips. One by one, they screamed their relief to the class. They had gambled with their dream, their weekend, and had won. They echoed one another; their feelings became kinder.

"I love you, Leonard."

"Me too, Len."

"I always loved you, Lenny,"

"Trixie's a lucky woman."

I was happy. I had wanted to sell them the realism of a story, and they were buying it. Who knew I was a natural con artist?

After passing the happy faces of three rows, the half-way point, I turned toward the blackboard and walked to Stacy, who sat in the first seat to the left of my desk. She dug into the can and pulled out a fist. Very slowly, her fingers stretched open. She opened one eye, closed it, and crushed the paper. I moved to the desk behind her. I offered the can to the boy, who closed both eyes and pulled the can away from me. "Give that back to me!" And when he shook his head and hugged the can, I heard Tessie Hutchinson's cry at the end of the story.

"It's not fair!"

When Tessie Hutchinson in the story realizes that she is the unlucky one, that she has the slip of paper with a black spot on it, she cries out, "It isn't fair, it isn't fair." Before the lottery began, she had thought it was fair.

"It's not fair! It's not fair!" Tessie Hutchinson was behind me. I turned to see Stacy crying into her hands. She was channeling Tessie. She hadn't read the story yet; she didn't know the line or the significance of its timing. Then I heard the students laughing as the townspeople do in the short story. I turned away from Stacy to see most of my students pointing at her. The students to the left realized they wouldn't have to draw from the can, so they began to laugh in relief. The students to her right realized that she was crying, so they began to laugh.

The exercise was wildly successful. We were playing out Jackson's vision; we were her town, her people. The townspeople in her short story also laughed at Tessie's misfortune. I turned to my desk and sat on it close to Stacy. She was sobbing into her hands, because the Governor of New York had ruined her weekend, and her classmates were rejoicing. I made a sixteen-year-old girl cry, and she was going to cry until Monday morning.

I leaned toward her and whispered, "Stop crying.... It's okay.... There is no homework.... You won't have to do anything.... I made the Governor story up." She couldn't hear me; she was crying too hard. I put my hand on her trembling shoulder and squeezed. This calmed her enough so that she heard Christina, who sat three seats behind her.

"Stacy, I'll come over tomorrow morning, and we'll get it done in half the time. Stop crying. We'll do it together. Okay?"

Stacy turned her grief stricken face to Christina, who was not laughing, and acknowledged her kind gesture. The class stopped laughing when Christina spoke up. She startled them, and me, with her kind offer. Out of thirty students, only one offered to help someone in pain.

She felt bad for a crying person (I don't believe they were friends outside of class) and realized that 2 people sharing 20 hours of work equaled 10 hours of work for each. Had others in the class realized this, the 20 hours of work could have been 5, 2 ½, and so on. They hadn't, but they understood that Christina was different from them. Did she reveal the evil in both the class—and me? My plan never anticipated an independent, kind voice. It's not possible to know if Stacy would have offered her Saturday for Christina or if she would have laughed at a crying classmate. The story takes fifteen minutes to read. When the students realized the brutal outcome and their resemblance to the townspeople, no one laughed. They were silent, embarrassed, because they had mirrored Jackson's dark portrayal of human nature. They didn't expect condemnation with revelation.

Whenever I think of Christina's unpredictable offer, I am reminded that I didn't teach books; I taught people. That important variable renewed me every year. In June, I said goodbye to smiling teenagers, who had enthusiastically shared their fresh perspectives on the year's literature. And in September, I greeted rows of unsmiling students sitting silently one behind the other—and welcomed their opinions and interpretations. Within days, we became comfortable with one another, and like the parent who takes his children to the zoo and sees the giraffe for the first time again, I saw the "classics" through new eyes. Those who criticize the teaching profession, pointing out the repetitive nature of the job and its subject matter, obviously have never taught. I never conducted a lottery again.

17

More Motivation

Another activity to stimulate interest in a literary work unexpectedly made me the victim. As a result, the truth of the play became more obvious to me than to my students. I had taught Edward Albee's "The Zoo Story" since the late sixties, always with great success. The play is difficult for young people, but the discussion afterward led us ultimately to an understanding of Albee's existential view that we can change our lives through action.

I always played Jerry, the lonely character who gives up his life to communicate with another human being. His death ironically affirms his existence. I chose his character to make my stage appearance (the only one of the year) because of his complexity—and my ability to read his very long monologue in one period.

Before we acted out the play, I broke the class into groups of two and three students with the instruction that they write a short scene in which the student playing Jerry must communicate with the student playing Peter in whatever way possible—despite Peter's wanting nothing to do with Jerry. I gave them a setting. Peter lives a comfortable middle-class life with his wife and two daughters. He enjoys reading his book on a bench near Central Park's Zoo in New York. Jerry is a down-and-out character, alone in the world with the exception of his landlady and her dog. Jerry lives on the West Side, and Peter lives on the East Side. Central Park separates their worlds.

I gave my students a period to come up with dialogue for Peter and Jerry's interaction that will be a failure or a success for Jerry who wants human contact from Peter who believes he has it all. Noisily, happily, they dragged their desks to the far corners of the room to safeguard the integrity of their original scripts and to brainstorm their titles.

When they were ready, each group drew lots to play their scene by my desk. It was always interesting to see what they considered to be an inducement for conversation—and even friendship. Sometimes the Jerry/student used information (Yankee game score), a gift (half of a sandwich), a threat ("I'll leave"), pity ("I'm homeless"), an insult ("You snob!"), etc. One group made them long lost brothers. They became great friends in five minutes, or one of them stomped off, cementing the socio-economic divide. No group was ever wrong, but some were more believable. When we read Albee's play the next day in class, they understood the characters' motivation.

In Jerry's monologue to Peter about his desire to befriend his landlady's dog, Jerry says that he has learned that kindness alone is not sufficient for communication between the dog and himself; Jerry gave the dog hamburger meat, but the dog continued to chase him up the stairs to his small apartment. Jerry has learned that cruelty is also necessary, so he mixes poison into the meat. Communication is achieved when the dog almost dies, recovers, and allows Jerry to enter the hall.

Jerry tells Peter that love and cruelty are the bases for understanding, communication. When Jerry finishes his story, he asks Peter what he thinks. Unfortunately, Peter is angry and confused by this bizarre story and exclaims, "I don't understand!"

"That's a lie!" Jerry furiously whispers to Peter. "I tried to explain it to you as I went along." But Peter's denial will force Jerry to be cruel in order to communicate; he forces Jerry to resort to violence.

For the dog, Jerry gives food; for Peter, the story of "Jerry and the Dog." Kindness alone does not work. Jerry then mocks, pushes, spits at, and punches Peter. He throws a knife to the ground and advises Peter to pick it up. When Peter does, Jerry runs at Peter and impales himself on the knife. Jerry has made his point. Yes, he will die, but Peter will never forget him. Peter of the East Side of New York City will never forget that people like Jerry exist.

In one class, I decided to emphasize the importance of violence in Albee's play through an improvisational scene with Bart, one of the students who always appeared to be comfortable with his position in the class. He had a wonderful sense of humor. Once, I remember lightly scolding the class: "Come on, folks. We're a little behind."

Bart thanked me. When I asked him why he had thanked me, he answered that he had appreciated the compliment: "You said we have little behinds." This was going to be my Peter, someone not easily aroused to anger.

Bart and I sat next to each other on top of two desks pushed together. I gave him the instruction to ignore me, to make it as obvious as possible that I didn't exist. The class sat in front of us. I made a joke, the class laughed, Bart didn't. I faced him and made a face; he looked through me. "You look very spiffy today, young sir." Nothing. So much for kindness. I couldn't hit Bart, so I whispered in his ear. "Why are you so ugly?" Bart ignored me. "Why don't you have any friends?" Bart looked down at the floor. "You're not very bright, are you?" Nothing. So much for cruelty. "I'd say you were as bright as you're ugly...."

Well, that did it; the anger kicked in, and Bart turned and pushed me so hard that I slid off my desk and fell onto another desk. I was shocked, the class was shocked, and Bart's fists were clenched on his lap. The outcome was more interesting to me than it was to the class. Yes, it illustrated Albee's formula (kindness + cruelty = communication) perfectly for us, as well as making something I accepted intellectually concrete. Suddenly, I had become Jerry—not the character in the play, but a person desperate to be acknowledged—and I felt existence in my fear of being hurt and in Bart's anger toward me.

These two pre-reading exercises were not failures; they were too good. They accomplished what the literature was intended to accomplish, but not in an abstract way that would have been intellectual and safe. If literature speaks the truth to the student about people, then the above pre-reading exercises forced the students to see the truth within themselves.

I worried that Stacy went home with the singular experience of being a hypocrite; Shirley Jackson had "all her readers" in mind for the Tessie

Hutchinson character. As for Bart's violent reaction, his anger was not perceived by the class as uniquely his; they all would have shoved me off the desk.

Not all my pre-reading motivation dealt with conscious or subconscious human response; some exercises simply allowed students to play and to appreciate the contexts of dramatic scenes. This certainly was my intention with the very popular and safe dramatization of a scene in *A Streetcar Named Desire*—my traditional Stell-off.

In the "Poker Night" scene, Stanley hits his wife, Stella, in a drunken rage. She runs to her neighbor's apartment upstairs and refuses to return. Stanley stumbles into the street and cries out to Stella to come back to him. She succumbs to his animal calls; Stanley carries her back to their apartment; the scene is brutal and sensual.

My directions were clear. Several male volunteers went into the hall and prepared. They would enter the room, look up to the ceiling, and cry out "Stella!" twice. They were to be drunk and heartbroken. The girls in the class voted for the best performance. The girls auditioned for Blanche, Stella's sister. Their directions were tamer; they had to convince the class that they "always depended on the kindness of strangers," words spoken to the doctor who takes Blanche away at the end of the play.

Usually, four or five boys volunteered. One by one, they staggered into the room, crashed against desks and chairs, and howled "Stella!" twice. The class and I laughed at each performance, which sometimes surprised us with its manic intensity. Boy after boy came in and usually did the same thing. Drunkenness outperformed passion every time. In 1978, two performances shocked the class, and me, with their caricatures.

First, Josh came into the room with the usual imitation of a drunk trying to maintain his balance. He looked up to the ceiling and howled his first "Stella!" When he lowered his head and caught his breath, Josh found a pre-made hole in his T-shirt. On the second howl, he made an apron of his shirt, exposing his chest to the screaming girls. The class chanted, "Josh is an animal! Josh is an animal!" There was one more student waiting outside the door, but the girls had made up their minds.

After the class had settled down, I gave Ian the signal to come in. He tripped into the classroom; we laughed. As soon as he reached the center of the room, he turned to the blackboard, so we couldn't see his face. He raised his shoulders and lowered his head. He stood like that for a while, head down, his back to us. Then we heard a low, slow growl that rose as he began to turn. When he faced us, he slowly lifted his head to the ceiling.

"What the hell!" someone shouted. "What's that on his face?" A huge piece of bloody roast beef dangled from Ian's mouth. He ripped the meat from his face and threw it at us, growling "Stella! Stella!" over our ducking, incredulous faces. Ian's roast beef was a clever allusion to the opening scene of the play when Stanley throws to Stella a package of bloody meat, symbolic of Stanley's animal nature; he had obviously done some research.

Those two scenes took place over twenty years ago. I don't remember who won the part, but both deserved to win. The exercise took only ten minutes, but the class was eager to read the entire play for the context of this memorable scene played by their talented classmates. Who needed Marlon Brando?

End-of-the-year review was never enjoyable because of very warm June classrooms and the drill-like nature of review classes. To introduce some fun into this unhappy setting, I created the game of "Beastie," inspired by William Golding's *Lord of the Flies*. I asked the students to sit in a circle, double rows when the size of the class was large; I was the Master Beastie. The day before, I warned them that they should prepare themselves by reviewing titles, authors, characters, settings, anything related to a literary work studied during the year.

If a student answered questions correctly, then he became the new Beastie. If a student answered incorrectly, he had to confess, "I'm so ashamed" and turn his desk to face out of the circle; he had to remain that way until one person, one Beastie, remained. After the applause for the ultimate survivor ended, everyone turned back into the circle, and the reigning Beastie began a new game. Usually, we played two or three rounds of Beastie before we returned to civilization with the class-ending bell.

I say civilization, because Beastie changed the students in the class. Many students developed a killer instinct. Like the boys on Golding's island, the strong enjoyed the power. They fired questions at their classmates. If it became obvious that students didn't know a question, they used questions like a machine gun and sat alone in the "circle" in a few short minutes. One year, the student I least expected to enjoy the game was a good-natured boy, very popular with the class. Hal's transformation from nice person to Beastie surprised even his best friends, who found themselves begging that someone else be chosen for a difficult question. Laughing, Beastie chose them.

My students played Beastie for thirty years. The game forced them to know the many *specific references* required by the New York State Regents Examination in June. In my final years of teaching, I no longer used this successful game for review. Since the students wanted to be Beastie, they prepared and knew the answers. In the late 90's, students became indignant if they had to say, "I'm so ashamed."

Despite their having agreed to the rules beforehand, some refused the playful admission, which ultimately every student would have to make but one, the last Beastie. Or they refused to turn out from the circle. The age of self-esteem arrived at our high school. Not all my students were touched with the look of "Be gentle," but all it took was one, and there were more—in Fitzgerald's words—"quivering on the horizon." This enjoyable, mock survival of the fittest game did not survive, because some thought it was "mean."

When I attended St. Catherine of Siena Elementary School in Manhattan, all the students sang in the choir on special occasions. I loved the experience, because we sang in the balcony, whose high view made being in church that day different from all the other Sundays. Instead of the congregation watching the little ones up front, we were looking down on them. The nuns demanded two things from us: When we were not singing, we were to be quiet, and those of us who could not carry a note should simply move our lips. Since the congregation could not see us up in the balcony, I guess we were moving our lips for God.

Once, in the excitement of the moment, I forgot and sang during one hymn in a rehearsal. After we had finished, Sister whispered in my ear. That evening, I told my mother about the day's special rehearsal and Sister's reminding me to simply move my lips. My mother approved and added her criticism; there were many things I did well, but singing was not one of them. There's nothing like the truth for motivation.

For two years in the early seventies, I taught "Speak Out," a new speech class for tenth graders. Since I knew little about the art of elocution, I was somewhat nervous about the assignment. By keeping a chapter ahead of them, I had a wonderful time with the class. Only a few students were nervous about standing in front of the room, and the rest relished the opportunity to ham it up. The speeches to persuade, inform, explain, etc. became speeches to entertain for many of these clever students.

If I were a teacher in my next life, I'd like to be a speech teacher. Of course, being a phys. ed. teacher, who never needs a red pen, is also attractive. "Call me Coach!" For the year, I sat in the back of the room, listened to speeches, often laughed, listened to student critiques, and then gave a critique: "Good!" "Very good!" "Excellent!" I was in teacher heaven: no papers to correct, few lesson plans to prepare, high grades. This was a unique high school course of talented students and entertaining speeches.

For the last speech of the year, the very popular "Heckling Self-esteem Speech," I decided to test their "newly acquired" skills (posture, volume, etc.) and their concentration for an unorthodox assignment. I gave them instructions to present a speech on the topic, "I am great." They could not use notes for the one-minute speech, and they had to maintain eye contact with the audience. Most important, they were not to laugh or smile.

For the audience, I had the following instructions: Heckle each speaker without making any sounds and without touching the speaker in any way. If the speaker did not smile or laugh during the speech, I added a point to the year's average. Today I think some students would find this assignment "mean." My tenth graders of thirty years ago thought, "Let me at 'em!," and enjoyed the assignment. They knew one another well, and the speakers' close friends, of course, gave them the hardest time.

Geoffrey, who was born in England, began his speech with "I am great, because …," and his friends threw paper missiles around him, but his girlfriend's exhortation to "Go home, Limey," on a sign decorated with hearts, brought Geoffrey to tears. No one bought his defense that he was crying, not laughing. Many students wore costumes, but Isabelle, waving her arms up and down in the rear of the room in a wet suit, mask, and flippers, was the queen of the ball and distracted many speakers.

Some students surprised me. I thought for sure their sophistication and intelligence would sustain them through paper airplanes, costumes, and "inappropriate" placards. But no. In the middle of declaring their "greatness," they screamed and collapsed on the lectern. One after the other crumbled with no intimation they were near the brink of hilarity. Finally, I noticed their collapses always followed their eyes sweeping the front of the room.

But now, Helen was at the front of the room. She would survive the heckling; she was my best student. Twenty seconds into the speech, I looked to the right at Isabelle in rubber doing the backstroke. When I looked to the front, Helen was no longer at the lectern. I called her name, and she rose from the floor and, cupping her face with both hands, ran to her desk. She was still laughing when the next student announced, "I am great, because…."

I quietly got up and edged up the side of the room to see the "killer" sign. As I was reading the ones I could see, I noticed that Scott, in the first seat of the middle row, became the speaker's focus. He was giving his maddest smile, which didn't affect the speech, but the movement of his hand did. He was slowly raising a hot dog perpendicular to the edge of the desk. If the speaker didn't see it, he wiggled it. Once the speaker saw it, he lowered it and smiled at the chaos he had wreaked. Fortunately, the bell rang, ending an excellent year with students who knew the difference between mean and absurd fun.

18

Race

The morning after the murder of Dr. Martin Luther King Jr. marked a milestone in my student-teaching experience at Roosevelt High School in the Bronx. I taught my first complete lesson to an eleventh grade honor class of girls, an observation not lost on me; I hadn't seen so many girls in a classroom since elementary school. And also, for the first time as a student teacher, I enjoyed myself.

My subject was Hawthorne's *The Scarlet Letter*, and I hadn't slept well anticipating this day; but Dr. King's death replaced my anxiety with sadness, then anger. In the education classes of the late sixties, college professors scribbled the word *relevance* across blackboards. Make the lesson relevant, and the students will eagerly learn. Compare poetry to rock and roll, and emphasize the beauty and power of language in the names of popular cars, and they will know "where you're coming from." The relevance of the students' concrete world would humanize universal truths. Driving a matador-red 1969 Pontiac LeMans, I expected women to discover my beauty and power.

That morning, the class saw a change in me; they saw confusion and anger. In the weeks leading up to this day, I had been an object of interest. I was the young male teacher who sat in the back corner of the room and graded vocabulary tests for their "real" teacher. During my short bursts of actual teaching when the teacher was busy with something else, I was a nervous, distant, hesitant, shy, reluctant class leader who aroused their romantic—or maternal—feelings.

But today was different. I wanted to teach. I was angry and I had something to say. I asked the girls if they had heard the news; many had. I asked for their reaction. Why him? He was pacifist. It would have made more sense if he were a violent Black Panther, we agreed. We spoke for several minutes about violence and social injustice. Then, I asked my class to consider the parallel between Dr. King and Hester Prynne of Hawthorne's novel. I hadn't related the hypocrisy and cruelty of her Puritan society to the racism of our society in my formal lesson plan, because it was written a week earlier; Martin Luther King Jr. was still alive. Leaving my apartment that morning, I hadn't considered using his death in my lesson plan.

Dr. King became Hester Prynne. The three scaffold scenes in the novel were my focus. I pointed out the obvious consequences of persecution and the lack of communion among the people of Salem, and the students saw the same problems in our world. We moved from Salem to Memphis to New York, from the past to the present. It was exhilarating. Within several days, I experienced anxiety about my first real lesson, then sadness and anger, which produced a "relevant," dynamic lesson.

When the bell rang, they applauded. Rarely in my teaching career have students applauded. Students will agree that "The class flew!" or "That was a fast class!" But these girls also knew it was my first complete lesson. I was no longer a student teacher/super student. After a passionate forty minutes, I had become a teacher, their teacher.

I discovered much about myself during that class. I was sensitive. I was passionate. Like Bobby Kennedy, I was connected to the world in a wise and relevant way. As I was enjoying the smiling company of several students at the end of the class, the principal's voice interrupted my euphoria with the grave announcement that the rest of the school day was cancelled and all teachers had a faculty meeting in the cafeteria immediately. The remaining students in the room and in the hall cheered. Students always react with the same intensity, even if they have no idea what to do with their freedom.

In the cafeteria, teachers smiled at one another. Like our students, we were happy. We smiled at the principal who had liberated the school. We had no idea what had prompted his good will. Maybe there was a ruptured pipe somewhere in the basement; and the school was going to fill up with water, class by class, until the six-story building sank beneath the Bronx sidewalk.

We stopped smiling when the principal mentioned Dr. King's murder, and we forgot about our gift of free time when he explained his reason for it. He feared some of our black students were understandably angry enough to become violent. He reminded us that some of our students were Black Panthers. After all the students had left the building, we could leave and return the next morning as usual.

I understood his concern, but I didn't believe for a moment that we were in any danger for a murder committed by a bigot in Memphis. But who was I to argue with administration? In the lobby of the school, looking for my keys and remembering my "Bobby Kennedy" lesson, I bent to pick up my attaché case. Before I could grab the handle, a black student jammed his shoulder into mine. He didn't stop to say anything, and I didn't stop to complain. I pirouetted on the shiny lobby tiles, stopped at my attaché case, snatched the handle, and walked toward the door leading to the street.

Bobby Kennedy would be assassinated in several weeks.

I grew up on the Upper East Side of the 1950's Manhattan, so my experience with African Americans was limited; I met Willy when I played baseball on Sheep's Meadow in Central Park. Today's New Yorkers call it the Great Lawn. He came from the West Side, pre-Columbus Avenue chic, for pick-up games. He was a terrific athlete and, of course, we bragged that the New York Giants weren't the only team to have a Willy Mays. But we saw Willy only on the field; we knew nothing about him. One day, he stopped showing up, and the team missed him. As for other black kids playing ball on Sheep's Meadow, there weren't any. They played in *their* section of the park.

We knew where they lived. Up north above 96th Street, Harlem was another country, and we were not travelers. Like other white people of the time, I admired the black entertainers and Jackie Robinson, and I didn't understand why some white people didn't like them. How could they be any kind of a threat to us on 71st Street between 1st and 2nd Avenues? And since my mother never said a bad word about them, I didn't dislike them.

In 1959, I became a world traveler, and I traveled every day. I went to high school one block from the heart of Harlem: Lenox Avenue and 125th Street. For four years, I rode the bus up Lexington Avenue, where it made a left onto 116th Street and then a right onto Lenox Avenue to my high school on 124th Street. After 96th Street, Rice High School students were the only white passengers on the bus. We sat in the back, copied homework, and smoked cigarettes until the bus driver threatened to throw us off. (It was cool to sneak a lit cigarette on the bus by "cuffing" it in a pocket.)

By 116th Street, I was staring at the people through the bus window. Growing up in the fifties was not exotic. We wore Keds or Converse sneakers and Lee or Levi's jeans. We smoked Luckies or Camels; we smoked Newport Menthols for a sore throat. If we "grubbed" a cigarette from a girl, it always had a filter, which we tore off to maintain our masculinity. Some years later, a few boys smoked Marlboros, the filtered cigarette for cowboys. Our world was simple, predictable, and white. The world outside the bus was exotic; it was not white.

Harlem, from the bus window in the fall of 1959, was my personal educational field trip. All the people on the street were "colored"—not black. We believed using the word *black* was being disrespectful. Stokely Carmichael changed all that a few years later with his stirring "black is beautiful" speech. After one week, there was nothing exotic about Harlem and its people. They were no more interesting to me than I was to them, and we ignored one another as we all went to work and school at the same time in the same way. Their world was simple, predictable, and black.

I spent four years at Rice and had a fist fight at the end of my first month there—with Don, a black boy in my class. We were freshmen, and the students were still getting to know one another. Don didn't want to make friends. Within a month, he had had several arguments, which led to the only other fist fight I remember at Rice; he beat up my friend Danny with some good boxing moves. A few days later, it was my turn. Class hadn't started yet, and the boy next to me and I were talking before Brother Murray came to class when Don approached and was about to hit me in the head with his book.

From my sitting position, I swung my arm to protect my head and knocked his book across the room. His fists went up; I charged. He never had a chance to outbox me. Fear and anger don't respect fancy footwork. I swung and swung and swung until I backed Don into the hallway, where students from the other classes left their rooms to cheer, "Hit him! Hit him!" I wondered if I was "him." I was no longer angry or afraid, because I knew I was winning, but I desperately wanted someone to end this fight. I was ready to hug Don, my arms were so tired. Finally, a couple of teachers pulled us apart. Exhausted and relieved, I followed Don into the classroom, and we sat on opposite sides of the room.

Before the class began, I received complimentary looks from my classmates, boxing tips from the teacher, and a disconcerting promise from one boy that the "white guys" would walk me to the bus stop. It had never occurred to me that a fight with a black boy in school would anger anyone. While the teacher explained the difference between a gerund and a participle, I imagined Harlem waiting for me on the corner. I knew they weren't there yet, but the word would spread quickly.

Sometime between the third replay of my being chased by a large mob and my inevitable capture, the principal knocked and entered the classroom before the teacher had a chance to open the door.

"How may we help you today, Brother Synan?"

"I understand fisticuffs shook our citadel today." They were smiling.

"You're not going to believe this, but the bloodied pugilists are in this room. And I believe they're waiting for their penance and absolution. See how contrite they are, Brother. Can redemption be far behind?" They could take this show on the road.

Playful sarcasm is a common way for teachers and students to show their affection for one another. Think of children pushing other children in a playground. In the school of the fifties, it might have been our only way to interact. I don't recall any "heart to heart" talks with teachers. They never used our first names; I was Mr. Leonard or Leonard. Today, very few teachers would get away with calling a student by a last name.

Hearing the syllables *fisti* in their sarcasm, I understood that Don and I were the subject of their merriment and that the gangs of Harlem would have to wait their turn. To confirm my suspicions, Brother Synan reached to his left side for his narrow, brown razor strap, which hung from his belt.

"Mr. Leonard, please come here and assume the position." I bent over the desk and must have betrayed my fear—and embarrassment—because Brother Synan assured me that he wouldn't feel a thing. The boys in the class laughed, and I tried to smile. He whacked me twice. As I walked back to my desk, he called Don to the front of the room. Not only did Don refuse his penance; he ran out of the room, and—I found out at lunchtime—out of the building.

The bell rang, ending the subject of my notoriety and sending us to lunch. I gave my sandwich away. How could a marked man think of food? How could white high school boys defend me against blocks and blocks of angry black people? Harlem was going to get its revenge. And Don was out there to identify me. In the cafeteria, the few black students, who attended Rice, sat together at the same table. It was a surprise to me to see one of the black seniors walk to my table and stare at me. This was going to be it.

"Are you the guy who beat up Don Brooks?"

"We had a fight." A little diplomacy here, I thought.

"Can I ask you a question?" I nodded. "Why didn't you give him a black eye?"

I didn't laugh—even when he did. Even when my friends at my table laughed, I didn't get the joke. His laugh told me that the black students in my school didn't hate me, that they didn't like Don, and that no one would be waiting for me outside school. This is my only memory of racial tension at Rice. For me—and the black students—the fight wasn't about race at all.

I spent the next four years at Rice without forming any friendships with black classmates. We spoke to one another in class, but it never went beyond a greeting or a request for the time. I went to Iona College in New Rochelle where all my friends were white despite the presence of black students on campus, and to Fordham University where my white world remained white; therefore, meeting Ronald James, an excellent math teacher at Gorton High School, proved fortuitous. For humanitarian reasons (he had been in the Peace Corps, after all), he decided to help me become a teacher. And he was to become my first, and only, black friend.

At times, during my first year of teaching, students saw the eyes of a deer frozen in a car's headlights. Two of my white juniors, Phil and Gary, wanted to be those headlights; they planned my October resignation. Using grades to give me leverage with disruptive students worked well in one of my classes. With these boys, it wouldn't work, because neither boy was passing my course anyway; they were Doc Holiday, Wyatt Earp's friend, who feared no shootout, because he was dying of tuberculosis and had nothing to lose.

It was over lunch that Ronald decided to help me. I wasn't eating and looked beleaguered, and he wondered why. In his usual direct manner, he asked me how I was. I told him about the two fearless gunslingers in my class just before my lunch period.

"We'll get them." There was no doubt in his voice. "We'll get them."

"How?" How could another teacher in a different room on a different floor "get them"?

"I have them next period."

"Are they failing math?"

"No."

"Are they bad in your class?"

"No."

Ronald never raised his voice. Students were not bad in his class. And since he had been in the Peace Corps, the problem children of the suburbs were easily manageable.

"They're good in class; I like them. They'll never know what hit them. Let's start today. Were they bad?"

"No, they were very good; they were absent."

"We'll start tomorrow. Whenever they give you a hard time, tell me, and I'll give them a hard time. No bathroom privileges, no small talk, no free time. Just work, work, and more work."

Crucial to Ronald's plan was that Phil and Gary make the connection between their behavior with me and his behavior with them, and he was not subtle about it. If we encountered them at lunch, Ronald asked me about their behavior. If my answer didn't satisfy him, he slowly shook his head and said, "I'm disappointed in you boys." After several oblique threats to them in my presence and his subsequent punishing classes, they realized the conspiracy and confronted us.

"You two are ganging up on us!" they whined.

Ronald smiled. "Why would we gang up on two good kids? Would we do something like that, Mr. Leonard?" He reminded me of Brother Murray and Brother Synan toying with us.

This frightened Phil and Gary, because we were not playing by the rules. Give new teachers a hard time and enjoy. They probably won't fail you. Get along with the old teachers. What else can you do? Veterans know what they're doing. But veterans have nothing to do with new teachers. Never, in eleven years of classroom politics, had Phil and Gary misjudged a new teacher's power. And for good reason. There aren't many veterans—teachers or administrators—who would resort to unorthodox disciplinary methods for a struggling new teacher.

Sometime in October, Ronald returned to his former amiable persona with Phil and Gary, because their behavior and their grades improved in my class. That month of Ronald's protection gave me the time I needed to gain confidence in a profession that does not give new teachers much time to learn.

Ronald's rescue mission had nothing to do with race. I was white, he was black, and the two boys were white. He just felt sorry for me. But for me, it had much to do with race. I became good friends with a black person, with someone from the world of Sidney Poitier and Jackie Robinson, someone from the world of Harlem, where I spent four white years in my insular high school. He was someone from the world of civil rights and its great leader, Dr. Martin Luther King Jr.

The romantic in me saw myself as the Robert Culp character to the Bill Cosby character in the popular TV series of the sixties, *I Spy*. The realist in me enjoyed not being a limousine liberal, who supported blacks from afar. Integrationists who send their children to private schools come to mind. Finally, I had a black friend, and I didn't seek him out to prove a point about myself.

I became so confident with my role as teacher that I accepted a position as a substitute teacher in New York City. The teachers there had gone out on strike with Al Shanker during 1968, and some voluntary make-up days were available during their Christmas vacation. The city needed substitutes, and I needed money to begin repaying my college loan. I went back to Roosevelt High School, the school in the Bronx, where I had student taught.

My first assignment was the gym. I was to open and close the locker rooms before and after each class. For the rest of the time, I was to sit in the principal's office for emergencies. Five minutes before the bell, I reported to the gym. No one needed to tell me that the day was coming to an end. I could find the locker room with my eyes closed. But I wasn't prepared for the challenge of opening and locking a door while holding my nose. Not having to take phys. ed. classes in any of my schools caught up with me.

My next assignment several days later tested my olfactory sense as well, but my exposure was not gradual; rather it was an explosion in the nostrils. I substituted for a science teacher who had left exact instruction for the students. They were to continue with their dissections of a pig. I opened the closet, as directed, and within moments longed for the locker room. Since Rice High School hadn't had biology labs for its students, I had never experienced the nasal invasion of formaldehyde.

The students knew what to do and did it, some even oblivious to the drastic change in our environment. I couldn't understand their acceptance of it. After a short period of careful breathing, I decided to ignore their education and gasped, "Please put your pigs back in the closet immediately." You never have to tell students to stop working twice.

Someone must have taken pity on me, because the following day was perfect: no lockers, no pigs. Just students who needed an English teacher. The class, for some reason, was all black, which was fine with me, because I had many black students—and a black friend—back in Yonkers. There was, however, one problem; we had no books. There were so few in the building the school wasn't going to trust a substitute teacher with them.

The students were quick to realize this problem and began to speak to one another. But I was a four-month tested professional who could ad lib a lesson—if I could get their attention. They preferred their conversations. I was faced with a classic teacher nightmare. The teacher stands before inattentive students; there is nothing he can say to interest them. Teachers who have this dream swear there is no prototype for this nightmare in their waking hours. I agree. I quickly conceived a plan.

While the students chatted, I wrote on the board the words *frog* and *nigger*. Like the click of a pen, their conversations ended. One group, then another turned toward the board. They were staring at me, and someone from the back whistled and said, "We got a crazy one here. He doesn't know what floor we're on." I looked down at my schedule for the room number, whose first number indicated the floor.

"We're high up." When I spoke, I was struck by their intense interest. But they weren't looking at me; they were watching a magician. How was I going to free myself from the chains before I drowned in the locked safe at the bottom of the piranha-infested river?

"Does it anger you that I wrote these words on the board?"

"Yeah," one girl to my right answered. "Who are you calling *frog nigger*?"

"No one. And I'm the frog."

"Why are you a frog?"

"I was born in France, but I'll explain later…. What about *nigger*? Are you angry that I wrote that on the board?"

"We're waiting to see what you're going to do," a girl to my left answered. "Maybe you got a death wish…. Maybe you'll hop like a frog out the window."

Everyone in the room laughed. And no one laughed more than I did. They were interested, and I was happy and relieved.

"Let's play a word association game. When I point to one of the words on the board, call out something negative." I pointed to *frog*.

"You!"

"Suicidal!"

"Sub!"

"Is that the best you can do with frog?" I pretended to be bored.

"We don't know any French people." Now they were frustrated; they wanted a reaction from me.

"We don't even know any frogs! This is the Bronx!" The laughing girl to my left was shaking her head. Then, the boy sitting behind her laughed. Good, I thought. The more laughter, the better.

"All right, try this." I pointed to *nigger*. Every student shouted out racial epithets, and when they topped one another, they laughed. At that moment, they were one and proud of it. Some students looked at me to gauge the effect the scene was having on me. So far, so good, I thought. This was going to work. "What would happen if you laughed every time a racist called you 'nigger'?" I wanted to make it clear to them that I was not a racist.

"He'd call us something else."

"But what would your laughing do to the word itself?"

"They would find another word."

"Let's focus on one word at a time. We all agree that the word itself is harmless, right? And we agree that the context of the word gives it its power. It's not the word, but the person using the word. You use the word all the time. I can use the word for discussion, but I couldn't call you 'nigger'—even if you understood I wasn't a racist. The word unfortunately has a life of its own." We were all in agreement; however, they were waiting for me to make a mistake.

"What do the police say about being called *pig?*" No one knew. "They say the letters in pig stand for pride, integrity, and guts. If they can contain their anger, their response to the hatred behind it, will people continue to call them pigs?" Of course, today it sounds anachronistic for someone to use the word.

"No! So why are you a frog, Frenchie?" someone in the back called out.

"French people eat frog legs … you bigot."

"Ugh! What do their legs taste like? … Why are you calling me a 'bigot'?"

"Chicken. Most people don't call French people Frenchie, unless it's a put-down."

"I'm not putting you down; I don't even know you!"

"How many racists know you?" The class was satisfied with that and waited for me to continue.

We spent the rest of the class sharing our knowledge of other racial and ethnic epithets (I was a *mick* as well as a *frog*), context, and word deflation. The groundwork was set for the rest of the week. I brought in my books by James Baldwin, Richard Wright, Ralph Ellison, Malcolm X, Claude Brown, and Piri Thomas.

I read the passages aloud, and they listened carefully to the truth spoken by these familiar voices that had the authority of publication—and street experience—behind them. And when I wasn't reading to them, I listened to them carefully. I had introduced them to the authors' worlds, and they had introduced me to theirs. I told them so and thanked them for our week together. They agreed it was a good week. When the bell rang, the girl to my left got up, shook my hand, and hopped toward the door. She turned and waved goodbye.

In January, I returned to my full-time job in Yonkers and to students who enjoyed a much nicer world than that of Roosevelt High School in the Bronx. They had plenty of books and supplies. They had beautiful classrooms with lacquered oak trim around the blackboards. I told the students we were lucky for our environment. They wanted to know about the city kids. Who were smarter? Nicer? I told them the city kids. I added that city kids were even better looking.

Since there were many black students in Yonkers, I emphasized black themes for essay topics and literature choices. I enjoyed working with black students, because they seemed more alive; they expressed themselves without inhibitions. I remember vividly, thirty-five years later, their stormy disagreements and their earthquakes of laughter, which sometimes knocked them out of their seats onto the floor. I never laughed so much in my life.

But I remember most their acceptance of a white teacher struggling through his first year. This memory captures a scene that played itself out behind my desk. I walked into my class to see two boys wrestling a girl to the floor. When Renee saw me, she yelled, "Mr. Leonard, get this nigger off me." The two boys ignored her.

Without deliberation, I responded, "Which one?" As soon as I spoke, all movement stopped. They became a sculpture of three stunned teenagers. Then they broke apart, rolling against one another, clapping their hands—and one another—at my unintended joke.

"Which *one?*" Renee howled. Since her appeal did not specify which boy to get off her, I asked for clarification. I was focused on the word *this*. I wasn't aware that I had implied *nigger*. I had grown accustomed to its use, because my students used the word frequently with one another. Only when Renee repeated, "Which *one?*" did I understand. They laughed, because I had entered their world of language at her inadvertent invitation. But they realized our classroom, our world, was safe.

Their intensity, which I understand falls into the dangerous category of racial stereotyping, was the great attraction of working with black students. By the beginning of my third year of teaching, I thought I knew everything there was to know about the art of teaching, racial harmony, and humanity. I was content. I knew firsthand that my black students performed as well as my white students. But the good life ended during my third year. The racial unrest in the country came to Yonkers, New York, concentrating its wrath on our high school.

In one of my twelfth grade classes, I was fortunate to have William as a student. In 1970, he was every black radical in the media. He wore a high afro and threatening dark sunglasses, but spoke with a gentle voice. He was very intelligent, and he enjoyed literature. He especially enjoyed exposing the different points of view in the class, which led to argument after argument. He motivated others to speak up, but he dominated the discussion, arguing with them or against them. He was the spark every teacher wants in class.

William: "Huck's a racist."

Michael: "But he helps Jim escape."

William: "For himself. He's lonely."

Patti: "When Huck hides the dead snake in Jim's bed, and its mate bites Jim, Huck feels bad and apologizes. A racist doesn't apologize to a runaway slave."

William: "He never lets on he did it, and he never apologizes to Jim."

Michael: "What about the time on the raft when Huck fools Jim with that story about Jim dreaming that Huck's lost?"

William: "Yeah, he apologizes all right, but it takes him fifteen minutes before he *humbles* himself to a *nigger*. And those are his words."

Patti: "Well, whatever ... he still does the right thing in the end."

William: "Yeah, for us, the readers. We know he's doing the right thing, but he doesn't. He really believes he's going to hell for helping Jim get his freedom. This is no Tom Sawyer fairy tale—this is a real story. Huck's going against all his upbringing, because he loves Jim, not because he thinks slavery is wrong. Huck's a racist."

William was also a black militant who believed the Civil Rights struggle justified violent action ("Look what they did to Dr. King, and he was a pacifist!"); but he tolerated me, so whenever possible, I used our discussion of literature to denounce it. I admitted that violence, in some cases, was understandable and effective; William approved this point of view. But he ridiculed my warning that violence had a life of its own, that it craved independence. He felt he could control violence, and once in a dramatic way, he did.

Fistfights and isolated fires broke out in the school, and William scheduled black walkouts that unnerved the white population in the building. The black students stood outside for a period of time and then returned to class. Sometimes, they had black assemblies, which admitted only black students—and black faculty.

During these walkouts, it didn't matter that I was a white teacher who taught Eldridge Cleaver's *Soul on Ice*; it didn't matter that we listened to Dick Gregory's records of comedic social commentary; and it didn't matter that I understood their rage. When my black students suddenly stood during a lesson and walked around me to leave the room, they refused to look at me when I asked for an explanation.

Fights were breaking out on a regular basis in the cafeteria. Lunchtime had become the worst period of the day. A week earlier, a boy accidentally hit a teacher in the back with a chair while the teacher was breaking up a fight; the injury required hospitalization. When the bell rang at the end of the period, I was relieved. In my classroom, black rage manifested itself only during the silent treatment of a student walkout.

My classroom, with its doors locked, acted as a haven for the students—and for me. Some students ate their lunches there. Their artwork covered the door window, permitting them to enjoy their free time in privacy—and peace. Some students painted murals, which they later used in their portfolios for college admissions. My yearbook staff members worked on the book. Everyone agreed that Hemingway's "clean, well-lighted place," his concept of order in a world of disorder and chaos, found a home in our classroom.

Opening the door one day for the first afternoon class, I was greeted by students settling in for *Alienation and Modern Man*, a twelfth grade elective. Unfortunately for my lesson, William was absent, and I would miss his enthusiasm. Fortunately, it was the last day of the week, it was a warm spring day, and the class and I had been together for nine months. We knew one another well. I liked them, and the class was predictably pleasant with that kind of comfort that evolves among people who support ideas with personal background information. The class ended with their cheery forecasts about the weekend.

I stood in the hall outside my room at three o'clock, enjoying the chatter that rose out of the flow of students. Some students called out to me in the Friday euphoria, and teachers waved to one another outside their rooms; all wanted to share in this ritualistic joy. Then, I heard a girl say she would never eat lunch in the cafeteria again. Many girls had already chosen to walk across the football field to the firehouse across the street where they could use the bathroom without fear of being assaulted—and extorted—by other girls. There had been a riot in the cafeteria. Some black boys and white boys threw chairs at one another. Most of the students, black and white, were caught in the middle. I knew who had given the command. I walked back into my room.

I sat at my desk, looked out the window, and enjoyed the calm and colorful homes across the street. This was my daily ritual; it was often therapeutic. The first time I saw Gorton High School with its tall columns presiding over its own green football field carved in chalk, I was reminded of a world I knew only through the window of the LIRR on my way to my father's new family in Huntington, Long Island, the world of beautiful homes and manicured baseball fields.

(We city kids didn't play ball on "professional-looking" diamonds; we shared one large, grassy field and used shirts for bases. Since several games were being played at the same time—and infielders from one game played alongside outfielders from other games—we often shouted "Heads up!" to warn players of another game's fly ball.)

The violence inside our school belied the beauty of its community, so I looked away from the window to the papers on my desk. When I heard a soft knock and William's gentle voice, I looked up. He was standing by the door, smiling under his sunglasses. He asked me how I was. I told him that the fight in the cafeteria ruined my weekend, and maybe even the year.

"It could have been worse; you could have been there."

"That's true."

"I hope you appreciate what I did."

"Appreciate what, William? What are you talking about?"

"I waited for you to leave the cafeteria. I waited for the next period."

What could I say? Thank you for throwing chairs at kids eating lunch while I was safely out of the cafeteria? He had come back to school to prove his point. He had controlled violence; he had controlled the direction of the riot. He had shown mercy for a teacher. He didn't know many of the people in the cafeteria; therefore, the assault was abstract, a black statement against white oppression.

"What would you have done if I had been in the cafeteria?"

"But you weren't. You were here in class."

The following year, 1971 to 1972, proved to be even more violent, and it would be my last at Gorton High School in Yonkers.

19

Championship Season

When I left Yonkers for Eastchester, I thought four years of teaching experience would make the transition painless. After all, I was a pro. I was wrong. My new tenth grade students, the reluctant learners in the building, didn't care that I had taught the most difficult classes in Gorton High School—and that students had liked me. Reputations do not precede new teachers in new schools. My new students didn't care that the Yonkers school system had acknowledged my competence with tenure. And I misinterpreted the significance of teaching in this better—more affluent—school district. I had to prove myself again. I had to relive my first week of teaching.

"My name is Mr. Leonard ... Quiet, please ... Yes? ... No, you can't change your seat ... Please raise your hand if you have a question; don't call out ... No, you can't go to the bathroom again ... Where's your homework? You *will* fail if you do not do your homework ... Quiet, please ... See you after school. For detention ... Of course, you'll come. I'll call your parents. Sit down. What's your phone number? Your number? I'll get it in the office ... No, you can't go to the bathroom again. Sit down."

It's true all teachers must prove themselves every September, but discipline is rarely a problem. Former students spread the word: "He's tough! He'll nail you!" But I always worried that I wouldn't repeat my success with students. *Teaching is an art form.* Good lesson plans, good classroom management skills, good grasp of the subject matter, respect for the students, etc., do not explain why "He's a good teacher!" They're elements for success, but teaching is not a formula. If teachers don't fully understand the reasons for success, how can they be sure they will succeed again? They find out in September.

But this was different. I was a new teacher again. I had to reestablish classroom rules. A long, penetrating stare didn't do it here in the wilds of Eastchester. These young people saw a chance for freedom. They had to test me. They had to do what they had to do. And I did what I had not done for four years. I didn't enjoy the role of unsmiling disciplinarian that warned the students I was "mean." I wanted to enjoy my students. I wanted to see their forgiving smiles when I made a bad joke. Rather than proving myself ever again in a new district, I decided I would die here in an Eastchester classroom.

To make matters worse, I had few friends. I knew two teachers, but we shared no free periods to unwind together. Unlike the Yonkers teachers who needed one another because of the discipline troubles, the Eastchester teachers had the luxury of being more independent and, therefore, reserved. As a result I spent all my free time alone in the library, making up new lesson plans, correcting homework, and missing the raucous male faculty room, where the Gorton teachers traded war stories.

During my first month at Eastchester, a senior, who recognized a lost soul when she saw one, became a friend. Theresa, the senior class president, sat at my library table one afternoon and introduced herself. Since Theresa was not my student, I didn't need to impress her with my classroom control; I could drop the mask. From late fall to Theresa's graduation in June, we had wonderful conversations about her interest in music and my interest in photography. And through Theresa, I met many other seniors. In the halls, students once again called my name and waved to me, and I was quickly feeling at home.

Theresa and I became better friends when she invited me in June to have dinner with her and her mother, Sylvia. Since I was taking students to the city for the Broadway play, *That Championship Season*—and didn't live in town—I appreciated the invitation. Like Theresa, Sylvia was vivacious and friendly. She served a wonderful meal and made me feel at home. Then, she reminded Theresa to "go backstage and say hello to Charlie and be sure to use my maiden name." I thanked Sylvia for her hospitality. Driving back to the school to meet my students in their "do-we-have-to-dress-up" clothes, I asked Theresa about Charlie.

"He's an actor. My mother and he dated before she married my father."

Over the years, I had taken students to see many shows: Joe Papp's production of *Hamlet* at the Public Theatre, *The Me Nobody Knows, Jacques Brel Is Alive and Well and Living in Paris, Equus* (my mother, who sometimes met us at the theatre, worried about the nudity and my job security), *Beatlemania, Our Town, The Wiz, Children of a Lesser God, When You Comin' Back, Red Ryder?, The Fantasticks* (several times!), and others.

The trips were always successful. For the students, they broke the suburban routine of driving around town or parking behind the mall. The bus ride to the city became a social event and sightseeing excursion with constant chatter. Once we pulled up to the theatre, I stood behind the driver, told the students exactly where the bus would be after the play, and handed out the tickets. For me, the pleasure of playing father far outweighed the work of planning—and the responsibility for fifty teenagers.

As soon as *That Championship Season* ended, the students boarded the bus, which waited for them on a nearby corner. They had loved the play, and their excitement and gratitude made me happy. When counting the students, I came up with one short—the nightmare of school trips. When I got to Theresa's name, I remembered her mother's request to see "Charlie."

As I was telling the driver that we had one student to go, I heard Theresa behind me. "I'd like you to meet Charlie." She was holding hands with Charles Durning, who was still wearing make up. Realizing that the actor on the stage was now on the bus, the students became quiet. Why was he on the bus? He waved to them, and some students applauded. He told Theresa he'd call her mother the next day, turned to wave again to the students, who all waved back, and left the bus.

Charlie did call Sylvia, who was divorced from Theresa's father. They began to see each other again and invited me to Shakespeare in the Park and a screening of his new film, *Dog Day Afternoon*. Eventually, they married. Whenever I see Charlie in a movie, I remember that wonderful dinner, which made me feel at home in Eastchester.

The summer of Theresa's graduation, she extended her concern for me to Rome. In 1973, she and her Roman family found me a room near St.

Peter's Church and showed me a Rome reserved only for natives. Soon after our return, Theresa and her mother moved with Charlie to California. I lost touch with them, but perhaps, like Charlie and Sylvia, we'll meet again. I hope so. I'll never forget Theresa's kindness.

20

Strikes

There's nothing like a strike for friendship and romance. I participated in two strikes, and both times my life was enriched—despite the severe penalties imposed by the state's Taylor Law. By not negotiating in good faith with the teachers' union, some Boards of Education gave the teachers no choice; they had to strike, and the district saved the salary money and received the fine money. In New York State, a teacher loses two days pay for every day not in the classroom. And the outlaw teacher loses tenure for one year. There is no penalty for Boards acting in bad faith. For my involvement in the two strikes, I lost fifty-eight days of pay, almost a third of a year's salary. But I have never enjoyed anything so much in my life.

The seventies was the decade of the strike. Thanks to Al Shanker and the New York City teachers' strike of 1968, the rest of the state teachers decided that they also deserved better salaries, which would allow them to work only one job at a time; most teachers worked evenings, weekends, and summers to keep up with the earning power of the rest of society. Veteran teachers have done so much to acquire the cost of living salary increases that young teachers today question the necessity of unions; they ironically believe the good salaries come from goodhearted employers. If they refuse to support the unions—supporting themselves, since they are the union—their salaries will stagnate, and they'll find themselves picketing outside their schools in 2020.

In the winter of 1972, the Yonkers teachers conducted their first strike. We picketed outside our schools for eight very cold days, watching the substitute teachers, the "scabs," take our places in the classrooms and *pretend* to teach. They allowed the school district to fool the public about educating their children. The TV screens highlighted administrative-conducted classes, but the students knew better. Once the novelty of watching movies and ridiculing the scabs wore off, they stopped going to class. We, on the picket line surrounding the school, knew that most of the classrooms were empty, because our students brought us the inside news with cups of hot coffee.

Coffee and thermal underwear prepared us for the cold weather, but the news that some of the scabs were *our* own college student-teachers, who received their state teaching licenses in *our* classrooms with *our* guidance, generated the heat we needed to be fearsome hecklers. We called out to them to stay home, to remember our contribution to their training; that didn't work. Then, we screamed at them, "Get your hands out of our pockets!" and "Get real jobs!" But nothing worked. Every day, the same sad-looking people endured our insults, making easy money—and postponing a settlement to the strike.

Exasperated with these young people who exploited our predicament, several of us left the picket line and drove to their school of education and spoke to the administrator in charge of student teachers. We explained that his students were helping to keep the building open, which led the public to believe that students were receiving an education; therefore, the school district didn't need to settle with us. He made it very clear to us that he couldn't interfere with the strike: Smiling and bobbing his head with the weight of wisdom, he sympathized with us, but whined, "Oh, my, no. We can't tell our students where to work or what to do. We can't interfere with their lives."

(This contradicted my student-teaching experience in 1968 when the professor in charge of the program warned us about participating in anti-war rallies with high school faculty and student protestors. "I don't want to see any of you protesting the Vietnam War. You represent our school.")

Our response to this college administrator was just as emphatic: "Oh, my, please don't send your students to Yonkers; we will not be able to work with your back-stabbing student-teachers in the future."

Each day that passed, we lost two days of salary. Teachers with families had to leave the picket line for other work. Those of us who remained out in the cold became angrier, and we warmed ourselves with the escalation of obscene insults and personal threats. Once we found out the names of the scabs, the insults became more satisfying and effective: "You're going to have ugly children, Grimwig!" and "We know where you live, Chuzzle-wit!" On one occasion, several strikers with an absurd sense of humor followed some scabs to a White Castle in the Bronx and picketed in front of the window to the bewilderment of the patrons eating hamburgers—and to the horror of the scabs.

On the eighth day of the strike, one teacher decided to frighten the scabs by physically intimidating a tall, athletic-looking young man; it helped that the striker had a black belt in Karate. The rest of us occupied the police with small talk, which worked well, until the policeman realized the tall, worried-looking young scab was hopping up the street toward the school. The black belt, walking next to the scab, was side kicking him at regular intervals. When the policeman intervened, the young scab broke away from his puppeteer and walked quickly into the building. Before he reached the door, the black belt reminded him that he'd give him "another lift after school." We never did see him; a contract was negotiated at noon, ending the bitter eight days of the strike.

Since teachers are always the weaker party in a strike, they benefit from the esprit de corps necessary to keep spirits high despite bitter cold weather and snow, daily loss of salary, biased news reports, and police-controlled picket lines. We had one another. A surprising advantage of the strike was that I became friendly with a school of strangers, who never smiled in the halls—or got in my way in the mailroom. I discovered that the unfriendly history teacher on the second floor was shy, but eager to make friends under an umbrella during a cold, wet afternoon.

I took advantage of our warlike existence to meet the female teachers I'd seen in the school corridors walking to their classrooms, the cafeteria, and the female faculty room. (Despite what enlightened people say about the benefits of integration of the sexes in public places, I found our male faculty room a refuge away from *responsible, mature* behavior.) I was especially eager to befriend Tina, whom I had seen but didn't know. After several days of steadying our "Good Schools or No Schools" picket signs on the windswept battlefield in front of the school, Tina and I agreed that every war needs a love story.

During our lunch break, we decided to act on our short, pragmatic flirtation. We ignored respectable social foreplay and the morality of a hostile public. We were anti-heroes, rebel-victims. We were lawbreakers. Our dignity depended on our acts of defiant free will. We would return to nature to create order in a world of chaos. We would create Hemingway's "clean, well-lighted place" in my friend's apartment, because he was picketing in another part of Yonkers—and I had his key.

When the strike ended suddenly the next day, Tina returned to her classroom, and I returned to mine, where we resumed teaching the great themes of literature with the composure of Hemingway heroes. We dated for several weeks until our romance succumbed to the realism of peacetime relationships.

Before entering the high school our first day back, teachers gathered in front of the steps leading to the building in a symbol of solidarity. On the steps leading to the doors stood the students, impatient with the locked doors, eager to return to normal lives. At eight o'clock, the principal opened the doors. He was happy to see us, happy that no one was injured while the public assumed that real teachers were not necessary for classroom instruction.

He and the assistant principal ordered the students to move to the sides of the steps; they grumbled and separated. He then signaled to us. In single file, we moved up the steps. Before the first teacher reached the door, the students began clapping. And they clapped until every teacher was inside the building. The press hated us, the politicians hated us, some of the parents hated us. But the students, who took orders from us, who were graded by us, and who, of course, knew us better than anyone, welcomed us like boxers pushing through the crowd to the ring.

It took no time for the routine of bells and student energy to tame the outlaw existence of the past eight days. I was happy to return to a predictable life. The peace, however, lasted only forty-five minutes. After the first period bell, from classroom door to classroom door, teachers were passing the news that a scab was substituting in the building. It was day one of the strike again, and we were ready "to walk"; we were going to call a wildcat strike if she remained in the building. The principal swore to us that Central Administration, not he, hired this notorious woman, who had smiled at our insults for eight days.

It didn't take much time for our threat to reach Central Administration. By the end of the second period, she left the building. We had lost our tenure and sixteen days of pay for standing in the snow and freezing rain for a small increase in our salaries. The students understood the significance of our stand. They gave their full support to us. For the first time, I realized that we had won. The public would believe us the next time we threatened a strike.

I left Gorton for Eastchester High School at the end of the year. I left students who liked me for students who didn't know me and to whom I'd have to prove myself. I left old friends, who watched me become a teacher and now respected me as a colleague. One friend asked me to stay, and I thought about it for a long time. I left my new "strike friends." I left an administration who gave me tenure, because I "passed" the three-year test. I would be tested for two years to regain tenure. But I had to leave. The racial tension was getting worse, and the strike convinced me this school system was not interested in education. Eastchester would never be Yonkers.

On January 25, 1976, the Eastchester teachers went on strike for twenty-one days, the record for teacher strikes at the time in New York State. Since Eastchester is a much smaller community than Yonkers, the strike was more personal. I knew our strike leaders well and respected them, and I became a strike coordinator with two friends, Lou Serico and Laura Thomas. Our first job was to rent office space for strike headquarters, which proved difficult once landlords discovered we were striking teachers. "Sorry, we found tenants for our space." Often, they wouldn't speak with us at all. Finally, we found a small storefront on the edge of town, where we set up picket line schedules and worked the phones to dissuade potential substitute teachers from becoming scabs.

We were also there for physical and psychological comfort. We supplied coffee and bagels for picketers. For inspiration we charted, with stars, the daily progress of the strikers (the honor roll)—and the names of the teachers who did not strike—on several poster boards stretched across an entire wall of the office. And, we kept the office open for teachers to meet and feel united in the face of the state's severe penalties against us.

We also kept the office open late into the night in case there was a development in negotiations, which would necessitate calling teachers to work the next day. Since I was single, I chose night duty, but Lou, Laura, and I actually spent days and nights in the office. I rarely drove to my apartment in the city. Often, friends invited me to their homes in the area, but on several occasions—when our negotiating team was meeting with the Board late at night—I slept on a folding table at strike headquarters.

I enjoyed almost everything about my role. I was more than an office manager. I imagined myself a dedicated union leader fighting for the "little guy" and would tough out the nights, sleeping on that table. On one particular night, I dreamt of hearing thunder. I sat up and saw tumbleweeds of fire roll across broken window glass under my table. Feeling the table become hot, I jumped off. I turned from the fire and ran to the back of the office, where I grabbed the bars on the window. Before I could bend the bars apart, I awoke to our negotiating team banging on the door. At three o'clock in the morning, they enjoyed my dream about union-busting goons more than I.

Hoping to hear good news—or at least accurate news—teachers came to the office throughout the day and night. In any strike, teachers always lose the battle of propaganda. The reporters interview union leaders, but often slant the news in favor of the establishment—in this case, the school district. If the scabs are showing movies, they are "adapting and creatively teaching," and "the education of the youngsters has not been disrupted." Some administrators support this interpretation to preserve their positions while gaining the benefits won in the strike: pay increases, benefits, etc. It's a no pain, all gain strategy for them.

As a result, negotiators frequently stopped by the office with facts for the membership. One afternoon, Marv Rothman, one of our two vice presidents and a negotiator, came to the office with the exciting news that he was just interviewed by John Johnson for WABC-TV Channel 7. Marv was a tough adversary. He never backed down from a fight, but he always believed that talking was more effective, and Johnson was willing to listen to Marv; we finally had a way to communicate with the public. We gathered around Marv for his preview of the 6 o'clock news:

Johnson: "Mr. Rothman, why are you on strike?"

Marv: "We are the second lowest paid teachers in Westchester County. Only Yonkers pays their teachers a lower salary. Unlike the City of Yonkers, the town of Eastchester is a middle and upper-middle-class community."

Johnson: "So this is about money?"

Marv: "Work is always about money. This is about paying our bills. The people who live here choose Eastchester over Yonkers and other towns, because they have the money to do so. People in Scarsdale pay more to live there, because they have the money."

Johnson: "But Mr. Rothman, you teach social studies, and you are breaking the law. How do you explain that to your students?"

Marv: "Well, you know, Mr. Johnson, it wasn't long ago that people broke the law so that black people would not have to sit in the rear of a bus."

We cheered. We clapped Marv on the back. Finally, we got our message out to the public, and Marv did it with history on our side. Since John Johnson is an African-American, he must have appreciated the response. We watched the news that night. John Johnson covered the strike. There were the usual interviews with parents who bemoaned our lack of respect for the law and commitment to their children. There was the insistence that property taxes were high enough. The piece ended with the usual frustrated faces of teachers screaming on the picket line. Marv's interview had been cut.

A month later, in a pharmacy on 86th Street in Manhattan, I ran into Bob Teague, another reporter at Channel 7. I introduced myself and told him about Marv's experience. I asked, "Was Johnson embarrassed? Was that the reason for the omission?" I wanted Teague's analysis. Well, the answer was simple; the editor, not Johnson, cut the interview. He didn't give a reason. That's the way it is, he shrugged.

What if Marv had stuttered and stumbled with his answer? What if he had been evasive? Would the public have seen the interview? Did the editor want the audience to reject this teacher, this union man, "who chose money over the law and the children"? But Marv did not give the anticipated answers. After all, network executives, wherever they live, also pay property taxes, and their teachers' salary increases would raise their taxes. And, of course, the public always loves a bargain. In Marv's words they wanted "Champagne at beer prices."

Watching the 6 o'clock news—or the absence of news—with Marv that night, we realized that we were important enough to be an omission and that we were at war. We were not striking just against the town of Eastchester. We were striking against all the districts in the state that were not paying their teachers fair salaries—and they were watching our strike. We were becoming the longest strike, and therefore a successful strike, in the history of New York.

If we were going to win this war, we needed the parents on our side. We couldn't count on the press to communicate with them. The picket line and the absence of professionals in the classrooms virtually closed the schools, but we needed to explain the reasons for our strike. We were more than babysitters, even though we borrowed the WNEW-TV Channel 5 logo, "Do you know where your children are?" for buttons worn on the picket line. But the parents learned nothing on the news. Driving by the school every day, they saw the same picket lines. They honked to support us, or they cursed our "pinko" strike, but many didn't know teachers were underpaid

The strike ended after twenty-one days, because some teachers panicked and broke the picket line. We had lost. The insurrection occurred after the Easter break, which negated the need for picket lines and moral support, and the advent of warm weather, which I believe undermined our unity and our determination to take on even the elements, if necessary.

Unlike the end of the Yonkers's strike, there were no crowds of students applauding our return the first day back. Unlike the elementary school teachers, we high school teachers didn't enter the building as a group; there was no illusion of conquering heroes. I went to my classroom, let my students in, and began teaching. During our first week back, the Acting Superintendent personally—and happily—delivered letters stating that we would be fined and that we had lost our tenure for one year.

The Board was jubilant; they had won. But they had won only a battle, not the war. We sent a message that had an influence in all our future negotiations. Teachers at blackboards—or walking up and down aisles—not administrators or Members of the Board, had the personal responsibility of educating students; we made the schools the most important buildings in our town. And since we were professionals, who demanded from the public the same respect that we had given to them and their children, we were a militant and proud union that would strike again if pushed to do so. After the seventies, there were very few teacher strikes in the state—and none in Eastchester.

Even if some parents didn't like us, the students did. They had a personal relationship with us, and no one could diminish their affection. That parents were shocked to learn that their Chester had cut a class or that Beatrice had cheated on an exam, was no surprise to us. Chester and Beatrice rarely shocked us, and we were prepared to fight for them.

I once went to a parent's office in the city, because his daughter, Jenny, feared he would never speak to her again after having found marijuana in her room. I explained that Jenny was depressed; she knew she had disappointed her father. I suggested he speak with Jenny, since her suffering was affecting her work. Our three years together in school gave Jenny the courage to speak easily with me about her "heinous" crime. The next morning the principal called me to his office to thank me for my interest in Jenny; her father had called him to compliment my professionalism. On her last day of school, Jenny gave me a teddy bear, which I still have.

We had to wait for June to receive our communal welcome back from those we cared most about, the students. They were gathered in the auditorium, prepared to enjoy the yearly slide show that was second only to the advent of the yearbooks in the students' hearts. They clapped and booed when images of their friends appeared on the huge screen, and they hoped they would be the next person to receive all this loving attention. This explained the reason for all the mugging that took place during the year when anyone raised a camera in the school. "Are you yearbook or slide show?" students wanted to know.

Often, teachers were the biggest mugs. Today, we stood in the dark at the back of the auditorium, waiting for our turn, but so far *we* were absent in *their* show. Suddenly, the auditorium remained dark for several minutes to give the audience its complete attention for the next song—"Revolution" by the Beatles. Then it happened. The strike! The revolution! We were on the picket line. We were waving our signs. We were shaking our fists. All the students screamed and hooted. They were saving the teachers for the last series of slides.

I didn't know what to make of their reaction; this was the first time the students as a group had a chance to comment on the strike. Would some students take the opportunity to condemn us in this dark auditorium? If they feared retribution from us, this was their chance, their perfect cover, to become a mob. Whenever a teacher became recognizable, did they cheer or jeer? I couldn't tell.

Then the music and the slides ended. The auditorium was dark and quiet for several long moments, and then speakers broke the tension with the theme of one of TV's popular shows about a beloved teacher, *Welcome Back, Kotter*. I will never forget the applause that coincided with the images of teachers in the classrooms, in halls, and in the cafeteria. If there were any doubts about our students' affection for us, their joyful response to us on the screen crushed them.

During the strike, the public and their representatives, the Board of Education, disappointed us with their disdain for our profession. The press shocked me with its manipulation of reality. But once again, the students were happy to see us and made our return to our classes less bitter. I had sworn during the strike to leave teaching soon, but thanks to the students, finding love is never difficult in this profession, and I taught for another twenty-six years in Eastchester.

I also found comfort, once again, in that strike fever led to romance fever, but this time my affair lasted more than several weeks; I fell in love with a teacher who made me laugh those late nights during the strike. This time, however, the romance survived six months in a strike-free world without anti-heroes. After the collapse of the strike, our feverish idealism sustained us, and by June, we decided to take advantage of a fly-and-drive promotional package to San Francisco in August. To pay for the trip, she worked an office temp job, and I worked—"shaped up"—on Canada Dry delivery trucks.

We flew into San Francisco, picked up a rental car, and drove up the beautiful coast to Mendocino. I was happy. I was with a woman who had lost her breath laughing at my dream of burning folding tables in strike headquarters. I loved Chloe, this woman, this teacher-outlaw who made me laugh, and I loved this late-afternoon world beneath its heavy gray-dark sky, because we were together, cozy in our warm, comfortable car.

At the end of the day, after several hours on the road, we decided to stop at a motel, one of many, just beyond Mendocino. Satisfied with the happy journey to Northern California, we pulled up to the motel. I went to the office *alone* to rent a room for two lawbreakers, *Mr. and Mrs. Leonard*, because my wild side didn't extend to renting a room in sin; I was an outlaw, not a libertine.

As I was signing the register, content with my lie in order to respect convention, "Thou shalt not rent a room with someone other than thy wife," I heard several joyful voices behind me:

"Mr. Leonard! Mr. Leonard!"

"What are you doing here? What are you doing here?"

"Is that Ms. Gervais in the car?"

"What are you doing here?"

"How cool!"

It was the Baldwin family from Eastchester. Last year, I had been their respectable high school English teacher, and now we were in a motel in the wilds of Northern California. My cosmopolitan manner that worked well with the motel owner vanished. Obviously, I was caught *in flagrante delicto* with an elementary school teacher.

While I was blinking and pulling my lips apart to smile, I waited for the inevitable questions: "Did you get married? Did you and Ms. G. get married? Are you on your honeymoon?" But they never asked; they were gone. I don't remember saying goodbye. I don't think they said goodbye. They had saved themselves—and me. Watching my eyes flutter from person to person must have been disconcerting for this very nice family on vacation.

Since I had already paid for our room, we were condemned to relive this awful memory the entire evening. I was sure Chloe was hiding under a blanket in the back seat, but no, she laughingly referred to life's surprising coincidences. Now, it was true that I exaggerated my significance in the moral universe of the Baldwin family, but Chloe would not see these teenagers in September when they would qualify as popular witnesses to an enjoyable scandal. "You'll never guess who we saw in a motel this summer!"

Of course, I was correct in my prediction. The seniors didn't waste any time to embarrass me in a playful way. On the first day of school in September, I stood at the blackboard with only one thing on my mind: Don't allow the heat to pass my collar and color my face.

"Mr. Leonard, were you in California last month?"

"Yes, I was, Maureen."

"Were you alone?"

"Yes, I was."

"You weren't with somebody?"

Do cats grin when they tap a mouse back and forth before the kill?

"No, I wasn't."

I knew she knew. She knew I knew. The class knew we both knew. I was President Nixon with my back to the blackboard. I was going to drive this girl crazy. She wanted to scream, "Give it up!" But she smiled.

"Are you remembering right, Mr. Leonard?"

I wanted to scream, "Forget it!" but I smiled.

"I don't know what you mean, Maureen."

Now, I liked this girl, and she liked me, but we had become opponents in a test of wills. She wanted to have some fun with me. Normally I never minded, but the sexual nature of the joke made it too personal.

She had incontrovertible proof that her childhood teacher and I were participants in the sexual revolution, a source of joy and ridicule for the class, but she never counted on my acting abilities. And she broke. The precocious, young feminist, whose bold and lighthearted attempt to expose a "role model," failed, and she surrendered in a fury.

"No! You were with Ms. G. in a motel. Patti saw you. Her whole family saw you."

The heat never rose to my face. The thought of this mouse, grinning back at the cat, inspired me, and I asked, "Why is your face so red? Are you all right, Maureen?"

I won. It was brilliant. I had lied magnificently. I successfully hid my personal life, which I kept private for the most part, and I didn't allow this student a sure thing. I had out-teased her mercilessly. That was the end of it, but she was very angry. I was sure lunch was going to be a disappointment for many students. But eventually she did forgive me. When students and teachers care for each other, classrooms become playgrounds where shoving is an act of love.

21

A Fabulous Reality

Many years ago, I saw a photograph of three school secretaries enjoying a Christmas party of a week earlier. I looked at Paula, the woman in the middle. She was smiling, because she was at a party, because one smiles at a photographer, or because she was having a good time. One hour after she and her friends had posed for that photograph, she would not have smiled for any reason. One hour later she walked into her home to discover that her husband had died from a heart attack.

I studied the photograph, which had captured a moment before the news of her husband's death, or perhaps the photograph captured the moment he died; maybe she was smiling while he was dying. Each time I looked at the photograph, the smile changed; it became ironic, mysterious, fragile. I didn't see the happiness that strangers would see. I studied that captured moment to understand time and death.

I planned not to attend another party, my retirement party, but my friend Marv persuaded me to go, if not for myself, then for my friends who wanted to celebrate my career. At the end of the party, we posed for a photograph. I recently saw this photograph, and I am smiling and Marv is smiling. One week later, Marv learned he had cancer; one year later, he died. I have become that secretary in the Christmas party photograph.

Marv's death was my first intimate experience with death. My father, grandmother, and aunt had died, but we were an estranged family. Close family friends died after a period of separation; I was prepared never to see them again. I was not prepared to miss Marv, and I remember him when I hear a joke or see a school building. When I need advice, I am reminded that I can't call him.

I met Marv in 1972. We taught together, traveled together, and spent much time together during the last year of his life. Since I no longer taught, I had time to be with him during his chemotherapy and his dying. At the hospital, I learned about the ritual of cancer treatment. I met kind nurses who explained that the two IV bags contained the chemotherapy and the water that prevented the chemotherapy from burning his veins. Marv needed methadone for the pain in his back, but he would ultimately require a morphine patch for "breakthrough pain." And it did break through. To be totally free of pain, he would lose clarity of thought; he chose the pain.

The last time I saw Marv, I drove him and Cissy, his sister and my good friend, to LaGuardia Airport for their flight to Atlanta, where he would learn that he was too sick and, therefore, not eligible for a new drug treatment. For the first time during his illness, he sat in a wheelchair, a wheelchair borrowed from the airline. We said goodbye and shook hands; Marv and I rarely shook hands, so it was our sign of affection. I watched Cissy push him into the building. One year earlier, Marv had run up the steps to McKinley's tomb in Canton, Ohio, boasting of his physical prowess: "Not bad for a geezer!"

When I think of Marv, I don't see him sitting in that wheelchair. I see him standing, always standing, in front of his classroom. The students loved "Marv!," which they shouted whenever—and wherever—they saw him. They enjoyed his stories that made history personal and real. His playfulness evoked smiles and laughter. Before he revealed a "news flash" about Calvin Coolidge or King Tut through the megaphone of cupped hands, he warned the students to hold onto their desks; and they did so with both hands. When they complained about the heat in his June classroom, he drew an air conditioner on the blackboard and pressed the button. When they said it wasn't working, he apologized and drew a plug in an outlet. "That better?" How could they say no?

If I had a question about history, politics, anthropology, medicine, finance, I called him. "What do you think, Marv?" From my divorce to my retirement, he found the patience and the wisdom to guide me with his deep, confident voice. During a twenty-five year friendship, he became my mentor, the male authority figure in my life.

During our last conversation, in which he could only whisper, he asked about a minor medical problem I was having with my foot. I was embarrassed. He was dying; he shouldn't be thinking of me. When I could no longer call him, I called his friends. We spoke about him, and that helped. Before Marv's death, I didn't understand how to help students who had lost a loved one. Fortunately, I learned from the students who depended on me in school—their home away from home—the lesson of listening.

Whenever someone died in our school community, mourning came in waves of tearful students, frightened students, shocked students in hallways, special assemblies, funeral parlors, and classrooms. Teachers tried to console them, and at the time, I thought I did as well as the next teacher. But since my experience with death was never intimate, I now know I didn't.

Back in the mid-eighties, Randy died in a terrible accident. The school did a good job helping the students cope with his death and with the shocking reminder of their own mortality. An assembly allowed some of his friends and teachers to speak to the students. I knew Randy, because his locker was next to my classroom, and we often spoke. That so many students appreciated the school's tribute to him was no surprise.

But I learned nothing about the power of communal grieving from that assembly. Randy had several close friends in my class. I had the chance to let them talk about their feelings for him and about their own mortality. Instead, I directed them to write in their journals, to use this quiet time to "create order" on paper. I thought the introspection would be good for them. But I really did it for myself. I thought I had to have answers for them. In effect, when I told them to work out the mystery of death on their own, I isolated them. At the end of the period, one of the girls complained bitterly that the exercise was "horrible" and swore she'd never spend time that way again.

Before every new unit, I welcomed a free-wheeling discussion dominated by student opinion. "What did you think of Bradbury's *Dandelion Wine*?" It was a rhetorical question. They would love it; they always did. Not Diane. She raised her hand like a sword.

"Bradbury doesn't know anything about death!"

"Why do you say that, Diane?"

"Great Grandmother's death is not real. That's not how it is; death is ugly and cruel, and Bradbury thinks it's beautiful. I hate this book!"

What could I say? Someone she loved had suffered before dying. I defended the book by emphasizing Bradbury's romantic theme that death is part of life. That knowledge almost kills Douglas, the twelve-year-old protagonist of the novel, who discovers he is alive, a fabulous reality—and, therefore, must die, another fabulous reality. Other characters die in the novel—one is even brutally murdered—but Bradbury chooses a quiet death for this character to introduce Plato's vision of an existence before life on Earth. Great Grandmother will die and awaken from the dream we all dream in this world.

Diane didn't buy it. She wanted realism. She wanted to read about the death she had witnessed; she wanted confirmation. How awful to read about a gentle death after watching someone suffer. How awful to be singled out for a unique experience that separates the bereaved from human sympathy. Diane's reaction put me on notice about the effect of our literary choices on the students.

On Parent/Teacher night, parents came, because some want to attach faces to names and offer their support to the teachers for the year, and some think it may be politically expedient. At the end of each presentation, they lined up, shook my hand, and told me their names. The next day, I usually didn't remember which parents came, because I was focused on the impression I was making. I did remember the mouths of parents and teachers locked in smiles throughout the building; my own face hurt at the end of the evening.

After all these years, I remember one Parent/Teacher evening when I shook hands with a parent who was killed in a car accident a week later. As usual, I didn't remember meeting her, but I knew she was there, because the next day her daughter Felicia, along with half the class, wanted to know what I had thought of their parents. "Better looking than their children," I told them.

Felicia sat in the second seat of the first row to the left of my desk; she was absent for several days. My anticipation of her return made me anxious. What would I say to her that would be meaningful? Would I say the wrong thing? What if she cried? When Felicia did return, it was far more difficult than I had expected. I said the conventional things. If she felt she had to leave the room, she could do so without my permission. She thanked me. But I was at it again. She needed to stay with us in class and feel our sympathy, and I was telling her to leave. When Blanche tells Stella, in *A Streetcar Named Desire,* that "funerals are pretty compared to deaths" and that the dying cry out, "Don't let me go!" and "Hold me!" I hoped Felicia would leave the room.

Felicia became the center of my attention, and my primary objective was to protect her. I began to screen our class reading. What would I do with *The Great Gatsby*? I loved the novel for its wildly romantic story. Of course, in my imagination, I was Jay Gatsby, loyal to the memory of Kathy, my first love. I tried to convince my students, year after year, that I deserved to be the voice of Keats—one of Fitzgerald's favorite romantic poets—when he says, "Beauty is truth, truth beauty."

To make Gatsby relevant, I told my students the story of watching my mother's 8mm film of my college graduation in 1967. I was the star, frame after frame: Angry young man with a crew cut waves off proud mother filming documentary. My mother converted the film to videotape, and for the first time in twenty years, we laughed at the stranger in the blue robe and cap. Who was I? Why didn't I smile? Was I angry about something? How did we get there? We didn't have a car. Where did we go for lunch?

Then I saw her. I forgot she had attended my graduation. Of course, she drove us there. Smoking a cigarette, she is sitting behind the wheel of her Chevy. Realizing that she is being filmed, she smiles through the car's open window. Unlike the star of this production, she is gracious. She has dark hair and dark eyes. She is very pretty. And she is very young. My college girlfriend hadn't changed in all these years, because I haven't seen her in three decades. When I think of her, I remember the girl who typed my college term papers and spoke with me for hours in her hallway. Unlike many suburban teenagers, we didn't have cars. Like the people on Keats's Grecian marble urn—and in my mother's video—Kathy has not grown old. And both Gatsby and I have been loyal to a memory, which has become our dream of youth. ("Ah, happy, happy boughs! that cannot shed your leaves, nor ever bid the Spring adieu …") The students wanted to find Kathy on the internet and reunite us. But look what happens to Gatsby, I warned, when Daisy and he resume their affair. They disagreed, of course. Kathy would "never reject the Great Leonard."

The students particularly enjoyed this revelation about my private life, because young people are romantic and curious about their teachers. And Fitzgerald's novel was for many a favorite of the year. After completing the novel, we spent many days discussing time and youth, idealism, and realism. But I was going to protect Felicia; I was not going to teach *The Great Gatsby*, since a tragic automobile accident plays an important part in it.

For the first time in fifteen years, I did not teach *The Great Gatsby*. And I dropped it from the course again when I taught Felicia's brother several years later. Although my intentions were good, for those two years, I deprived my students of Fitzgerald's poetic revelations of love and youth, and their reactions to these favorite themes. Fortunately, for me and the students, I met a wonderful student ten years later who taught me the value of community and the value of literature during the grief of losing a loved one.

Tracie was in my eleventh grade class for three months when her father died. Once again, I decided to "protect" a student. I spoke to her guidance counselor and other "health experts" in the building who confirmed my belief that the themes of death and dying would upset her. They told me that Tracie needed a "break" and a "respite." The work would remind her of her father. At the time, I took the opportunity to ask a wise doctor for his opinion.

"No. Nothing you can say, or she can read in your class, is worse than her loss. On the contrary, you would be helping her work through her suffering. It's there; you can't ignore it. She must mourn the loss of her father. You can't avoid the one subject she needs to confront to remain the well-balanced person her parents raised."

My many educational courses never included such practical, important advice. Obviously, Tracie was thinking about her father. In one of our discussions after his death, she told me that, days before his death, he had reassured her about college and the money that would be available for tuition. She was not to worry. He spoke to her about the reality of her education and the reality of his death. And I believed that he would have wanted his daughter to receive realistic support from the people around her.

That made sense to me. If I exposed her to authors who struggled with death, then my class would become a comfort for her. Before reading Robinson's "For a Dead Lady," I gave Tracie the if-you-need-to-leave speech. She never left the room. She recognized—and appreciated—the truth in Robinson's poetry.

I read a study recently that stated men are less sympathetic than women. That may account for the higher depression rate among women. Women worry not only about their family but also about the sick little boy down the hall and the widow on the third floor. While I was correcting papers in the library one day, I overheard a conversation that supports this theory.

Boy: "Hi, Tracie. How are you?"

Tracie: "Not great."

Girl: "Her father died last week.... I feel terrible, Tracie."

Boy: "Me, too."

Tracie: "Thanks."

Boy: "Are you going to do Jazz Co this weekend?"

Tracie: "My mother wants me to. She says my father would want me to."

Girl: "How's your mom doing?"

Tracie: "It's tough. I'm worried about her."

Boy: "Did you do the math homework, Tracie?"

Tracie: "Not yet. You?"

Girl: "Sorry about your father. Please say hi to your mom for me."

Boy: "Look at the third problem."

The girl was a sympathetic friend; she understood Tracie's need to speak. The boy was a friend who didn't. Or did he believe that Tracie needed a break from grieving? I couldn't tell. I'm not sure about my own motives, and I'm inside with them. Did I want to give her a break as some of my colleagues suggested I should, or did I want to protect myself from all those feelings that surrounded these students in pain? Later, mourning Marv's death confirmed the lesson I had learned from Tracie, who drew comfort from the truth in literature and from her parents.

What if Tracie had rejected the author's sentiment as false? Well then, this would have given us reason to discuss the matter together as a class. That could only be therapeutic for Tracie and educational for the class. If the poem, the short story, the novel, or the play is not truthful, then it is not literature. I once asked my creative writing students to compare the endings of two novels: *A Farewell to Arms* and *Love Story*.

They agreed that Hemingway's character reflects the shock, anger, and acceptance of Catherine's death in an honest way when he says, "… it wasn't any good. It was like saying good-by to a statue. After a while I went out and left the hospital and walked back to the hotel in the rain."

On the other hand, they felt that Erich Segal exploits his readers' feelings in the last scene between Jenny and Ollie in her hospital room.

"No, Oliver," she said, "really hold me. Next to me."

I was very, very careful—of the tubes and things—as I got onto the bed with her and put my arms around her.

"Thanks, Ollie."

Those were her last words.

In 1994, Liz Lichtman wrote a poem in honor of her father, who had recently died. In my creative writing class, Liz read it to her classmates and received the praise she deserved. The poem was emotionally honest and effective. After class, I asked Liz to submit the poem to *Forum '94*, the school's literary magazine. She wouldn't. She didn't feel it was good enough. Perhaps, she felt it didn't accurately reflect her feelings about her father. But after her reading, everyone in the room was connected. She made all of us feel her loss. The magazine editors convinced her to submit, and the entire school read her tribute to her father in the June issue:

Father's Day

I pushed the tape in and stared at the screen.
I saw my sister niece sister brother-in-law mother sister brother DAD.
I pushed the "Rewind" button quickly,
DAD rehtorb retsis rehtom wal-ni-rehtorb retsis ecein retsis.
I pressed "Play."
sister niece sister brother-in-law mother sister brother DAD.
We sat on the couches, talking and laughing,
STOP.
REWIND.
PLAY.
sister niece sister (click) "Fast Forward"
brotherinlawmothersisterbrother DAD.
PAUSE ...
DAD.
The still figure with the crooked-toothed smile stared at me.
I sat and stared back.
It was perfect.

I met Liz's sister, Loni, during my last year of teaching. I depended on Loni to begin my class. Between periods, students enjoy the five minutes of freedom that exists between bells by cramming their thoughts into loud, excited conversation. At my signal, Loni placed two fingers into her mouth and cut the room in half with a loud whistle. It always worked. The sharp silence gave me the time to say, "Okay, folks, let's start."

At one point in the year, I began my poetry unit. Most teenagers enjoy writing poetry despite their protestations that they hate poetry, don't understand poetry, and can't write poetry. I proved most of them wrong, year after year. Their real fear, I believe, is rejection. Who can blame them? Writing poetry doesn't allow the author to hide behind characters in a setting somewhere not in a classroom.

I wanted them to work with the typographical free verse structure, sometimes called visual rhythm. (Everyone has read E. E. Cummings in school.) The poet arranges words to affect the reading in some way. In the past, I used Liz's poem, since students are more easily convinced that they have the ability to write poetry after reading the work of a former student. I decided to speak to Loni about her willingness to read her sister's poem. I had come a long way, thanks to my experience with Tracie. I asked her directly if it would be difficult for her to read a poem about her father. She said she wanted to read it.

The class sat in the usual circle for the reading. Before Loni began to read, I gave the background of the poem. They understood that they were not going to listen to a poet who lived somewhere else at a different time. They were going to hear a poem from someone who graduated from their school six years earlier and who wrote honestly about her loss. They also understood that Loni suffered the same loss. Her whistle wasn't needed today.

Loni began to read. In the middle of the poem, she began to cry. She stopped reading. She tried once again to read but couldn't. She gave her copy to a friend who read the poem while the class sat quietly, and some of them began to cry. I had never before felt the emotional intensity that united this class. One by one, emerging from thoughts of their own losses, they told Loni the poem was beautiful. I asked the rhetorical question, Was the feeling in the poem honest? Yes. Yes. Yes. They knew the difference between sentiment and sentimentality.

But I was not comfortable with Loni's emotional reaction. When I approached her after class, she was surprised. She insisted that she had read her sister's poem for her father and for her sister. She took full responsibility for her tears and complete ownership of those feelings. They were there, she expressed them, and they made me uncomfortable; they were honest and deserved validation, but at the time, despite my progress in the world of bereavement, I was still unsure of myself.

On my way to the cafeteria, a student from Loni's class stopped me in the hallway. Josie said she had written a poem about herself, never to be read in class, but after witnessing Loni's open and free nature, she wanted to read her poem. The next day, Josie read her poem about her weight problem and society's disapproval of anyone who didn't meet its standard for beauty. Thanks to Liz and Loni, Josie found the courage to share her pain. Once again, the students in Loni's class came together to comfort someone.

In my retirement, I have become familiar with the internet, which makes the world much smaller than the world of my youth when neighborhoods supplied us with everything we needed. Since I grew up in the Lenox Hill section of Manhattan, I was at home with the Italian, Irish, and Czech streets of the Upper East Side. Very often, a girlfriend introduced a new boyfriend to the streets of her neighborhood, and when I fell in love with Kathy, I discovered Yorkville, the neighborhood north of Lenox Hill, where many enjoyed the many "exotic" German restaurants.

When Kathy and I ended our two-year inter-neighborhood romance, I never saw her again, because we lived ten city blocks apart, and then her family eventually moved to Far Rockaway in Queens. Her parents' decision to relocate the family prevented any meeting between us and, therefore, preserved my last memory of her to be resurrected by my mother's 8mm graduation. News of her marriage did reach me years later.

Last year, I discovered the Social Security Death Index on the internet, where I confirmed the deaths of my father, aunt, and grandmother. Since I hadn't attended their funerals, seeing their names on the screen became a public confirmation of their deaths. I decided to see if college and old neighborhood friends were alive, but without dates of birth, happily I didn't find anyone.

I decided to look for Kathy. Last year, a friend from Long Island telephoned me with the news that the obituary of Kathy's mother appeared in his local paper, listing the "Late Kathleen ... loving daughter." Using her date of birth and her married name, I found on the Social Security Death Index that she had died on October 15, 1999 in Merrick, New York, forty miles from our neighborhoods in Manhattan; she was 51 years old. I still imagine the girl in my past, smiling for my mother's camera, but now I can also imagine her children—and perhaps her grandchildren—grieving with their classmates and teachers.

22

Fistfights

In the summer of 1984, I took a summer creative writing course in Cambridge and then had the pleasure of touring London for three days. One evening, as I was eating dinner in a quaint storefront restaurant in the Bloomsbury section of the city, two large, well-dressed men in their late twenties began to fight in the street before our window.

Of course, I had seen many fights in my lower-middle-class neighborhood and in schools, but this fight was different. Middle-class men in gray suits were punching each other, and the fight lasted for some ten minutes. No one broke it up. We in the restaurant stopped eating and watched in shock this dinner-theater/reality TV performance.

When both men fell against the restaurant's window, the waitress calmly drew the curtains. I had lost my appetite long before she acted on her questionable motive. And then we listened to the men curse each other and grunt until I supposed they were worn out, because there was complete silence on the other side of the restaurant's curtain.

But I stared at the curtain, which had become the radio of my pre-television childhood, and waited for the climactic swell of music and the men to crash through the window in the fight's last gasp. After five minutes of silence—on both sides of the curtain—I decided it was safe to leave. I refused the dessert that came with the meal, paid the bill, and prepared myself for the bloody battlefield.

When I opened the door, I saw no dead people. There was no blood on the window or on the sidewalk. No torn clothing. No broken glass. No police. Just passersby. Enjoying the mild weather, people were casually walking home from work past a charming storefront restaurant. But I was not so carefree. I was nauseated. I had broken up many fights as a teacher but never experienced this nausea. School fights lasted no more than a minute or two; and boys in jeans—not mature men in business suits—fought in school hallways, not in public streets. Later I began to understand that the adrenaline counteracted the nausea. Breaking up a fight in school, I was a participant, not a spectator eating shepherd's pie.

That evening, I realized that fighting and breaking up a fight share some of the same emotions. When I had to break up a fight, I was afraid that I would be hurt; I was angry that I might be hurt; and when it was over, I was happy that I wasn't hurt. And sitting alone in my classroom afterward, I experienced a peaceful fatigue. Seeing and hearing the men fight, however, made me only fear that someone else would be hurt. I didn't fear the men; therefore, I never became angry.

I remembered a fight I had broken up between two young students, probably freshmen or sophomores. The first step is to shout, "Break it up!" Everyone shouts, "Break it up!" and, of course, the fighters never do. The second step is to shove oneself between them, using the arms to push them apart. Since these two boys were small, I pushed them apart easily.

I thought the fight was over, but then one boy charged the other boy. Irate—without thinking—I swung my open hand into his chest, knocking him into a locker. Like a drunk in a TV western, he slid to the floor. At the time, I remember thinking that I had just "punched" someone in the chest and "enjoyed" the experience—the release of the tension. For an adrenaline moment, I had become one of the boys.

I have broken up many fights over the years, but I remember four fights vividly. They were memorable for different reasons: In the first fight, I was very fond of the boys; in the second, I was not fond of them; in the third, I defended a girl from female extortionists; and in the fourth, I didn't know some of the boys, because they came from another school district. In the first three fights, I was a growling, grunting participant; in the fourth fight, I failed to get beyond "Break it up!"

I met Bruce my first year at Eastchester. He sat in the corner of the room near the window. He was a quiet boy, who never participated in class discussions. He did his homework and passed the tests, but if I called on him, he politely waved me off. He didn't seem to have any friends in the class, but I knew the students respected Bruce. If he had to answer a direct question, they listened. Since they rarely showed any interest in one another, I was impressed. After class, I made conversation with him whenever I could, and he tolerated it with quick, short answers, then hurried out of the room.

One morning I found a note from the principal, calling me to a meeting about Bruce in the guidance office at three o'clock. I was to bring my grade book. When I arrived several minutes late, the principal, a guidance counselor, and several teachers had already begun the meeting. My new-teacher input would make little difference to these veterans. As soon as I sat and opened my grade book, the principal looked at me.

"Well, Mr. Leonard is here. Tell us what you know about Bruce. How is he doing in your class?"

"He's doing 80, 82, this quarter. He has one of the highest averages in the class."

"What about his behavior?" The guidance counselor placed his face in his hands and rested his elbows on the desk; he wanted me to know that I had his full attention. In fact, everyone seemed overly interested in me, and I began to think the meeting was about my progress as a new teacher in the school.

"Good. He's quiet, polite. He minds his own business." From the incredulous expressions surrounding me, I gathered Bruce was not a star student in other classes. Nothing mystifies teachers more than someone else's success with a troubled student.

"His probation officer wants our report by the end of the week. Has Bruce threatened anyone in your class?" The counselor began to scratch his temples with his fingers. Bored, he considered his questions rhetorical.

"No, not at all. He doesn't even speak." What was going on here? Probation officer? Were we talking about the same boy?

"He's a very disturbed boy; we have to watch him closely. If he acts out in class at all, make sure you get back to us immediately." He looked at all the teachers but saved me for his final warning. "He needs careful monitoring." Apparently I was the exception in his report; Bruce had not exhibited any murderous tendencies in my class. As a new teacher, maybe I was not a reliable witness. Maybe I didn't recognize a killer when I saw one.

I was having problems with Bruce's class, not Bruce. We didn't agree about my classroom management; for example, I wanted the students to raise their hands before answering questions and never to interrupt one another. This was too much discipline for them, and they were going to let me know it through our weekly "rap" session with the head of our special program for these "Professional Career" students. PC was the latest euphemism for reluctant learners.

The five PC teachers and the ninety PC students met in the administration building across the street from the high school. Administration had decided to segregate these students to enhance their sense of unity and self-esteem; fortunately, this process lasted only two years. Since there was a rug in the room, the students sat on the floor, an affirmation of individuality, and we, the teachers, on chairs in front of them. The head of the program opened the meeting:

"How is the week going? How are your classes?" Satisfied that she understood their special needs, she smiled warmly.

"Mr. Leonard doesn't let us answer questions." They were wasting no time telling her. I looked up. Finding my accuser, I wasn't surprised. Dana was a poor student who would benefit from my downfall.

"You never shut up, Dana!" Jason wasn't going to allow her to sandbag me. Jason was my best student.

"If you raise your hand, he'll call on you." Everyone turned to find the voice. I couldn't believe that Bruce, who never raised his hand, disapproved of the "problem solving" agenda of this meeting. And that was enough for the rest of my students. For the remainder of the meeting, the discussion turned to excessively warm classrooms, too much homework, and the perennial favorite of "rap" sessions—the boring lunch menus.

Everything changed after our meeting. Because of Jason's—and Bruce's—defense, the class behavior improved; they raised their hands, and the students and I began to like one another. But Bruce remained aloof. Among his classmates, who now felt comfortable to speak freely in my presence, I learned he had a reputation for being a "tough kid," someone to be feared. Tough kids idolize tougher kids. Before the year ended, I found out why.

One day during fifth period, I heard the familiar loud, angry sounds of a fight in the hallway. Before my students had a chance to react—to run to the door and scream "Fight!"—I was already shouting "Break it ...!" I saw Bruce kicking a student who lay on the floor covering his face with both hands. I stepped in front of Bruce. Since the fight was over, I used my "settle down" voice, gently pushing Bruce toward a wall. He didn't resist. But while reassuring me that the fight was over ("Okay, okay, Mr. Leonard"), he continued to address the boy ("You're lucky, Jesse"). I found out later Bruce had broken Jesse's nose.

Since he had a history of violence, the Board of Education conducted an evening meeting to determine Bruce's future. While other witnesses gave their versions of the fight, I waited in another room. I remember thinking that my testimony was going to hurt Bruce. I knew that Jesse was a good kid, one of my favorite students, but I also knew that he was a funny kid, and I never saw any indication that Bruce had a sense of humor. Perhaps, Bruce hadn't meant to break his nose—and Bruce hadn't hurt me. In fact, he had tried to calm me down. "It's okay, Mr. Leonard ... the fight's over." I felt bad for Jesse, but I didn't want to betray Bruce.

Then, it was my turn; a Board Member opened the door and called me into the formal boardroom. The mood was somber. Everyone turned to watch my entrance, and the principal asked me to take the empty seat across from Bruce. I assumed the man at his right was Bruce's lawyer. I wondered if Bruce's fate at our school depended entirely on my testimony, which I realized was being videotaped when the room suddenly became very bright.

Was Bruce a problem in my class? No ... Was Bruce passing my class? Yes ... Did I see the fight begin between Bruce and Jesse? No ... What did I see? Bruce was kicking Jesse ... Did I see anybody else hit Jesse? No ... Did I stop Bruce from kicking Jesse? No. When Bruce saw me, he stopped ... While I was restraining Bruce, did he resist me? No.

The President of the Board turned to Bruce and asked what he thought about my testimony. Looking down at the table, Bruce answered, "Mr.

Leonard's a good guy." The room was quiet. I don't think anyone expected this answer. I didn't and I felt terrible. This was a boy who had defended me at that "rap session," but I had to testify against him. And he understood. He went out of his way to confirm my reliability—and admitted his guilt. The President of the Board thanked me, and the lights dimmed. Bruce never came back to school.

Unbelievably, two weeks later, I broke up a fight involving four bullies in Bruce's class. In all my years of teaching, they ranked at the very top of my hope-you-fail-in-June list. It was a dangerous fight to break up because of the fists, elbows, and heavy black motorcycle boots jutting out from the cursing jumble of boys on the cafeteria floor. I was about to leave the cafeteria when I heard them. I've never seen a fight begin. The cursing was thick and low. I placed my lunch on a nearby table and removed my blue blazer and glasses—a ritual Lou Serico found amusing, but sensible, because teacher salaries were not generous.

I was in no great hurry to break up this fight. Their boots looked like weapons. And I didn't like any of these boys. I didn't care if they hurt one another. But I had to intervene; I was a teacher, and I was there. I circled them and picked the one whose fists and boots did the least flailing. I grabbed Rory from behind, pinning his arms to his sides—and with the magic of adrenaline—I plucked him up and away from the cursing mess beneath us and pushed him toward the wall. Over the years, I learned the benefit of subduing a student by pressing him, face first, against a dead end; but when I looked over Rory's shoulder, I saw students against the nearest wall. I felt my grip loosening, changed direction, and pushed him through the door leading to the small room off the cafeteria. This was our room, the teachers' room, where fifty teachers ate their lunches in a space meant for thirty. I ran Rory between two rows of tables and made a hard right to avoid the long table at the end, which ran perpendicular to the two rows.

Rory quickly gave up the struggle. He didn't know who had paralyzed him with strength of steel, and then he found himself facing fifty shocked teachers. Confusion replaced his fury, and his shoulders sagged. He was the figurehead of a frigate cutting through waves of angry and fearful faces. And this was also confusing for the teachers. Since I had pressed myself against his back, they saw a student with four arms and four legs, attacking them without provocation.

"What the hell!" Several teachers reacted appropriately.

"What does he want?" One teacher sought a reasonable explanation for this invasion.

"Get out!" One teacher was a problem solver.

"No students are allowed here!" One teacher remembered the rules.

I heard the complaints, but I was still breaking up a fight. I wasn't aware that Rory had given up the struggle, but then the teachers saw my battle face. Some of the men stood to help me, and some incredulous voice wanted to know, "Why is Mr. Leonard bringing that boy in here?" Like the waitress in London who closed the curtain, my last critic believed that fights ruin the appetite.

Later in the day, Rory complained that his forehead had opened the door, but he dropped his complaint to preserve his reputation. As usual, the students always admire a teacher whose new role surprises them; my performance belied my persona. For the rest of the day, I was a hero, a very tired hero. Despite the boys' suspensions, I never met the parents. They probably didn't like them either.

Actually, I met only one parent whose children had a fight in school, and she wanted to beat me up. She was the mother of twin girls who attacked another girl. I was sitting in the teachers' room in Gorton when I heard the screaming; I knew girls were fighting, because girls use their mouths as weapons. When girls are not biting, they scream their hearts out at each other—and at bystanders who try to separate them. When boys fight, the female bystanders sound the alarm with a soundtrack of screams and tears. I threw my book onto the desk and ran into the corridor, where I saw three very angry girls.

Breaking up a boy fight is physically more dangerous, but the Velcro effect of a girl fight is absent. Girls grab and pull, and always remain connected. They leave very little room for the teacher to squeeze between them to push them away from each other—and since all their movable parts are dug into each other—they can't be easily pried apart. If the teacher wants to yank one girl up out of the fight, he yanks up two girls. Boys are a battle; girls are a war.

One teacher alone can't separate three girls, but I was able to distract them long enough for help to come. This was the battle before the war. The twins were taking turns pushing and punching Denise, who was screaming. "Leave me alone! Buy your own! Buy your own cigarettes!" Like stalking lions on a PBS special, the twins were flanking her, forcing her toward the wall behind her.

I stepped in front of Denise. I pushed one of the snarling girls away from us, and they let me have it. Rarely have students directed such language at me, and when they have, they were cursing the world around them in the heat of a fight. This was different. These two hadn't lost control of their tempers, because someone had pulled their hair. They were angry with me, because I was interfering with their quarry, which I found out later involved extortion; they preyed on girls in the bathrooms. I remember thinking that these two squat, snarling girls not only looked alike but also sounded alike. When their cursed me, they echoed each other.

"Mind your own business, ya bastard!"

"Mind your own business, ya bastard!"

When I ordered them to go to the principal's office, they became indignant and frightening with their two-heads-are-better-than-one strategy. These girls were not the Doublemint twins; they were not doubling my pleasure.

"Why? Tha' bitch started it!"

"Why? Tha' bitch started it!"

Finally, some teachers came to our rescue. Growling, the girls were escorted to the principal's office. I returned to the teachers' room. Recuperating in our one recliner, trying to understand their ferocity, I could clearly hear them.

"We didn't do nothin'!"

"We didn't do nothin'!"

At the end of the day, I received a note from the principal to attend a meeting with him and their mother in fifteen minutes. It's never pleasant meeting parents of failing or disruptive students. Despite the contemporary emphasis on teacher/parent cooperation, the emphasis may become adversarial with parents' requesting better grades or more lenient punishment. Once, a father threatened me with a lawsuit for not allowing his daughter to do a book report on a movie: "But she also read the book."

Opening the door to the principal's office, I saw the unhappy principal behind his desk and triplets in the chairs to the right of his desk. The twins and their mother looked exactly alike. They shared the perpetual snarling face and low-to-the-ground combative stance. I knew the one on the far left was the mother, because she was not wearing jeans. The principal asked me to sit.

While I turned to locate a chair, I heard one of the twins. "This tha bastard ..." I sat and looked up. The one not wearing jeans was speaking. "... who pushed you?" The *mother* was speaking. Unless one of the twins was a ventriloquist, mother and daughters also shared the same voice. I looked toward the principal, and he looked toward them. Together, mother and twins assailed my appearance—and sexuality.

I knew to keep quiet; these people wanted an argument. And since my principal had no interest in a fistfight, he said nothing. Realizing that mother and daughters were not interested in my professional opinion—and fearing they wanted to attack me—I stood to leave. Before I reached the door, I heard, "Where ya going, faggot?" As I was passing the principal's secretary, I heard again,

"Where ya going, faggot?" Twin One or mother.

"Where ya going, faggot?" Twin Two or mother.

The principal never suspended them. They received a three-day detention. That was the punishment for attacking a student and threatening a teacher. Fortunately, for me—and Gorton High School—they also made the mistake of calling the president of the Yonkers Federation of Teachers a "faggot." He recognized their special needs and engineered their transfer to an appropriate learning environment. They never came back.

I did see them once more before I left Yonkers for Eastchester. On a busy street in Yonkers, I had stopped for a school bus. While I patiently watched children tell parents about their day and hand over book bags, I saw the twins and their mother. Walking in a row, forcing people to step into the street, they were six cars in front of me. In a few seconds, they would see me.

Children were still on the school bus. There were cars behind me, and I couldn't turn to the left or to the right. They were now three cars in front of me; in one second, they would see me. Even near-sighted teenagers in the suburbs can identify every passenger in a moving car at night. I knew they would drag me out of my car—or shake me out—so I dropped onto the passenger's seat. Only when I heard the car horns behind me, did I sit up, check out my rear view mirror, and follow the school bus down the street.

The last memorable fight took place at a carnival on our soccer field in Eastchester. There had been rumors that boys from another town planned to crash the festival; it seemed that one of our boys had broken the golden rule for all neighborhoods of my childhood: Thou shalt not date outside thy neighborhood. The teachers were placed on high alert for angry-looking boys we didn't recognize. I ignored the warning. Students often predicted war with another town. "Mount Vernon is coming!" or "Yonkers jumped our guys at Nathan's last night!" But whooping students in their school colors never invaded our citadel.

I was a married man in 1978 and enjoyed showing off for my new wife at school functions. A carnival at school was the ideal place for it. And this was a soccer field, not a dark auditorium. There were no rules to enforce, no back talking. Everyone was in a good mood. Girls calling across the field, "Hi, Mr. Leonard!" and boys shaking my hand would prove to my wife that I was the most popular man in Westchester County—and that she was the luckiest woman.

While I was being humble to a complimentary parent, several boys rolled into us. Immediately, a circle of students and townspeople gathered around them. This was my first, and only, fight outside the school building. But we were on school grounds, and we teachers had to break it up.

Walking around the boys, I looked them over and chose one. I couldn't tell if he was one of ours. I reached down to grab him. Once I had him, I slipped and fell to my knees. Holding on to him, I tried to regain my balance to haul him up when I felt clamps dig into my sides. Arms and legs seeking ground, I was slowly lifted off the pile into the air. I had to let go of the struggling boy beneath me.

Bewildered, now standing, I turned to the voice behind me. "Are you all right?" Mr. Pearl, one of the school Board Members, stood behind me. "Are you hurt?" When I looked down, the boys were gone; other teachers had broken up the fight.

Mr. Pearl thought he had saved me. On the way home, I explained to my wife he was well meaning, but mistaken. I had broken up many fights. Really. I knew what I was doing. "Teachers break up fights all the time; it's part of the job. Mr. Pearl overreacted; I know what I am doing. Really."

"I know you do, Richard, but for a while there up in the air, you looked like an confused crab."

Sometimes a confused crab becomes a raging bull when even the best plans fail to anticipate human behavior. While I was making last minute adjustments to the day's lesson plan, two boys in the eleventh grade stomped into the room, dropped heavily into chairs, and made angry noises. At first, I thought, post-lunch depression. I looked up to see them, three rows apart, mumbling at the same time. Maybe a difficult math test, I thought. The second bell for class to begin had not rung yet, so I looked down at my plan again.

Soon, the mumbling grew louder, and I looked up again. The boys were making faces at each other. The bell to begin class rang. I stood, placed my lesson plan on the filing cabinet/lectern, and heard one of the boys say, "You idiot!"

"You're the idiot, Todd!"

"You're a slob, Hank!"

"Come over here and say that, fool!"

I was about to play peacemaker ("Calm down, guys.") when Hank stood and pushed his desk into another desk. "Let's go!" Todd flipped his desk onto its side, and they moved toward each other. Rolling my seat back against the blackboard, I stood and ran to them, pushing them apart and shouting, "All right, cut it out! Now!" With clenched fists, both boys looked up at me.

"He's serious! Look at him!" Both Todd and Hank were laughing. The other students in the class were laughing. I was the only one not laughing. They had triggered the fight reaction in me and discovered a "raging bull" beneath a teacher's façade. Only after several minutes of listening to their laughter and mimicry ("All right, cut it out! Now!"), was I able to smile and lie.

"I knew you guys were kidding."

"You did not, Len! We nailed you! You should have seen your face!"

They had nailed me.

23

Yearbooks and Literary Magazines

Advising the staffs of yearbooks and literary magazines, I worked with the most interesting—and dedicated—students in the building. Unlike the members of school clubs who meet periodically to decide the logistics of a fundraiser or a school trip, my editors and their staffs met several days a week over seven, eight months. Unlike the athletes and the performance artists, who do spend many hours practicing and rehearsing each week, the editors did not receive cheers or applause from fans at a game or theatrical event.

The literary magazine and the yearbook publish poems, stories, photographs, and artwork of the other students in the school, who receive more attention than the editors themselves. For much of the time, the only audience is the custodian, who cleans the empty building after three o'clock. Once the books and magazines arrive, the editors receive compliments from their advisor, friends, parents, a few teachers and students, and at times, administrators. The yearbook understandably receives more attention, especially from the seniors, because their faces are the main attraction of the publication.

During thirty-two years, I advised seven yearbook staffs and forty magazine staffs. Of the two, the yearbook was more enjoyable, because the photographs were the main objective; copy was secondary. As a result, staff meetings were noisy with the excitement of teenagers at the end of a school day. They joked, gossiped, and flirted with one another; they worked and played, and I enjoyed them.

For the magazine staff, the text was the only objective, and silence was necessary for their concentration. After a full day of classes, they came to my room, enjoyed soda and snacks first, and then got down to work. Sitting in a circle, they would proof and pass copy to the next editor. I sat behind my desk with my copy, listening to their comments about diction, syntax, characterization, and the logic of a passage. Most of the time, they worked quietly. I enjoyed and respected the staffs of both publications, but I admired my literary magazine staffs. For them, the sole motivation was artistic.

My advising students about literary magazines and yearbooks was ironic, since my only student participation in extracurricular activities had been limited to a month on the high school swim team (chlorine allergy), one college intramural softball game (quick elimination), and posing twice for senior portraits. Staying after school while in college was impossible because of my job at the liquor store.

My first professional extracurricular experience took place my last year at Gorton High School. For the yearbook staff and me, the experience became a way to deal with the racial tension in the building. The violence was becoming so bad that colleagues were transferring to other schools in Yonkers. During my last year there, the yearbook became my salvation, and that of editors, both black and white. When not working on the yearbook, they ate their lunches, did homework, and socialized in my room.

For the art staff, the walls of my room became their canvas. When Dorothy, Janice, and Jennifer were not in their other classes, they sat atop ladders at their "walls" in my room painting murals of animals and small children. The symbolism was obvious. While I taught, they painted. After two days, my students forgot they were there, but I didn't. I watched monkeys and zebras appear in the landscape above the windows and the blackboards. When they painted above the blackboard behind my desk, I taught from the back of the room.

Sometimes, after long stretches of balancing on the ladders, the girls sat above us and listened, reacting to a controversial comment. I was able to judge the success of my class by the motionless brushes. If they turned and sat on the ladder to listen, I knew it was a good class. The painting lasted for five months, and two girls took photographs of their murals to use in their college-admission portfolios.

And I exploited them—with their permission. When Dr. Driscoll and Dick Krell came to Yonkers from Eastchester for that most important observation of my career, I asked the three girls to paint while I taught my two lessons; they were the only people in the school that knew of the observation. I wanted to create the impression that I was the most versatile of teachers, the main event of a four-ring circus.

They were going to observe my second and third period classes; therefore, at the end of my first period, I waited at my door. I saw the principal escorting them toward me and—since I hadn't informed him of the visit—he looked more nervous than I did. I wasn't sure they would come to Yonkers after my pro union/strike argument with Dr. Driscoll, but he was polite and professional. He shook my hand and said, "Let the show begin."

The students were discussing a chapter of Black Panther Eldridge Cleaver's book, *Soul on Ice*, which might not have been acceptable in Dr. Driscoll's white school district. But we had been discussing the book for a week, and I had to continue. I didn't mind using the girls to make me look good, but the lesson had to be honest. Most of my students were unaware of their presence. Those who were didn't care. Today, I remember nothing about the lesson. I only remember thinking that Dr. Driscoll and Dick watched the girls on their ladders as much as they watched me.

At the end of the second observation—a conventional discussion of Edwin Arlington Robinson's poetry—the juniors left the room at the bell, and the men stood and spoke together. Did the safe Robinson poems atone for Cleaver's book? I walked to the back of the room, where they were waiting for me.

"Excellent class!"

"Thank you, Dr. Driscoll." I didn't ask which one.

"You've got the job." He shook my hand.

"Great. Thank you. That's great."

"Who are the girls?"

"They're the yearbook artists. I'm their advisor."

"Why are they painting on your walls?"

"They're creating a world for themselves." He didn't ask for an explanation. If he had, I would have told him that he had just created a new world for me. But he didn't. Thirty years later at a graduation party for a mutual friend's daughter, I had the opportunity to explain and thank him again.

Dr. Driscoll must have said something about the wall painting to my new principal at Eastchester, because he offered me the newspaper, an offer new teachers fear to refuse. "Yes, sure, I'd love to advise the newspaper staff." ("And your shoes could use some polishing, too, your highness, my highness.") Usually new teachers receive the toughest teaching assignments.

My first extracurricular assignment at Eastchester High School nearly changed my life. My never having advised a newspaper staff was not a problem; my not knowing the editors was. At our first meeting, the editor in chief and his staff introduced themselves. I admitted my ignorance of journalism, but insisted I would quickly learn the fundamentals. Intelligent and enthusiastic seniors, they reassured me about sharing their experience with me. After our meeting, I felt more confident about my role as a first time newspaper advisor *without tenure*. I found the school's textbook on journalism and studied it diligently.

My obsessive-compulsive nature—coupled with the rebellion of the sixties—had demanded scrutiny of literary magazines and yearbooks at Gorton. In a photograph, I discovered a boy, almost hidden by his friends, giving the finger to the yearbook photographer. We needed to use the photograph, so we colored in his finger to match the background. Now, he was giving us only the knuckles. More than ever, I searched for the hidden obscenity.

But the year went well. My classes were good, and the newspaper published several editions. Mrs. Elvove was correct when she predicted I'd love the students in Eastchester. In June, the happiest month for all teachers, I received my last, and positive, observation write-up from Dick Krell, a kind man, who mentored his young teachers to professional maturity. I missed my old friends in Yonkers, but I felt comfortable in my new school.

Walking down the hall toward my classroom, and whistling out of tune, I heard my editor's voice and looked to the left. He and the newspaper staff were in an empty classroom, collating our last edition. They had pushed ten desks for the ten pages of the newspaper into two rows and walked around the desks, picking up the pages to be stapled by the editor in chief at a table off to the side.

I walked into the room and offered them "a hand—two hands, in fact"—but no, they had all under control. I told them that I was perfect for the job; I had been "walking in circles all my life." They nervously laughed as people do when they want to be polite. I was going to help these great kids on this glorious June day with my positive observation write-up in my pocket. I said no more.

I found page one and began my walk around the desks, picking up pages 2, 3, 4, 5, 6, 7, 8, 9, 10…. At the last desk, I looked down at page 11. I picked it up. Everyone in the room stopped to look at me. I had never seen this excellent drawing of our high school in flames. In bold letters beneath the drawing was the caption, **End Oppression Now!** The week before, I had proofed ten pages of the newspaper; I had never seen page 11.

"Harold, what's this? What's this?"

"What?"

"Right, what?"

"It's an editorial comment on our society."

"Why didn't I see it?"

"We didn't have time."

I picked up the entire stack of page 11—and the stack of stapled papers—and brought them to the principal's office for his advice (I knew very little about high school freedom of the press)—and his forgiveness. When the principal saw the page, he requested the rest of the newspaper. No one ever saw the June edition of *The Eaglet*. Since I had given up my Yonkers's tenure to teach in Eastchester, I had no legal right to a hearing to explain what had happened. But the principal did not fire me. He understood the rebellious nature of the times and the cleverness of the deceitful editor.

Today's young teacher/advisor may have to defend himself against an editor's parent who complains to an administrator that the child's self-esteem has suffered irreparable damage. But this was 1973, and parents understood that their children were not fragile, perfect human beings; and if they didn't understand, they still didn't try to convince an administrator.

I was a lucky man. If I had not been walking down the hall at that time ... if I had not heard Harold's voice and turned to my left ... if the classroom door had been closed ... if they had completed collating the newspaper ... if I had not ignored their polite laughter at my corny jokes, my teaching career would have ended that June. If the community had seen the newspaper, even a strong principal would not have been able to defend me, and thirty years later, despite the influence of Henry David Thoreau's and Mary Karr's memoirs, I would not be writing this book.

The following year, I did not advise the newspaper staff. I wanted nothing to do with extracurricular activities—at least, not until I had tenure again. But several months into the school year, Debbie, one of my eleventh grade students—and a gifted poet—asked me to advise a literary magazine. I made it clear that I—not she—was ultimately responsible for anything inappropriate that I missed in my proofing. After my speech about the cowardice of rebellion without responsibility, Debbie laughed and swore that she wrote poetry, not "vehicles for violence or obscenity."

David, a precocious tenth grader and excellent poet, Georgine, a talented eleventh grade artist, Debbie, and I resurrected the school's literary magazine, *Forum*, unpublished for several years; it became my extracurricular activity until my retirement in 2000. During those years I never worried about rogue editors; my staff did. Teenagers crave structure. They want their classes and their clubs to be meaningful. Once the advisor defines the objectives and the rules for an activity they respect, the editors and the staff resemble cult members in their loyalty.

One year, I needed to convince Catherine and Gwen, two intelligent—and witty—yearbook editors, that a caption beneath a photograph of a teacher holding papers in his outstretched hand was not appropriate: "I've graded your testes." The girls rejected my judgment. "But that's what he says when he hands back our quizzes." When I asked them if all their family conversations were appropriate for public consumption, they quickly agreed, "We need a new caption."

In 1985, the yearbook became an important focus again. I was very fond of the yearbook senior editors who needed an advisor. I had been their eleventh grade teacher the year before, and they quickly convinced me with affectionate appeals. "Come on, Len! Please! Please! We need you! Come on, Mr. Leonard! We love you, Len! Come on! Come on, Len!" I was also an easy mark for cake sales, Valentine candy and flower sales, and sponsorships for charity walkathons. I hadn't advised a yearbook in four years, but I remembered the speech about *their* responsibility to *Le Souvenir, their* yearbook, the most important book for seniors in June.

They were a great staff, conscientious and fun-loving; I looked forward to being with them at the end of the day. We worked four days a week. When we had a deadline, we worked five or six days. We had a layout staff, a copy staff, a business staff, and an art staff, each group essential to the success of the book. If someone couldn't make all the meetings, he or she was asked not to come back. Since athletes followed the same rule, there were none on the staff.

Brian, one of the best artists in the school, had missed many meetings, and the editor in chief wanted me to speak with him. When I explained to Brian that we needed him at those meetings, he listened quietly. He agreed he wasn't being fair to the others. He would come to all of them, and he did for a while. After the second week, he stopped coming. That was enough for the editors to "fire" him.

During our next meeting in the hall outside my classroom, he again listened quietly and nodded his agreement that the editors needed their staffs to meet the deadlines. I told him how sorry I was to lose such a fine artist. He thanked me for the compliment and asked if he could still submit the nearly completed front endsheet. "Of course, Brian. And make sure you sign it. I'm sure it's great, and you deserve the credit." He promised to bring it in by the end of the week. "Thanks, Brian." He was an artist who couldn't give the time, and we wanted to publish a yearbook. Nobody was wrong here.

True to his word, he brought in a beautiful drawing of the school—in the morning—to avoid the staff members. I thanked him. He smiled and we shook hands. The staff loved the drawing. When they saw him in the hall, they told him so. In June, when Brian opened the yearbook to the first page and saw his drawing, he must have enjoyed his revenge. Beneath the placement of his name, which I had insisted he sign, Brian camouflaged a message to us in dots, some darker than others: "Fuck You."

Unless the reader knew where to look, he wouldn't see it. What was the point (or dots) of Brian's sendoff to the yearbook staff if no one saw it? He had, therefore, confided his secret to only one person. And one person was enough to direct the student body to his displeasure with us. But he had seriously underestimated the staff's reaction; they wanted revenge.

They went to the principal and demanded that he not graduate with them. They wanted to block his college acceptance by revealing his disloyalty to his high school. They wanted revenge for the desecration of a year's work. I understood how the editors felt.

The principal asked Brian and his parents to meet with him and me in his office. His parents were shocked. After Brian's tearful apology, I returned to my room, where the staff was waiting for the verdict. I didn't mention the tears. I said that his parents, whom they knew, felt awful. I conveyed their apologies to the staff, which they graciously accepted. Then they happily returned to the scrutiny of *their* yearbook.

They decided to have a yearbook party that night for the seniors only, a tradition that's been difficult to maintain because of the immediate gratification students demand today. Once the students spot the yearbook truck, they surround the staff with questions of when and where. And once they find out that the yearbooks will be in the cafeteria, they sit there and wait; some will even cut class to find their pictures.

But in 1985, we still had the luxury of postponing the day of distribution. With great concentration—and a history of planning school parties—they decorated the cafeteria with streamers and balloons. They handed out pens, the color of the yearbook, to each senior for the ritual of signing his book. Once the underclassmen receive their books, they sit in the cafeteria, in halls, and classrooms writing their fondest memories and best wishes for people they know—and hardly know. Teachers of difficult classes love the silence.

Despite several complaints from students who didn't like their pictures, our censorship of their captions—or the limitation of one candid picture per senior—the staff enjoyed the overall positive reception of the book. Smiling students slowly flipped through the book again and again, enthusiastically sharing their favorite pictures and captions with friends and teachers.

The party was a success. The seniors received their books and had a great time. It was late, but we had one job left; we had to take the decorations down. When the editors realized that they hadn't blown up all the balloons and that we still had helium in the tank, they decided to share their joy with the principal. He had demonstrated his sense of humor during the year by shooting a water gun at surprised students and teachers in the hall. The plan was simple. With the aid of a custodian, and my approval, they planned to stuff his small office with balloons. After an hour of teamwork between the helium tank and his office, they pulled his door shut.

Unhappily we never saw the confusion on his face the next morning when he pushed the door open and walked into fifty or more red, green, and blue balloons bouncing lightly against him. According to the principal, he quickly pulled the door shut, popping a few balloons, and escorted worried-looking parents into the conference room across the hall. "Someone stuffed my space," he apologized.

I never met a yearbook staff that wasn't devoted—and clever. To publish a good yearbook, they had to be. In 1980, the editors miscalculated the number of spreads they needed for the school's teams; we had two blank pages and no teams left. What to do? It was too late to knock the spread out. But they solved the problem quickly by making up four teams: Varsity Equestrian, Varsity Fencing, Varsity Swimming, and Varsity Frisbee.

The editors went to the local stable and took photographs of strangers on horses. That evening, they went to the local pool and had a parent photograph them in a backstroke-racing position in the water. The following morning, they posed with intramural fencing equipment in our gym. And finally they joined other students on our campus to capture the spring rite of frisbee.

Identifying members of a team or a club is always serious business. Since many students in the lower grades are unknown to them, they relied on contemporaries and faculty advisors. Identifying athletes of imaginary teams was playtime for this imaginative staff, and I enjoyed the fun.

Some of the coaches didn't find the inclusion of exotic fictitious teams humorous. Many in the school were initially surprised by the existence of these teams, and the community was impressed by our local talent—until they read the names: Jean-Paul Chantillier, Alfonse Achtung, Salsa de Tallerines, Boris Vensinov, and Oowang Golamma for (what else?) fencing; H. Thornton on Heyfield's Great Guy, Q. Applebee on Northern Royality, K. Wheeler on Tuckerhill's Silver Shadow, and C. Stevenson on Starheart's Morning Mist for the equestrians. If these unfamiliar names didn't reveal the comic intent of the spread, the names of our student swimmers certainly did—T. Smith, T. Doe, T. Jones, T. Clark, and T. Bone.

In 1988, the staff needed a face for a faculty position and used my mother's work ID photo. Seeing the faculty section, the superintendent immediately called the principal about this very attractive Shannon O. Shenanigan, who taught Botanical Arts—and whom he didn't remember hiring.

I advised my last yearbook in 1988. I had a wonderful group of teenagers who wanted to do what all previous staffs wanted to do: Publish the best yearbook in the history of Eastchester High School. To accomplish this, they chose the theme of time, which is ambitious for teenagers with a short past and an all-consuming present.

They found a 1938 yearbook in the library and decided to celebrate the fiftieth anniversary of that book. The teenagers of 1938 were proof that time wrought many changes. The jackets and dresses, baseball uniforms, and hairstyles of these mature-looking young people, who sat in the recognizable classes and cafeteria, confirmed their place in a world unlike the present. Juxtaposing the senior portraits of 1938 and 1988 in the beginning of their yearbook, the editors felt like historians.

One of the editors recognized a graduate from the class of 1938; she worked in the cafeteria at the cash register. We saw her every day when she charged us for our lunch, but Vicki graduated from our school in 1938; we had her senior portrait to prove it. Today, she was not only an employee in our school but also the grandmother of seven Eastchester students.

Suddenly, those 1938 faces with fixed smiles became the editors' grandparents and neighbors. A century was no longer an abstraction. (When I turned fifty, I announced to my classes that I was a half-century old. The following year, I was a half-century plus one year old.)

Of course, they understood that their grandparents had been their age at one time. Through photographs in torn albums, they had traveled from the present to the golden past of teenagers lying on beach blankets or sitting on car fenders "built to last"; but for the first time, they traveled from the past to the present by viewing a portrait of a graduating senior of 1938 whom they knew as Vicki. A teenage girl became a grandmother "overnight." For the rest of the year, time became more than a theme for a yearbook. It became a revelation they wanted to share with the school.

Even though the yearbook demanded time and diligence, it seemed more play than work. The magazine *Forum* seemed more work than play. I had great respect for the teenage editors, because *Forum* was much less a social activity. They enjoyed one another's company, but very limited socializing began and ended our meetings; everything between was silence. They loved the unglamorous and solitary work of editing poems and stories, and I often referred to the magazine staff as the track team of the school's clubs. Very few people support their teams at track meets.

Publishing the magazine was far more difficult in the seventies than it is today. We used typewriters, which made mistakes more difficult to correct. Sometimes a staff member needed to retype an entire page to correct a simple error. As a result, our book never surpassed thirty-two pages.

How often could someone type a page? Today's *Forum* never falls below a hundred pages.

In the pioneer days, we spoke to the printing teacher, who taught us the mechanics of making negatives of the pages, printing them on a drum, sliding the pages through the folding machine, and finally stapling them. For several years, the editors ran the operation from beginning to end and loved the process, which gave them complete ownership of the magazine. Covered in ink, they made mistakes, laughed, and learned the beauty of complete artistic control. Their only dependence was the source of the paper. Sometimes the student government donated the paper; sometimes, someone on the staff had a friend or family member in business who supplied it.

One year, we had to work during the awards ceremony, taking place in the cafeteria directly above the print shop in the basement. Since *Forum* always attracted superior students, they had to attend the ceremony; one editor after another ran up the stairs to the cafeteria to receive his applause and awards with ink-covered hands, turned, waved to his parents, and ran back to the print shop.

Reading the program for the evening and watching the ceremony, the junior staff members, stationed at the doors and the stairs, screamed to each other the names of the next editors to be honored. "Christopher!" ... "Christopher!" ... "Christopher!" ... Christopher handed the sheets of paper to Jarod and ran upstairs. "Megan!" ... "Megan!" ... "Megan!" ... Megan handed the work off to Lois and ran up to the cafeteria, passing Christopher, who had handed his award to his parents in the cafeteria, on his way back to the print shop. With the return of each editor, we screamed, "Roll the presses!"

I used a need-to-be-in-the-print-shop excuse that year to avoid attending the award ceremony. The year before, in front of hundreds of people, I sat with colleagues behind the lectern. I watched teacher after teacher present the certificate of award and kiss the recipient on the cheek. By nature I'm not a kisser—one of my favorite Seinfeld episode reveals Jerry's distaste for kissing people—but I didn't want to cheat the female recipients of the congratulatory experience.

That night I presented the English awards to all the students in the school. A petite girl approached the lectern to receive the award for her excellent work in the ninth grade. I extended the certificate and leaned forward to kiss her; she reached for the certificate but leaned away from me. When she did grab it, I decided I was not going to let go before kissing her cheek. I leaned farther forward again. Being a tall man, I towered over her; she still hung on to the certificate.

Since I had never returned to an upright position, I simply moved my face closer to hers; she moved her head down away from me. She became a small c under my large C. Once again, in defiance of perception or logic, I bent farther forward to reach her cheek; and in defiance of gravity, she bent farther backward. When the back of her head was near the floor, I gave up. I released the certificate, she backed quickly away from me, and a very quiet audience explosively—and gratefully—applauded her award and her escape. I never attended another ceremony.

A year later on the award-ceremony night, the superintendent walked into the print shop. Everyone said hello and he smiled. He picked up a page from one of the stacks and read aloud part of a poem. Placing it back on the stack, the superintendent smiled again. "We missed you upstairs, Mr. Leonard." Was he referring to last year's performance? Did he want an encore?

"Sorry to miss it." Was it still going on? Did he come to get me? "We need to make this deadline. I'm sure the kids and the parents understand."

"It's over, but come up for coffee. The parents would love to see you."

"Really sorry to have missed it, but if we're going to get this magazine out before June, we can't stop working." My editors and I knew this was an exaggeration; we were nearly finished. The superintendent saw a dedicated advisor.

"We don't have *Forum* in the budget, do we?"

"No. That's the reason we're here. We can't afford to send it out."

"Next year, you will. Next year, it's going out. You people do great work; you deserve the district's support." The following year, the magazine went to a professional printer, and I had to find another excuse to miss the awards ceremony.

The magazine was never the same. Financial support—and technological support from our creative and patient computer teacher Ray Pace—permitted and encouraged us to publish bigger books; the 1994 edition of *Forum* contained 175 pages. The magazine comprised more student writers—and more work—from each writer. Computer proofing motivated us to proof everything four times, and the editing became more than correcting grammar and spelling mistakes. If a work needed major stylistic revision before the computer age, we didn't accept it for publication. After, editors rewrote entire sections—with the authors' permission.

We entered our "professional looking" magazine to contests, such as the Columbia Scholastic Press and the National Council of Teachers of English (NCTE) magazine contests. *Forum* did very well, and I shamelessly used the high ratings to publicize our work and justify the expense of the magazine. My creative writing course itself benefited from the magazine's publicity.

But I missed the early days of publishing the smaller *Forums*. There was more control when the magazine never left the building, and the contests became too important. When pre-contests editors returned from college to visit, they criticized my including artwork to meet the ranking criteria of Columbia and the NCTE. They believed literature did not need artwork. But I wanted excellent ratings, and my good friend Sue Mariano, an inspirational and nurturing art teacher, came up with the perfect solution: From this point on, artwork and text would never share a spread and, therefore, never lead the reader to look for a correlation; and every drawing, poem, and short story would retain its raison d'etre. For ten years as our art advisor (without ever receiving a stipend), Sue made *Forum's* artwork an annual rite for her fine young artists.

I continued to advise the little magazine, *Twixtujons*, which showcased the work of my creative writing class. It was named for my room, 101, between the boys' and girls' restrooms. To make sure people got the joke, we called ourselves The Stereoflush Press and adopted two bathroom doors next to each other as our logo.

(When I taught Orwell's *1984*, my students considered changing the name of the room from Twixtujons to Miniluv. In the novel, Mini-luv—the Ministry of Love—tortured and indoctrinated people in room 101. Since there were no windows in Miniluv—and my window shades were always down—I thought the change of name was a good suggestion, but teenagers delight in their traditions and continued to call the room Twixtujons.)

In 1994, I stopped publishing *Twixtujons* against the wishes of my industrious *Forum* editor in chief, Christina, who showed me no mercy in marathon proofing sessions; she produced the largest *Forum* in the history of the school. *Forum's* new professional look attracted many student submissions, which required too many hours of work involving selection and editing.

I was very fond of my editors. I'm fortunate that some have become good friends. After graduation few students visit former teachers. When I was with them, I never considered our relationship finite in most cases. I didn't miss not having children. Being around the students—especially the editors—satisfied me.

One day last year, I encountered Diane, one of my favorite editors. She was a very kind person who befriended students in class when no one else would. In the course of two years, I saw the positive effect Diane had on them. Quiet students participated in class discussions, and many of them developed crushes on her.

In Diane's yearbook, I signed my message with the word "love," commonly used by female teachers without suspicion. When Diane read it, she looked confused, and when I saw her at graduation and offered congratulations, she thanked me. But she seemed somewhat distant. I worried the entire summer that she had misinterpreted my affection for her. I never signed a yearbook in the same way again.

That was not the case in Gorton High School in 1970. Lucy, one of my graduating seniors, had no reservations about asking me for an explanation of my inscription in her yearbook. "Why did you write this?" She looked troubled. I took her book and read what I had written the day before: "Don't fall out of any beds."

"What is it?"

"What do you mean, 'Don't fall out of any beds'?" She squinted for an explanation.

"You broke your collar bone when you fell out of bed last semester."

"Oh, yeah." She laughed at my joke, innocently made at her expense, took her book back, and rejoined her friends.

I recently met Diane on the street of a nearby town, and she seemed happy to see me. I saw no signs of confusion in her eyes. Would she ask me the meaning of my inscription? She didn't. I thought of mentioning it but decided a clarification was no longer needed. As we were saying our goodbyes, I pinched her cheek, a spontaneous, but unmistakable sign of affection for all the editors of *Forum*, *Twixtujons*, and *Le Souvenir*.

24

Challenges

When I met Joe, he told me to "go ... yourself." I didn't hear the second word. I was able to fill in the blank, but I wanted him to say it again; I dared him to say it again. I had seen him around the building, but I didn't know his name. Knowing a student's name always gives the teacher an advantage. He was a junior and a troublemaker. He wore tight T-shirts, even in the winter, which made it clear year-round he was very strong. Students—and some teachers—feared him. Joe didn't fear anyone, certainly not a teacher, certainly not me.

Since my room on the first floor was in the corridor leading to the cafeteria, I became the "noise police." My students did not find it odd that in mid-sentence, I ran to the door, yanked it open, and stood in the hall, like Superman, arms akimbo. Over the years, I was the law-and-order teacher on the first floor, the sheriff of the badlands leading to the cafeteria.

"Quiet! There are classes going on!"

"Sorry." Most students listened to teachers. But Joe was an outlaw, a desperado, a tough kid, who didn't see an impressive figure with arms akimbo.

"Quiet! You with the T-shirt, quiet!"

"Go ... yourself." In the past, students had lashed out at me, then apologized or run away from me. This was different. Joe didn't lash out; he was very calm. He didn't apologize, and he didn't run.

"What? What did you say?" He ignored me. "What did you say?" He looked straight ahead and said nothing. He wasn't going to disturb his lunch with an argument. I followed him into the cafeteria, where he decided to sit—to ignore me—until I went away. Then, he would buy his lunch and eat in peace. "What did you say?" He was winning this battle. I was lashing out. I was invisible. At the tables around us, students watched.

I leaned over, positioning my face several inches from his, placed one hand on his chair and one hand on the table in front of him, and through my teeth, I challenged him. I challenged him to say it again. And I challenged him to commit himself to something much more serious. "What did you say?" He never opened his mouth. He never looked at me. He fixed his eyes on something on the wall and remained calm. I had never met anyone like him.

Fortunately, he chose to say nothing. As a result, we both won; we both saved face. My authority didn't make him say it again. My authority made him afraid to say it again. I straightened up and remembered I had students waiting for me in my classroom. The crisis was over. I turned from Joe and saw Jimmy, the school electrician, watching us.

"Do you believe this kid, Jimmy?"

"Yeah. That's Joe."

"He could become a real problem."

"He is a real problem. That's why I'm here."

"What do you mean?"

"I was afraid he'd kill you."

I had been in difficult situations, face to face with boys, who ultimately backed down, because my position and/or anger convinced them it was the wise thing to do. But this boy did not back down; he hadn't even acknowledged my existence. I never wanted to see him again.

In September of the following year, I saw him sitting in my classroom; Joe was a student in my twelfth grade class, the last period of the day. Neither of us showed any signs of our common history. Joe, however, lost no time demonstrating his idea of school; I was not going to restrict him in the halls—or in my classroom. He sat directly in front of my desk, but it didn't concern him. He spoke to the person on his left and right. He didn't care if I stood in front of him. If I gave him detention; he didn't come. When asked why, he answered he had better things to do. His classmates loved him. He entertained them. He tortured other teachers for his and their amusement. His passing gas sent students shrieking to the window. He looked around and then criticized their immaturity. I was schizo-phrenic about ending my workday. For some reason, if a teacher has a difficult class in his schedule, it's always the last period.

At this point in my eighteen-year career, I considered myself a good teacher, having needed no help from the dean's office. The following axiom is incorrect: An excellent teacher does not have discipline problems. I warned Joe, "Cut my detention again, and I'm sending a referral to the office." He cut again, I sent the referral, and he had to serve Saturday school or face suspension. He served Saturday school often but never cut detention again. When he came for detention, which was frequent, he ignored my attempts at "reaching him" and "relating to him."

"Do you like baseball?"

"No."

"Do you like football?"

"No." Of course, he did; he was a terrific fullback on our football team.

"It must be hard playing a sport you don't like. I know you're very good."

"Great!"

"It must be hard to be great." I had him.

"For you, maybe." I hated Joe.

I received the good news on Monday morning. Joe had broken his leg in Saturday's game so severely that people on the opposite side of the field heard the crack of the splintering bone. He would miss two weeks of school. I no longer dreaded the end of the work day. Without their leader, this student from Teacher's Hell, the class worked and behaved. At lunch with my friends, I was honest about my lack of sensitivity. "I hope the doctors recommend a long and thorough rehabilitation for Joe's leg … poor kid."

I knew, however, he would return. He was a powerfully built boy, and a broken leg would not prevent his hero's return to school. I decided to be political; I'm not saintly. I went to the hospital. In the gift shop, I bought a football magazine and prepared for possible humiliation. He was in a pri-vate room, and his leg was in traction. Since he was watching television, he didn't see me enter the room. When I said hello, he turned his head toward me. He didn't have a chance to hide his reaction; he was sur-prised—and pleased—to see me. "What are you doing here?"

I tossed the magazine on his bed. "How long do you have to hang around here?"

He pointed at his leg. "Hang around!" He surprised me with his laugh-ter; it wasn't directed against me. We were sharing a joke. And that was it. That was our breakthrough. And at that moment, I began to like him. He told me about the game and his touchdowns, and he delighted in making me squirm with the sound effects of his leg breaking. "They heard it twenty miles away."

The class welcomed him the following week with a standing ovation. He smiled broadly. I was uncertain about our new relationship until the first test. When I told him to turn around, he did. When I told him to keep quiet, he did. Our new relationship didn't transform Joe completely. He was still rebellious; he enjoyed the attention, but he was no longer rebelling against me.

Joe's idea of a good time manifested itself during a visit from his guid-ance counselor, who had also been his football coach. Their mutual respect was confirmed with a handshake, and I expected Joe to keep a low profile during our conference at my desk. While the class worked on an assign-ment, the counselor and I reviewed grades that could prevent a student from graduating. Suddenly, the counselor fell against me, forcing my chair to roll to the blackboard. The class looked up. "What's the matter, Ralph?"

"Look!" He pointed at Joe, who was quietly looking down at his note-book. I looked back at Ralph.

"What?"

"Look!" Tears filled Ralph's eyes. Joe looked up at me. Then, he looked down at his desk. I looked down and saw it. Joe had stuck a twelve-inch ruler in his sweatpants. When I looked up, Joe sat back with his hands behind his head and smiled at us. I smiled back at him and pointed to my *Dead Zone* sign. After seeing the Stephen King movie with Christopher Walken, I referred to my detention list as the *Dead Zone*. When I looked in the direction of the sign, my students frantically swore to behave. Joe removed the ruler. And I didn't give detention. How could I? I had laughed. To cover myself, I gave him a quick warning about proper behavior; I knew Joe wanted a five-minute lecture to spotlight his latest antic.

Joe became my first arm-wrestling challenge at Eastchester High School, a tradition that continued for the rest of my career. I challenged the boys yearly to give blood to the Red Cross; girls always outnumber them three to one. Focusing on the strongest boy in class, I bet him I would fill my pint bag with blood before he could. Then, pointing to my heart, I added, "They stick the needle here." (Students surrounded my cot in the gym to time the bloodletting.) Since Joe refused to give blood, I challenged him to arm-wrestle.

"Let's go!" He stood up.

"No, no. Not today, Joe. It has to be the last day of school. The humiliation is going to be so great that you won't come back to school for your diploma."

"You're stalling, Leonard!"

"No, Joe, I want you to graduate. After I give you my diploma, we'll see who's stronger."

When the last day of class arrived, I handed out the LT diplomas. At the end of the ceremony, Joe rolled up his sleeve and approached me. "Let's go!" For the entire year, I had told them I was unbeatable. For the entire year, I pantomimed bending his arm back, sometimes using only my pinky.

"All right, let's go. Give me your parental-release form, the one you drew up with your family lawyer."

"I don't have any release!"

"Sorry. I can't arm-wrestle you without one."

"You liar ... You're crazy!" Appreciating my last joke of the year, Joe sat down and laughed along with the rest of the class. "I knew he was crazy last year when he wanted to fight me in the cafeteria." He winked at me.

I sat back and admired this clever boy who made my life miserable in September. He had taken my arm-wrestling tease and built upon it. Joe was a legend in school long after he had graduated. There were stories of fights in which he threw people through saloon windows. Since he was never a bully, many young people in our town looked up to him. I met him recently in front of the stationery store. He picked me up, shook me like a rag doll back and forth, and growled to his friend—and the neighborhood—"I love this guy!"

Not all discipline problems work out, and my failure to communicate with Greg was a spectacular failure. Unlike Joe, Greg didn't seem to be a problem at first. He seemed much older than the other students in the class. He was tall and sullen; there was talk that he lived in another town and used a relative's address to attend Gorton. This deception occurs more often than people think, costing homeowners higher property taxes to pay for the town's schools.

Greg wanted to impress me with his maturity. He was far cooler than anyone else in the class, which comprised mostly younger girls. He spoke out of turn and interrupted them. When I asked him to wait his turn, he humored me with a smile. "Of course, Mr. Leonard. Whatever you say."

"I do say, Greg. I certainly do." The next time he interrupted a student, he intercepted my reprimand with both hands in the stop position. He never learned the rules of the class, because he didn't respect the class or me. If I explained a correction on one of his essays, he argued that the correction was my "opinion."

For one assignment, Greg maintained that his style reflected the way people in his world spoke. I explained that I respected his world, but he needed to know two styles—one for his world and one for the State of New York. When he pointed out the absurdity of my suggestion, I pointed out the necessity of a New York diploma to graduate.

Greg's arrogance was tolerable until he began complimenting the girls in class while leering at their body parts. They told him to get lost, but his persistence unnerved them. For the first time in my memory, girls needed my protection against a boy's attention.

"Len, he creeps me out. Make him stop." Tammy was waiting for me after school. "He points at me and says stuff." I told her I would speak with him. She made it clear that if he didn't stop, she would tell the other boys. Since he was a newcomer in the school, she understood the boys' obligation to protect their territory.

The next morning before class, I met Greg on the food line in the cafeteria. I asked him to join me at an empty table, where I calmly told him about the complaint from one of the girls in the class.

"That's what a man does. He looks at beautiful women."

"But, Greg, you have to be cool. You look away when they look at you. And you definitely don't describe your fantasy to them."

"You look at women."

"Sure I do, but I don't drool."

"All right, I get it." I thought that went well.

A week later, the complaints were loud and clear from two other girls. For the first time in my life, sexual harassment was a problem in my classroom. I spoke to his guidance counselor, who agreed his behavior was particularly offensive and dangerous. Not only was he a threat to the girls, but also to himself. I learned that his being an outsider already made him unpopular with the boys in the school. After a meeting with his counselor, Greg kept a low profile in my class for several days.

Then one day I overheard Greg maliciously tease a girl with a slight mental retardation. I think seeing her smile at him enraged me. She had no idea that she was his new victim; she liked the attention. Regrettably, I had lost my temper many times, but my blowup with Greg resembled nothing in the past.

"Greg, get out of my room! Take a walk to guidance. You're no longer a student in my class."

"What did I do?"

"You know exactly what you did. Take a walk, Greg!"

"You disgust me, old man! You're a rotten teacher!" He yanked open the door and slammed it into the blackboard. Rotten teacher, I understood. The "old man" part disturbed me.

As soon as the bell rang, I walked toward the guidance department. Greg was waiting for me near the stairwell. He called out for to me to stop; I ignored him. He tried to placate me. There were going to be no more talks. He demanded to know my intentions. I warned Greg to "get away from me."

His guidance counselor decided to place Greg with another teacher with whom he had had a good relationship. I like to think the "old man" was too much man for him. Everything was fine until the principal returned with some of our students from the annual student-exchange trip to Belgium. Discovering someone had solved a problem without his consent, the principal came to my room.

"You can't make a decision like this."

"I didn't. His counselor and I did."

"But I'm the principal."

"You were in Belgium."

"He's going back to your class."

"He's a threat to the girls; he can't come back."

"He's going back."

"If he's coming back, I'm telling the girls that it was your decision. I'll tell the girls the principal demands he return."

"You can't do that!"

"Why not? You *are* the principal, and you *don't* believe he poses a threat to the girls in my class; therefore, he's coming back."

The principal never sent the boy back. I knew he wouldn't. Like some administrators today, he wanted the power, but not the responsibility. I also knew the girls and I would enjoy a good year. And fortunately, I had tenure that permitted my educational decision and protected me from retribution; I could not be fired without a hearing.

25

Tenure

One morning in the faculty room, I overheard Bob Liftig, our especially altruistic—and courageous—teacher/union president, have an unusual conversation with a young teacher. He'd had this conversation many times with people who didn't teach, but Ken did, and Bob had to convince him that tenure doesn't protect bad teachers. He had to convince "one of us" that the union—we, the teachers—should not be the scapegoat for lazy administrators.

"Don't get me wrong. I appreciate tenure's taking the politics out of grading. But if it protects someone who doesn't teach? And Bob ... you know who I mean."

"I do know, but *all* teachers—even our friend in room 477—deserve due process if they have tenure."

"Oh, please! She can't control her classes, and if she's not showing them movies, she's dismissing them early. The union ... uh, we ... should do something."

"Like what?"

"Fire her!"

"Don't hire—therefore—can't fire. Unions make sure the reasons are educational. For instance, should a teacher be fired for putting on lipstick during class?"

"Yes, *he* should."

"Come on, really? Should she?"

"Absolutely!"

"Why?"

"She's awful!"

"Not an educational reason. I bet you could teach and put on lipstick at the same time. Think due process, Ken."

"It takes too long … due process. Lipstick, I don't know."

"She deserves less time for a hearing than a bank robber?"

"Then, what do *we* do about her?"

"You mean *administration*."

"You can't always blame administration. What about the union?"

"You're right, but tell me something, Ken. If a teacher is bad, the union gets the blame. Why doesn't the union get credit for a good teacher?"

"All right, all right. If you were the principal, what would you do?"

"Observe, observe. And if necessary, observe again. If I see lipstick in her hand during a *good* lesson, fine. Maybe she needs a prop. But if the kids are watching a movie every time I come in, well…."

"Well, what? Pull the plug? She's got tenure."

"Speak with her. If she doesn't correct the problem, document it. Have other administrators come in. The assistant principal, one day; the chairperson, the next."

"What if she doesn't care?"

"I don't think so, Ken. She'd care. Teachers care about multiple observations. But more important, it's worth the effort."

"Seems like a lot of work."

"Making up lesson plans and correcting term papers and essays at home? Not a lot of work?

"That's my job. That's what teachers do."

"And the administrator's job?"

"Who observes lazy administrators, Bob?"

"We do, Ken, but we don't hire them."

26

A Clean, Well-lighted Place

In the fourth grade, Sister Jean Marie made me feel special when she leaned over my desk and enclosed the two of us—and her swinging crucifix—within her habit, a holy place, and gently corrected my spelling. I felt safe and special. With fifty students in one room, the nuns were always protective but rarely gentle.

When my parents' divorce became contentious, and my father threatened to abduct me again and take me to his home on Long Island, the nuns protected me. For several weeks at the end of the school day, nuns stood on either side of me in front of the school and waited for my mother, who worked at New York Hospital down the street. When she arrived at the school, the nuns handed me over and returned to their classrooms. After my mother's safely escorting me home, she returned to the hospital. My father, himself a product of the good Sisters, understood the odds and never came near the school. If one nun could control—and protect—fifty boys and girls, what would two nuns do to one man to protect one child? Their holding my hands made me feel special.

In F. Scott Fitzgerald's novel, Jay Gatsby's "rare" smile "concentrated" on Nick Carraway, making Nick feel special; it "believed" in Nick as much as Nick wanted to believe in himself. I believed I was special when my teachers made eye contact with me. If their eyes moved across mine, they were speaking to me. If they lingered on mine, I imagined they waited for my insightful reaction to their comments. Then, I'd vary my expressions for their gratification. Narrowed eyes indicated my appreciation of a teacher's profundity. *Hmm, very interesting.*

Even in grade school all the students recognized the special students. Most of the time, the teacher looked at and spoke to them; and these weren't the ones who always raised their hands or stood by the teacher's desk after class. They were good students or interesting people. They didn't seek the teacher's attention, but we called them "teacher's pet" and worse. We didn't know it, but we wanted to be in their place. We wanted the teacher to look at us.

I discovered very early in my career that "speaking" to students made me a better teacher. I made the effort to acknowledge every student in the class. I quickly learned their names, made eye contact, and listened to them. I was not a Jay Gatsby, but I was the teacher, the leader of the class; I was special to them, and I let them know they were special to me. I complimented the students and gave them honest reactions, not perfunctory self-esteem boosters. And I never had a problem admitting to students that an idea of theirs had never occurred to me.

When Ann Marie pointed out that Emily never speaks to her dead brother, Wally, in the cemetery scene in Wilder's *Our Town,* I shook my head and congratulated her. "In all the years I've taught this play, no one ever noticed that; I never did. You're right. Emily speaks to Mrs. Gibbs, Mrs. Soames, Mr. Carter, and Mr. Stimson, but never to her brother, whose appendix burst on a Boy Scout trip years earlier. What a terrific observation! And," I deadpanned, "don't ever show me up again, Ann Marie!"

Teasing students also makes them feel special. Actually we teased one another. From the beginning of the school year, I laced my lessons with personal asides. When we discussed the transcendental movement and Emerson's disdain for materialism and society, I'd mention my 1969 Pontiac LeMans, which cost half my gross teacher's salary for one year. I still lived at home, of course.

"What color was it? Wait, I know ... You're a tan kind of guy."

"No, I wanted women to wave at me from the sidewalk. I wanted them to perceive my sensuality and power; I bought a red car. When I drove my eight-cylinder car down the street, women saw a matador-red kind of guy."

"How many women did you meet?"

"I never met anyone."

"What about Trixie?"

"The car didn't impress Trixie. She saw me au natural."

"Len!"

"No, I'm not talking about my ... Yes, I have subtle muscles ... Who's groaning? Raise your hands!" They all raised their hands. "Listen, Trixie knows her Ralph Waldo Emerson. She believes '... nature is the opposite of the soul. One is seal and one is print.' Trixie saw my soul and fell in love with ... Oh, stop groaning ... All right, then, how many of you want to know more about Trixie and me?" Smiling, they all sat back and raised their hands. A personal teacher story is almost as good as an early snow dismissal. "Then read Emerson's 'The American Scholar' on page 167 for Monday ... Stop groaning, or it'll be for this Friday. See you tomorrow, folks—and thanks for coming."

The next morning, I told the class that I had had a disturbing dream. Did they want to hear it? Of course, they did. I hesitated until they insisted. The dream was intimate. Could they be discreet? Of course, they could—sure, until lunch with their friends.

"Well, I dreamt of this woman who fancied me...."

"Fancied! I think he and Emerson took buggy rides together." Doug turned to his friends for the smiling nods.

"Maybe, in a former life, he was Emerson." Andi wanted a piece of the action.

"May I continue?"

"Sorry, fancy pants." There was no stopping Doug today.

"Well, I asked this woman if she would go out with me. She made it very clear she found me attractive."

"Mr. Serico told us you took your sister to the prom. Did she find you attractive?" Doug loved digressions.

"Never mind his prom ... Come on, Len. What did the woman find attractive about you?"

"She pinched me." They yelled. "I better stop here ... I made a mistake. I think you might be too young for this." This always worked. A few of them folded their arms across their chests, but the rest shouted, "You can't stop now! You always do that! We'll never listen to you again." Yes, I did stall, because they loved the tease.

"All right, quiet then. Where was I?"

"She pinched your butt!"

"She pinched my arm."

"How long did it take her to find your muscle?" Unlike Doug, Andi never turned to gauge the class response; she watched my response.

"She was trying to whisper in my ear, Andi. She was petite, so she was pulling herself up my arm to my ear. She pinched me on the way up."

"What did she whisper?" Their heads moved forward.

"I don't know. I was so excited, I didn't give her a chance. I asked her for a date before her lips reached my ear."

"What did she say?"

"She laughed and said, 'No way!'"

"What! Get out! Why wouldn't she go out with you?" Now Andi was angry. I was *her teacher*. "You're not that bad. Besides, how could she turn you down? It was your dream; you dreamt her!" Andi, the school's most talented writer, was ahead of me.

"She never told me. But I think I know why." I paused for several seconds.

"She was the woman of my dreams, the one who goes out with men in matador-red cars, not soulful men who are awake and teach Emerson to drowsy students. I was dreaming the truth."

"You're an Emerson kind of guy."

"I am. Therefore, don't ask me about Mr. Serico's knitting lessons."

"Mr. Serico takes knitting lessons?"

"I said don't ask! Let's get to work."

Students are shocked to hear a teacher poke fun at another teacher in the building. When the teachers are obviously playing a game, the students appreciate the contest of wit and the display of friendship. Lou Serico—a superior history teacher with a warm fatherly appeal—and I delighted them with half-truths and outlandish lies. We've been friends since our days in graduate school at Fordham where, I complained to my students, he had received a fellowship, and I hadn't (true). And to make matters worse, I would have received his fellowship (not true) had he played for the old Washington Senators. But no, he chose a college diploma over a professional baseball contract (true).

"What would you have done, Mr. Leonard?"

"Well, I'm standing here."

"But were you good at sports?"

"What do you think?"

"You're no Mr. Serico. He's a big man—and some athlete." Anyone who watched Lou play in the annual faculty/senior basketball games knew this. And Lou's prowess became the talk of the school when he broke up a fight despite the cast on a broken leg—incurred during one of those games.

He even saved my life once. Standing at the top of the bleachers, we were cheering our students on to a football state victory. It was a wintry night, and when a strong gust of wind blew across the field into us, I lost my balance; but Lou's hand snapped out and grabbed me before I fell behind the stands. The next day when the students asked for confirmation of the story—and my "flight weight"—I told them he exaggerated my near death experience (not true).

"So come on, Len. What did you give up for a diploma?"

"I like to think of myself as a multi-talented contender, a nouveau post-renaissance man, but—unlike some people—it's not my style to boast." (Not true.)

During a typical school year, our students learned that I took my sister to the prom; Lou bought sport coats at the local hardware store; my mother interviewed my girlfriends; and he studied ballet during the summer months. More enjoyable to them was their becoming players in our game and revealing to me in the middle of a class Lou's latest announcement: "Mr. Serico said you cry during movie love scenes. That's sweet, Len." They'd sit back and smile, but I'd ignore the bait. The next day I'd surprise them with a random reference to his plant-growing trophies and passion for puppy photography. Lou and I never spoke about any of this.

When Lou visited my classroom on his way to the cafeteria, I'd stand next to him and ask for a "candid opinion": "Who's better looking? Please be brutally objective." Tapping my grade book against my chest, I made my preference clear; but the unanimous show of hands always went to him. I immediately opened my book and pretended to write, and they hooted and laughed. Their joy was witnessing our friendship; our joy was making the school a safe place, a home away from home.

Sometimes, to make students feel special, I broke the rules. My strict Catholic education gave me a model to follow during the anarchy of the late sixties. Students must be orderly for the class to be effective. But over the years, I realized that exceptions might be made with certain classes. I can't say the same for my Catholic high school days.

With their heat-seeking rulers and straps, Dominican Sisters and Irish Christian Brothers were renowned disciplinarians. How else could they control large classes during the boomer-generation years? But we lacked the internal motivation to behave once the external motivation (smack in the head) disappeared. When Sister or Brother stepped into the hall, we celebrated our freedom with paper airplanes and punching contests. My public school students never needed to celebrate my stepping into the hall. When I returned, they were quietly speaking with one another.

In 1968, I was the reincarnation of a 1959 Brother. With the exception of the creative writing class, I stood behind a filing cabinet, and the students sat in straight rows with their backs to the windows. I didn't like to compete with nature. They raised their hands to speak. They didn't interrupt one another; no one, not even I, interrupted. The rules were simple and clear. There were others, but once the students understood them and trusted me, I eliminated many.

Students love cameras, falling snow, a bee in the room, an absent teacher (at least, for a while), assemblies, a personal teacher story (not too many), early dismissal, postponed homework assignment (unless they already did it), postponed tests (unless they know the material), visitors to the classroom, structure with occasional digressions, rigorous work within their reach, fire drills, and humor. I combined the last two during our first fire drill. I informed my new students that during a real fire, contrary to fire-drill instructions, I was to be the first one out of the room. But most of all, they look forward to a favorite class, where they feel special and safe.

When I retired, I received thoughtful letters of congratulations from old students, who flattered me with memories of our time together. Joan, now living in Australia, thanked me for making the class "safe." She felt safe to express her thoughts, however different. I don't think a student can feel special before she feels safe. I felt special—and safe—when Christina, *Forum* editor and class leader, sitting near my desk, whispered "Dickinson" after I had mistakenly said "Wharton" to the class. She was protecting her teacher.

If I allowed one student to break a rule, I allowed everyone to break it. If the class accepted the change in routine, I ignored the rule. I like to think that I was consistent, that students never complained to classmates about my having favorites. There were times I would let students sit at my desk next to the filing cabinet/lectern where I stood; they had forgotten their glasses and couldn't see the blackboard. But if the smiling student had no visual problems, but needed attention, I said nothing. My teaching wasn't affected, and the other students didn't seem to care. If they cared, a different student developed vision problems the next day. And that was fine.

Since I lacked the perfect handwriting of the nuns, I rarely wrote on the blackboard. Dictation and handouts spared my students' eyesight. When the students complained that Mr. Serico had better handwriting, I told them he was a latent nun. Sometimes, students sat at my desk to decipher my hieroglyphs.

When Lynn, a quiet student who didn't seem comfortable with me—or the other students in the class—sat on top of her desk, I wasn't sure about this change. Certainly, during plays, the students and I sometimes sat on desks and performed from our "stage" for the other students, but Lynn was breaking new ground. Her elevation was not a distraction to the class; she sat in the last seat of the row. It was a distraction to me.

What if all the students wanted to sit on top of their desks? I liked the democracy of rows. I liked seeing the students' faces equidistant, one behind the other. Standing at the front of the room, at the side, and at the corners, I saw order, equality, and safety. Surveying their fields, farmers must feel the same way. And during my rookie year when I taught in several classrooms, didn't the veteran teachers warn me to "keep the rows straight" in *their* rooms?

Perhaps my staring at Lynn one day prompted her cheerful defense. "I'm short. I can see better up here." She surprised me—and pleased me. For the first time, she initiated a discussion.

"Why not sit here?" There was an empty seat in the first row.

"It's different here. It feels good. Can I stay here, please?"

She didn't block anyone's view, and she wouldn't upset my sense of democracy—too much. And the other students didn't seem to care; she was an outsider, not a trendsetter. Balancing her notebook on her legs, she sat bowlegged on the desk to make my class "feel good." Once on top of the "world," her demeanor changed. She became happy.

"Well, it looks uncomfortable to me, but all right. Just don't fall asleep up there. It's a long way down, and I don't have insurance." It was a running joke in my class that certain students needed seatbelts to prevent lecture-induced accidents.

Lynn sat on that desk for the rest of the year—and the following year—even when the students and I sat in a circle for the creative writing class. With her new-found confidence, she became a leader. In creative writing, I depended on my students' constructive criticism and support to motivate revision of their work. Most students never write for their peers. They write for their teachers. In the creative writing class, they wrote for my grades—and their classmates' respect. The students appreciated Lynn's reaction to their work.

Not everyone, however, approved of Lynn's special treatment. Antonette Alfonsina, an excellent guidance counselor, informed me that Lynn's "unorthodox classroom behavior was unacceptable" to her father who wanted Lynn to sit in a chair. I ignored the complaint. I explained that a smiling student on a desk was preferable to a sulking student behind one and that she became a class leader after having abandoned the chair. I made the correct decision with Lynn, who was comfortable with her unique position in the class and who eventually became an editor of the literary magazine during her senior year.

Unfortunately, I didn't always understand the special needs of students. With Meryl, I broke the rules the first time a decision had to be made and followed the rules the second time. My second decision was wrong. She was a conscientious student in my eleventh grade honors class. She did all her assignments, took excellent notes, and enjoyed the course material; but she couldn't raise her average above an 80% for the quarter.

To remain in the honors program, the student must maintain an 85% for the quarter. I ignored the criterion if the student demonstrated a sincere desire to remain in the program. Often, students fought to stay in it for social reasons but refused to do the work. When their grades fell below 85%, I removed them by the first quarter. Since Meryl worked to her potential, I didn't apply the 85% rule. She deserved the enrichment of an honors curriculum.

That first decision made two people suffer, Meryl and me. I dreaded correcting and returning her papers, because she rarely received 85% or better. When she succeeded, we were happy, but her grades were rarely "good enough," and she couldn't mask her frustration. Understandably, she was upset, and I worried about her emotional well-being. After several assignments, I couldn't look at her. I cowardly slipped the graded test or essay—facedown—onto her desk and hurried to another desk. She was never angry with me, only with herself. Ironically, students who didn't make the effort directed their anger at me: "Why did you knock me out of honors?"

Unlike some students (and their parents) today who do not believe that criteria for AP courses pertain to them, Meryl understood that advanced placement students had to qualify. (The sudden increase in the percentage of students taking AP courses has resulted in good publicity for administrators and good public relations for school districts; however, national magazines erroneously use enrollment numbers, not *scores* on AP exams, to rate high schools. Is it any wonder that, to accommodate this influx of new AP students, many teachers are forced to water down curricula?)

When the time came to recommend Meryl for senior AP English, I couldn't; I worried about her frustration level. I knew she would do very well in an academic English class. After all her hard work, she deserved to smile over papers marked with A's. Meryl understood my reasons but insisted she preferred the challenge of AP work; she would be "okay." I disagreed. Beginning in September, Meryl would be in an academic class. Students and parents are more willing to accept that placement for science and math courses.

I saw Meryl frequently. As she passed my classroom on the way to lunch, she'd stick her head in and wave her latest success at me. "I got another 98%!" But she always added, "The work is too easy!" When she received her first report card, she came to my room and held it in front of my face. She had received 99% for the quarter. I congratulated her, but she would have none of it. "It doesn't mean anything; the work is too easy. I'd rather get a lower grade and learn something." I believe she would have received a grade of 2/5 on her AP examination. Did I make the right decision denying her the AP experience? I thought so. I worried about her emotional resilience, but what if I misinterpreted her sighs and frowns.

One thing was obvious: Meryl would not feel special unless her grades were meaningful. Students like inflated grades, but soon scorn an "easy marker." Meryl resented the high grade. For her, the grade was not evidence of good work, but evidence of an easy class. Unlike students who accept lower grades in AP classes for inflated self-esteem and/or school transcripts, Meryl was a superior student.

After my experience with Meryl, I spoke openly to diligent students—and their parents—about the frustration of low grades. I knew I would never inflate a grade to appease anyone. I wanted them to know the grades might not improve, and I wanted to be sure they weren't being hurt by their "failure" to improve, to do as well as the other high-achieving students surrounding them in their honor class.

I once had another student like Meryl. He was an excellent "math/science person" but fell short of the 85% criterion to stay in the honors class. I observed over the years that good "math/science people" usually do well in English, but "English/history people" sometimes have difficulty with math and science. Gabriel was an exception. At the end of the quarter, his mother called for a conference. I knew of her reputation; she was very active in the district and had special parental powers.

Like a lawyer, I prepared my case and brought my grade book to the guidance office, where she and the counselor were discussing Gabriel's college options. We shook hands, and she thanked me for the meeting. I wanted to thank her; I appreciated the respect.

"What can Gabriel do to raise his average?"

That was always the first question. I didn't know. As far as I could tell, he did his best. He was a good student but not an honor student; however, he would be a ninety student in an academic class.

"Can he do extra-credit assignments to raise his average?"

That was always the second question. No, I wouldn't agree to that. Honor students shouldn't need extra-credit assignments to remain in the program. I allowed only students with learning disabilities to do extra-assignments. Gabriel's mother looked annoyed.

"Gabriel likes the course material, and he has friends in the class. He'd like to stay with you. He'll work harder, and he understands that he may never achieve above an 80%."

She was being respectful—and practical. She knew I was an "old timer," someone with enough experience and independence perhaps to survive a "connected" parent. She was saying all the correct things; I appreciated her honesty. I complimented Gabriel's diligence, but I wanted her reassurance that he was not being hurt emotionally.

"He's satisfied being a top student in math and science. Actually, his staying in your class would be emotionally good for him." In that case, I decided that Gabriel could remain in the class, but if she noticed any change in him, we would meet again. We shook hands goodbye. I hurried to my next class.

After the last student left the room at the end of the day, I sat in my chair, rolled back, and crossed my ankles on the desk. I wonder if the Sisters ever crossed their ankles on a desk; the Brothers did. I felt good about the day. The classes went well. I had no papers to correct and no lesson plan to prepare for tomorrow. When the guidance counselor came into the room, I prepared myself for a reality check.

"Gabriel's mother thinks you're a sensitive person."

"For letting Gabriel stay?"

"For worrying about him. She never expected that. You caught her off guard. She's a tough lady."

"She seemed reasonable."

"She can be Dragon Lady."

And when I met the principal on my way to the parking lot, he surprised me with his hardy greeting. "How did you win Gabriel's mother over? How? She's the toughest parent in the school district."

"I paid her!"

"Not with your limbs, I see."

Driving home, I thought about the day. My decision about Gabriel was a good one. His mother assured me he was fine with low eighties. I thought about that parish priest, Father Reilly, in the eighth grade who recommended my going to a vocational high school, even though I never demonstrated any technical aptitude; I was just not a good student at the time, and he didn't know what to do with me. Fortunately, our pastor Father Shay, at my mother's request, recommended an Irish Christian Brothers' school, which recognized that I was neither scholar—nor mechanic.

Times have changed; the power has flipped to the other side. Some of today's "important" parents (board of education, PTA, etc.) remind me of Father Reilly. They don't appreciate a middle ground, a place for average students to be comfortable in a class of their peers. Gabriel was a math/science honors student, not an honors English student. His mother and I came to an understanding that worked well for Gabriel.

Sometimes, making a student feel special requires unorthodox attention. Jane Nason is that rare person who reaches everyone; Jane at times was a teacher's teacher. When teachers argued about a line of poetry, they asked for Jane's interpretation. When teachers criticized an answer on a state examination, they asked for Jane's confirmation. When the principal had a question about his letter to the community, he called Jane into his office. And when Jane argued with a colleague that Finny shook the branch, resulting in the death of Gene, in the novel *A Separate Peace*, she telephoned John Knowles, the author. He agreed with Jane. He then asked her out to lunch; she didn't accept.

More people attended Jane's retirement party than any other retirement party in the district's history; people admired her professionalism and kindness. Jane's career was solely an academic one, despite an appealing offer from the *New York Times* to work in its editorial department. When she warned her students, "I wield a wicked red pen, and that's an alliteration," they laughed and learned their grammar and sentence structure.

In 1973, Jane and I shared a classroom for a year and chatted between classes. I liked this attractive woman with the long blond hair immediately. She was honest—and direct. "Richard, your breath is bad. Garlic," she whispered. She was also discreet.

"I had Szechwan last night." I covered my mouth and leaned back.

"You have to be very careful to brush well." She treated my breath as if it were a sentence fragment.

"Thanks, Jane." I was grateful. She took a chance. Not many people would have warned a colleague about bad breath; I never have.

Jane's students saw the same honesty. If she scolded a student for looking out the window rather than at her, he knew the reason. This was *their* time, not *his* time. Her lesson plans were thorough and important. Jane was the hardest working teacher in the school, because she wanted her students to do well in college. And in life.

I think I heard Jane at her best one afternoon while I was on hall duty assignment. We teachers policed the halls one period a day. I heard shouting, which was common in a school of the early seventies. I looked to my right just in time to see a textbook crash against the wall opposite Jane's classroom. Then, I heard a door slam shut. Before I could stand, I saw a loose-leaf binder fly into pieces before it made to the wall and heard the door slam shut again. I was now two doors away when Shirley, a tough talking girl, stumbled out of Jane's room. "Don't you ever speak to me that way again, young lady!" The door slammed shut.

"Don't you push me!" Shirley screamed at the closed door.

The door opened. "And don't come back until you apologize!" The door slammed shut.

By the time I reached Jane's door, it was over. Textbook and loose-leaf paper covered the floor, Shirley had stomped out of the building, and Jane was teaching behind the closed door. "No, Bobby. Fielding did not write *Pamela*. You're thinking of Richardson. Fielding wrote *Shamela*. That's okay; that's a common mistake, Bobby."

Before the day was over, Shirley returned to school and apologized to Jane. Fear of school punishment didn't exist in those days. Our assistant principal refused to alienate our "alienated" students, so teachers handled their own discipline problems. Shirley recognized Jane's honest approach to her students. When I met Shirley in town years later, she reminded me of that afternoon: "They'll never be another Miss Nason. There's a teacher! I love that woman."

And good teachers love their classes and quickly personify them as nice, smart, lazy, funny, and so on. Listen to a discussion in the faculty room, and you'll hear most teachers agree about the personality of a class. They trade comical stories about some classes and commiserate about others. All the teachers who taught this one senior class agreed: "They're sweet kids!" and "I love that class!"

I met them in their junior year. They were special, because they were nice to one another since elementary school. Like old friends, they understood and accepted individual temperaments. I admired these students when they insisted that a classmate pose with them for a photograph at the end of class; Jeff wouldn't, because he had criticized them during a class debate. But they knew he was a sincere and passionate person.

Earlier in the period, three students were guiding the class in a discussion of Hawthorne villains and heroes. I had assigned this task for many years. Unlike many student-directed assignments, this one made the group passionate; the ensuing discussion reflected the point of view of their essays, which I had already graded. Two weeks earlier, I had assigned the essay to identify the nature of certain characters in Hawthorne's "Minister's Black Veil," "Young Goodman Brown," and "Rappaccini's Daughter."

Hawthorne believes human beings are innately evil and share secret sin; therefore, they should accept one another. A Hawthorne villain suffers from the sin of pride and alienates/isolates others for presumed intellectual or moral superiority. On the other hand, a Hawthorne hero forgives and loves others. (People who live in glass houses should not throw stones.... Let he who has not sinned cast....)

In "Young Goodman Brown," Brown is the villain, because he rejects his wife and the inhabitants of his village when he sees—or dreams—of a witch's ceremony. A close reading of the text reveals Goodman Brown's misinterpretation that the community reveres its evil state. They do not; they acknowledge it. In effect, he denies his sinful nature and isolates himself from the community. Like Brown, many students in their essays condemned the community.

Once the students handed in their papers, I broke the class down into six groups, each of which picked a character from a "hat": Beatrice, Giovanni, Dr. Rappaccini, Dr. Baglione, Minister Hooper, and Goodman Brown. The members in each group, then, had to agree about the morality of the character—villain or hero—and develop an argument based on textual evidence. When the interpretation was unanimous within the group, the evidence was presented to the other groups. They, in turn, agreed or disagreed with the textual arguments. Sometimes the argument was heated, since it was the thesis of their essays that I had already read. The students were hoping to improve their grades.

When Jeff argued his group's position on the villainy of Giovanni in "Rappaccini's Daughter," he ran into strong opposition from several groups. In his thorough way, he presented the evidence. They rejected it. They believed Giovanni was a hero. After all, Beatrice poisons *him.* They had not read the short story carefully. Beatrice has no idea that her breath is poisonous to him, and she never allows him to touch her. When Giovanni curses Beatrice and wishes she were dead, his cruelty stuns her. When the class agreed Giovanni was a hero, Jeff was stunned.

"Don't you see! Beatrice wants to protect Giovanni. She does *not* know she is poisoning him. And she believes he *will leave* her, and the garden, someday to 'mingle with thy race, and forget that there ever crawled on earth such a monster as poor Beatrice.' Look at page 207 in the text! Beatrice is not a villain! Giovanni is!"

The class ended and Jeff dropped into his seat. Unlike the students who welcomed the bell for lunch, Jeff looked disturbed. I understood. Many times, I wondered why a lesson plan had failed. The students were packing their books when they saw the camera. There was no reason for its appearance. No holiday. No weekend. No birthday. Someone just wanted to take a picture of the class. "Mr. Leonard, please take a picture of us."

Students love cameras. They take pictures of one another and the class—with or without the teacher. Today, disposable cameras are omnipresent. Whenever one appears, they shout, "Come here! Come here!" or "Take our picture!" Girls meet cheek to cheek, and boys make faces and muscles. They want to make the moment last; they want to be the moment. I've seen students run across the room at the sight of a camera. In my classroom, they wanted to stand beneath **The Mob is Ugly** sign above the blackboard to remember—and be remembered. I focused the camera.

"I'm not going to lose my eyesight, am I? It doesn't get uglier than this!" They ignored me.

"Come on, Jeff!" I turned to see Jeff in his seat.

I shook his shoulder. "Jeff, get over there!"

"I can't. It was wrong of me to lose my temper."

They didn't hear him. He spoke to me. But they had known Jeff for many years and respected his intelligence—and passion. And they were very fond of him. "Jeff, come on. We wanna go to lunch!"

Finally, their insistence convinced Jeff to join them. He had lost his temper, but they, like Hawthorne heroes, had forgiven him. I took the picture and complained of a burning in my eye. "Another picture will blind me for sure." When a colleague entered the room, the class screamed for me to squeeze him into the group.

"I think we just got uglier, Len!" Bob wasn't going to ignore me.

Today, it's my favorite school picture. When I look at it, I remember this class. I remember their honesty, exasperation, anger, forgiveness, unity, and love. Teachers loved this class, because the students were good to one another and made the room a safe place for everyone.

I love school buildings. They contain many worlds, many stories, past and present. When Marv and I chaperoned school events at night, we'd walk around the eerily empty building and joke about the ghosts of former teachers who roamed the halls and visited *their* old classrooms. When we passed our rooms, we couldn't imagine other teachers behind our desks. But someday, of course, old man Rothman and old man Leonard would also roam these halls; we would become those teachers with the funny hairstyles in dusty yearbooks.

Schools are rich with the worlds of students and teachers who come and go, year after year. What building contains as many stories, relationships, conflicts, dreams as a school? Schools must have more ghosts than a castle. But I imagine only a few teachers appreciate the spiritual nature of a school. For most people who pass through schools doing their time as students, an empty school at night must be like a museum with blank walls—or a department store without merchandise.

In 1990, I visited a school building built in 1893 in Hot Springs, South Dakota. In 1961, it had become the Fall River County Museum. The woman at the desk was baffled by my interest in her childhood recollections of Civil War veterans doing military drills in the school's circular lobby on national holidays. Why wasn't I asking questions about the pioneer Americana on display in the classrooms? The cracked blackboards and the old desks, crammed in a room on the top floor, meant nothing to her. I wanted to know about the long, narrow coatrooms in the classrooms. Did the children play in them? Did they play tricks on their teachers? What about her, this woman who admired the old soldiers seventy years ago? I was speaking to someone for whom the Civil War was not several pages in a history book. She and her classmates sat in rows of desks, listening to their teacher and thinking of the upcoming weekend. Nothing changes in schools. "But aren't the spinning wheels and the other collectibles interesting?" she wanted to know.

Another incident reminded me how much I love school buildings and classrooms. As part of an ongoing training program, ten teachers from our school visited a major corporation in the area. To prepare students for the corporate world of the future, this company invited us to see and hear its vision of the perfect workplace. The more important lesson of the day was unintentional; it confirmed my suspicion.

First, they stressed cooperation. The representative showed us a company-motivational poem that emphasized the power of the **We** over the **I**. Second, they praised the importance of technology. Frequently, they conducted meetings via videoconference, so people in different locations could communicate screen/face to screen/face. That explained the empty—and chilly—corridors of the company.

I was not receptive to any of this. I didn't care for their poem that contained abstraction (cooperation), after abstraction (unity), after abstraction (sacrifice) without any concrete, sensuous image that described the world outside the building. I didn't care for a world that depended on screens for interpersonal relationships.

I also didn't care for the way the representative treated us at the beginning of the tour. She led the *ten* of us to a room with *nine* folding chairs. She served us coffee and tea in paper cups. Since she hadn't checked the equipment in advance, when she flipped on the projector switch, nothing happened. No motor hum, no light. One of the teachers looked under the table to discover the problem; the projector's cord lay unplugged.

The company's representative laughed at the oversight. But she—and her company—had not given us the respect reserved for their clients. I knew we were not special to them and looked forward for the tour to end. When we left the huge and under-heated complex, where people teleconferenced from their offices, I wanted to get back to my school, my classroom, where students made me feel special, where Walt Whitman's "beautiful, curious, breathing, laughing flesh" surrounded me.

27

June 23: My Last Day of School

I began to teach in 1968, and like all new teachers, I "traveled" to several rooms on different floors, where the veterans gave me a bottom drawer in their desks for storage—and a stern warning to keep the rows straight. When we met at the doorways between periods, they lamented the golden years when principals "knew how to run a school" and students were wonderful young adults who never would disrupt classes with sit-ins and class boycotts to protest war, civil rights injustices, and school regulations banning pants for girls. And "their" students never used marijuana or LSD. The veterans began to retire in 1968, the end of an era.

Despite the metamorphosis occurring in education, I found my career challenging and satisfying. With the advent of PowerPoint presentations, differentiated-learning workshops, administrative hierarchies, and the marketing of Advanced Placement courses for public relations, however, I now lamented my golden years. When slippery whiteboards and foul-smelling, greasy markers replaced the dusty blackboards and chalk in my classroom, I retired in 2000, the end of an era for another generation of teachers.

I had had a wonderful thirty-two years in the classroom; and today, June 23, I was sitting under this tent, away from the sun's glare, waiting for the distribution of diplomas to begin and my last day of school to end. The senior class president and the GO (General Organization) president sat on the stage next to the administrators and town dignitaries. The president of the class approached the podium and began calling our names in alphabetical order to receive our certificate of recognition.

I wasn't nervous. I didn't have to make a speech. All I had to do was enjoy the spotlight. Since I had carefully watched the four retirees before me ascend the stage and return to their seats, I was comfortable without having had a rehearsal. The seniors had rehearsed several times, but, of course, we were the adults.

As the reading teacher was returning to her seat, I heard my name. I stood with the rising applause. It pleased me that I had received more applause than she. But somewhere between my seat and the stage, I realized that I had taught many more students and, therefore, knew many more clappers in the audience. So much for my sudden popularity.

I quickly walked up the steps and shook hands with the president of the class, who handed me the certificate of recognition. I smiled at the GO president when she mouthed, "Kiss me." Why hadn't the other teachers kissed her? Had they kissed her? Had I been daydreaming? And had she really mouthed for me to kiss her? While I was considering these questions, I heard a hoarse whisper. "Kiss me." I leaned over to comply before she had a chance to find the next name to call. She air-kissed me—or sighed—and announced the next name.

When I turned to leave the stage, the class president directed me to a different set of steps, which led to the side of the stage. I stopped to wave to the students, something I normally would never do. I have always remembered the photograph of Joe DiMaggio's bowed head while he ran the bases after a home run. *Be humble.* But that wave, that sign of appreciation to the students, waiting for their diplomas, would be my last communication with them.

Reaching the bottom step, I looked to the left. Before I began to walk back to my seat, I saw the next retiree approaching the stage. My acceptance had taken more time than that of my predecessors. Had I continued, he and I would have met somewhere between the stage and the seats. I didn't want to detract from his applause—and I thought returning to the seats together would look awkward. Before my appearance on the stage, the class president had always waited for the teacher to sit before he called the next name. I, therefore, turned right and walked out of a tent, where thoughtful seniors devoted part of their graduation ceremony to honor us retirees. I now stood behind the stage beneath a bright sun, the only person—as far as I could see—not under the tent. What were the students thinking? Where did Mr. Leonard go? He disappeared. And what were their parents saying? "I saw him go up the steps. He waved to us, remember? Look, his seat is empty!"

I looked for an aisle back into the tent, but since it was a very hot day, crowds of relatives and teachers gathered at its edge for the shade. I passed clogged aisle after clogged aisle. Looking for an opening, I was the naked man in a towel locked out of his apartment. And walking around the tent, I was the child in search of the biggest horse on a carousel. I came upon the orchestra students, many of whom were not graduating this year and were, therefore, bored with the proceedings. They were happy to see someone who looked more wretched than they.

"Hi, Mr. Leonard. What are you doing out there?"

"I'm trying to get back in."

"Why did you leave?"

"I took a wrong turn."

"You must've been going pretty fast."

My appearance amused them. They sat to the right of the stage. One minute I was walking across the stage away from them, and the next, I was standing behind them, a man with a mission. I wished them a good summer and moved on. On my third turn around the tent, I imagined a lesson with students I'd never know.

Teacher: "Yesterday we were discussing literary devices. Let's start with the point of view in this scene."

Student: "It's in first person. You're in the narrator's mind the entire scene."

Teacher: "But there's third person too, right? The audience sees him go up the steps, kiss the GO president, and disappear. They even say his seat is empty."

Student: "No, they don't. He's imagining that. The reader sees from one point of view. His. Nice try, Leonard."

Teacher: "But imagine—from the third person point of view—the narrator would be able to be objective and give an aerial view of someone quickly *walking around a yellow-and-white striped tent, which then would look like a moving carousel."*

Student: *"Yeah, that's a great image, but you can't have both first-and-third-person points of view in the same scene. You taught us goodly."*

Teacher: *"But isn't it better to 'Show, don't tell'?"*

Student: *"Len, a naked English teacher? Get the Visine!"*

Student: *"Two bottles! One for each eye."*

Teacher: *"You're right. In this case, better to 'Tell, don't show.' And the metaphors? Do they work for the narrator?"*

Student: *"Definitely. He loved being a teacher. That's who he was, and this graduation is his last day with students. Without teaching he'll be naked—fortunately figuratively speaking."*

Teacher: *"And the child-finding-the-biggest-horse image?"*

Student: *"He never says that he finds a horse."*

Teacher: *"He found his horse; for thirty-two years, he taught."*

Student: *"But he won't ever teach again. I think the carousel symbolizes his years of teaching … his past."*

Teacher: *"In <u>Catcher</u>, why was Holden 'damn near bawling' watching his sister Phoebe going around and around on her brown, beat-up looking horse at the carousel in Central Park?"*

Student: *"That's the best book ever, Leonard. Holden loves Phoebe's youth and innocence…. Was the narrator thinking all these things while he was walking around the tent?"*

Teacher: *"What do you think?"*

Student: "He doesn't mention Holden, but he's imagining this lesson, so he must realize his walking around the tent—and trying to get back in—must mean something more than just walking around a...."

Finally, an aisle opened up. Since names were still being called out, I waited. So far, my timing got me into this mess. I was hoping better timing would deliver me to my seat without calling too much attention. "Hey, look everybody; he's back! Where did he come from?"

Seize the day! Like a considerate movie latecomer, I quickly squat-walked down the aisle and slid into my seat. I applauded with gusto for the next teacher—and myself. Then I noticed that he was receiving a longer and louder applause than my earlier rousing welcome to the stage. Probably taught more students. Probably.

Under the warm, cheerful light of the yellow-and-white tent, the abrupt chords of "Pomp and Circumstance" made me sit up, and I heard "Wild Thing." Did my students hear it? I watched the boys and girls in their blue-and-white gowns move up and down steps. With each round of passing graduates, I watched parents behind cameras rushing up and down aisles, again and again, as their smiling children turned and waved. I would never see this again.

One of the greatest pleasures—and honors—for some teachers is to have a former student become a teacher. Over the years many of my students have, and most are English teachers. Few things please me more than hearing from them. When Chris Fiore became a teacher at my school, I like to think I was being somewhat of a mentor—my last important teaching experience. Even though Chris was a natural and an immediate success with the students ("I want Fiore for English next year! All the kids in his class say he's a great teacher!"), he respectfully listened to me and the other old timers who ate lunch in my room. ("Try using the Delaney book for attendance, Chris. Or "Never go to your mailbox at the end of the day.") Unlike most adults who leave behind some of their special teenage qualities, Chris—today, a husband and father of three children—retained his openness, honesty, and generosity, and he quickly became a trusted colleague in the English department—and a close friend.

I knew Chris was special when, as a senior, he studied creative writing. He was a superior student athlete who worked hard and did well in both worlds, but it was his approach to life that made him special. In the writing circle where students sat to read their poems and short stories aloud—and needed the support of their classmates—Chris was kind, positive, and encouraging. ("Please reread the last two lines, Eileen. They're beautiful.") On the soccer and baseball fields and basketball court, he was aggressive and merciless. Watching him move back and forth between these two worlds, I saw the whole boy in perfect balance with all the contrary lines of his talents overlapping. There were no shadows of doubt; he knew himself well and demanded from himself complete dedication in everything from his writing poetry to his stealing second base and heading soccer balls.

Unlike most favorite students who disappear after graduation, Chris waved at me whenever I passed the window of his after-school job. During his college years at Fordham University, he worked at the village bank. I'd pass the window, and he'd signal for me to come in. We'd talk about school and his future, and on one occasion, I complained about getting up at three in the morning to catch an early flight. (Poor me, I was going on vacation.)

"I'll take you to the airport, Mr. Leonard."

"No, I'll take a cab."

"That's crazy. Why spend all that money?"

"Chris, we're talking about very early morning."

"So what? I have to get up sometime." When I took the cab, he wasn't pleased.

And that's Chris today. If you must do something, do it. Don't complain. Get it done. Period. And now that I'm retired, he's still getting it done, teaching—and improving—my creative writing and American literature classes, as well as advising the literary magazine, *Forum*. And, of course, he's still involved in the world of athletics, coaching basketball and soccer; and recently he became the Athletic Director for the district. Teenager, adult … poet, athlete … student, teacher … student, friend. The overlapping lines of his talents and character are sharp, deep, and dark.

And despite several years of collegiality and summer-backyard parties, he still calls me Mr. Leonard.

Remembering my early teaching years, I think of Martin, Roger, Jane, and Marvin, and appreciate how lucky I was to have them near my classroom. And when I think of my later years, I realize how fortunate I was to share some of my academic experiences with a talented teacher down the hall. My old-timers enjoyed helping someone who needed their advice, their guidance, and I hope they thought I had become a better teacher.

Last January, the wonderful English actress Helen Mirren told Morley Safer of *60 Minutes* that she never regretted not having children; she preferred having her freedom. I remember thinking that I felt the same way. Mirren continued to say she enjoys the children in her extended family. Well, I never regretted being childless, because I also enjoyed an extended family. And my family grew every year. September strangers became smiling teenagers, and class after class, I met thousands of young people. Perhaps, they were the reason for my not having children; they returned my affection year after year.

And now years later, some of those waving boys and girls in blue-and-white gowns have become my close friends.

Teacher: "Speaking of carousels, remember reading Rainer Maria Rilke's "The Merry-Go-Round" last semester? Of course, you do. That's why you're my favorite class."

Student: "You say that to all your classes."

Teacher: "Never!"

Class: "You do!"

Teacher: "Let's not bicker. Listen to the last stanza. Would Salinger agree?
And all this hurries toward the end, so fast,
Whirling futilely, evermore the same,
A flash of red, of green, of gray, goes past,
And then a little scarce-begun profile.

And oftentimes a blissful dazzling smile
Vanishes in this blind and breathless game."

Student: "Both are really comparing life to a merry-go-round. I used 'breathless game' in my yearbook caption."

Teacher: "You're an old soul. And you're in good company; Salinger admired Rilke's work. And what about the narrator?"

Student: "Maybe he thinks he's vanishing ... like that smile in the poem, and like ... as ... his friend Marv said, he'll become a ghost roaming the school at night with ... Len, that can't be the bell already!"

Teacher: "Sadly. Next time, we'll work on the memoir. Terrific class, folks. Have a safe weekend, enjoy the homework—no groaning, please—and once again thanks ..."

Teacher and Students: "... for coming!"

About the Author

For more information about Richard Leonard, please visit www.RichardLeonard.net.

978-0-595-44387-1
0-595-44387-7